117:4 · October 2018

The Authoritarian Personality

Robyn Marasco, Special Issue Editor

AGAINST the DAY

City Plaza: The Best Hotel in Europe
Loukia Kotronaki and Olga Lafazani, Editors

Robyn Marasco

Introduction

In the immediate wake of World War II, a team of researchers, including most famously Theodor Adorno, set out to understand the psychological roots of fascism. The result of their research, *The Authoritarian Personality*, was published in 1950. There are many reasons for returning to *The Authoritarian Personality* that have nothing to do with Donald J. Trump, but the real trouble with his tabloid narcissism is that we have all become participants in it. A glaring weakness in his character is also his greatest political strength: the uncanny ability to make it all about him. So contagious is this self-absorption that even the opposition is formed by it, by the consoling and congratulating idea that Trump is the exception. The historical precedents that he follows, the social conditions he reflects, and the structural disrepair that enabled him to assume the American presidency—all of these get buried under the generalized narcissism of our current political moment.

One of the many things we learn by returning to *The Authoritarian Personality* is that "Trumpism" runs deep, historically and psychologically. Its current avatar is a television brand and a social media celebrity, without ideological substance beyond his personal ambition, but "Trumpism" is

The South Atlantic Quarterly 117:4, October 2018
DOI 10.1215/00382876-7165818　© 2018 Duke University Press

a discernable force in American political history. The descriptive sections of *The Authoritarian Personality*, which detail the pervasiveness of racial prejudice and paranoia among middle- and working-class white Americans in the mid-twentieth century, provide caution against any Trump exceptionalism. But they also give an account of just how powerful his base of support is, despite record unpopularity and a governing party ambivalent about its own leadership. That support is drawn from the historical and psychological depths of white supremacy in America. Indeed, one of the most provocative arguments put forth in *The Authoritarian Personality* is that the affective and ideological energy for fascism comes mainly from racism. Other elements surely matter—class alliances, political opportunities, the state of the state—but fascism takes root in the soil of racism. Would it be appropriate to call Trump the F-word? Historians remind us of the profound differences between Mussolini's dictatorship in Italy, Hitler's Germany, and Shōwa Japan, each of these "fascisms" distinct from the other. But the diversity of national political movements does not cancel the underlying momentum that drives and unites them: an ideology of race, attached to an idea of the nation and national greatness, that authorizes every inhumanity. Neofascist movements, surging in the United States and around the world, may differ from their twentieth-century predecessors in any number of ways, but the ideology of race remains. It has new targets and new means of organization and new forms of expression, but murderous racism defines this new fascism as much as the old.

The Authoritarian Personality is a social scientific treatment of American-style fascism, which the authors understood to be distinct in many ways from European fascism, but probably not in ways that ultimately matter. Adorno originally intended that the book be called *The Fascist Character and the Measurement of Fascist Trends*, to reflect the political problem at its heart, as well as his main theoretical contribution (the so-called F-scale). The final title was one of many compromises between Adorno and his coauthors: Else Frenkel-Brunswik, Daniel Levinson, and R. Nevitt Sanford. They were academic psychologists working at the University of California, Berkeley. Max Horkheimer knew Sanford's work and initiated a project collaboration between his Institute for Social Research and what was known as the Berkeley Public Opinion Study Group. Their project was to examine the psychological basis of anti-Semitism. But, as Adorno notes, their research gradually moved away from the psychology of anti-Semitism and toward "the relation of anti-minority prejudice to broader ideological and characterological patterns" (Adorno et al. 1950: 297). And they moved, at the urging of Adorno and the Institute, from psychology to social theory, from individual prejudices to collective patterns.

The structure of *The Authoritarian Personality* provides some insight into its content. The principal authors adhered to a division of labor and responsibility for the material, which is reflected in the book's table of contents. Sanford worked on case studies and statistical analysis. Levinson created the project scales and offered some psychological analysis. Frenkel-Brunswik developed the personality variables and classified interview material. Adorno gave theoretical interpretation to the empirics and put specific data points into a larger social context. Each author drafted a section of the book, in addition to the section—"The Measurement of Implicit Antidemocratic Trends"—that they wrote together. It is a composite text more than a systematic treatment. Anchored in case study and interview material, the book reflects the aspirations of early critical theory to empirical social science. But it is also a highly theoretical work that aims at a reconstruction of the psychological structure of the potential fascist. *Potential*, because the point was not to expose Nazi sympathizers, but to identify the type of person who might be susceptible to fascist ideas. They were trying to figure out why some individuals embrace a fascist worldview and others do not. They believed part of the answer could be found in different personality types. And they believed Freudian concepts were key to unlocking these types.

Beyond the field of political psychology, where it remains a canonical text, *The Authoritarian Personality* has not received much scholarly attention. Those working in the tradition of Frankfurt School critical theory have taken greater interest in Adorno's philosophical and cultural criticism. There are some notable exceptions. Peter Gordon's (2017) recent essay, *"The Authoritarian Personality* Revisited: Reading Adorno in the Age of Trump" provides very helpful historical and intellectual context for the book and a substantive engagement with its arguments. Gordon argues that the book is torn between two conflicting frameworks: one that posits fascism as an individual problem, a personality disorder, and another that treats it as a social structure and historical condition. Gordon sees these positions as in conflict, where the authors of *The Authoritarian Personality* might have seen them in (dialectical) relation. Gordon believes these positions roughly correspond to the division between a psychological and a social-theoretical approach to understanding fascism— or, the views from Berkeley and Frankfurt, respectively. But it might be that the tensions in *The Authoritarian Personality* are also sources of strength: in this case, the foundations for mapping social and psychological patterns.

Other tensions are equally significant. For instance, the authors begin by distinguishing between *potential fascists* and *professed fascists*, noting that their empirical data dealt only with the former. The United States had just concluded a war against fascism as the research team launched their study, so they found no one among their test subjects in California willing to identify with fascist parties or causes. But the case of the potential fascist is almost more menacing in some respects, as it suggests that fascist movements, even when marginal, draw from an ample reserve of fascist sympathy. The authors were focused on the fascist character, but we might be equally concerned with the antifascist character—not as a mirror image of his or her enemy, but as an altogether different type. The authors were criticized for failing to consider "left-wing authoritarianism" (Stalinism) as a disorder no less dangerous than right-wing authoritarianism or for failing to see that authoritarianism knows no left-right distinctions whatsoever. But we might conclude from reading *The Authoritarian Personality* that authoritarianism is a political structure *and* an ideology, that it is ideology *and* affect, and that it is an affective structure that gets produced in ideology and the organization of the state.

Returning to *The Authoritarian Personality* today, in light of neofascist formations and the intensification of state violence against black and brown people, may mean significant revisions to its conceptual framework and research methods. But it also offers an opportunity to reflect on the politics of critical theory and advance the project of its "decolonization." This politics, as I see it, is a consistent antifascism—sometimes called revolutionary socialism, sometimes called "genuine liberalism"—that is always linked to a critique of capitalism and bourgeois society. Decolonizing critical theory means challenging its Eurocentrism and its express or tacit assumption that Europe represents the pinnacle of progress and humanity. But advancing a critical theory of neofascism might also require keeping eyes on Europe, on the political reaction to the refugee crisis, on the resurgence of Far Right and nativist political parties, even on the political fortunes of Silvio Berlusconi (Trump before Trump, and with more vowels) or Recep Tayyip Erdoğan (Trumpism between East and West). It might require turning eyes to Israel, to make sense of how the Arab or the Muslim has displaced the Jew in neofascist discourse, which is not to say that anti-Semitism is any less a part of it. Or it might require looking at American politics with fresh eyes. For example, would it make sense to place #BlackLivesMatter in a discernible tradition of Black antifascism, a tradition that says that the police are not just any type of pigs, but *fascist pigs*? Would this approach help us to see that the F-word has always had a polemical use? And would we then be able to worry a little bit less about how much Trumpism is like or unlike Hitlerism, and more about how Trumpism is like the fascism that has long found a home in the United States?

The Authoritarian Personality everywhere begs the question of an *anti-authoritarian personality*, but its answers are unsatisfying, if in part because the authors rightly see psychology as an effect of society. They believed anti-authoritarians to be rare types, but not a single type, too diverse a group to incorporate into their study. More importantly, with enough disorder to go around, even among the low scorers on the F-scale, the authors were reluctant to hold up any type as an ideal. They rejected the false equivalence of fascism and antifascism, as well as the implicit golden mean to which this false equivalence appeals. But they also refused to romanticize their subjects, even the ones who did not fit their models.

Whatever its limitations, *The Authoritarian Personality* remains integral to recovering the political theory of the early Frankfurt School and indispensable to contemporary critique. It was this basic conviction that prompted my call for papers in early 2016 for a conference to be held at Hunter College, CUNY, in November, just four days after the election. Many of the essays in this special issue were first presented at that event: a full weekend of intensive discussions of *The Authoritarian Personality*, more effective than any therapy in managing the mixture of emotions that we felt at the time. This dossier offers a revaluation of an understudied masterpiece of social science. It aims for some theoretical clarity and political vision beyond the counter-reality principle by which we are presently governed.

References

Adorno, T. W., Else Frenkel-Brunswik, Daniel J. Levinson, and R. Nevitt Sanford. 1950. *The Authoritarian Personality*. New York: Harper and Row.

Gordon, Peter E. 2016. "The Authoritarian Personality Revisited: Reading Adorno in the Age of Trump." *boundary 2* 44, no. 2: 31–56.

Robert Hullot-Kentor

Metric of Rebarbarization:
Real Time in *The Authoritarian Personality*

America now exists primarily in order
not to know what it is thinking.
November 9, 2016

Undreamt Nation

The central focus of Theodor Wiesengrund Adorno's philosophy is a critique of the primitive from
the perspective of the primitive as the single possibility of what might be other than primitive.
Adorno so exactly says this, one sentence to the
next through the whole of his work, that there
would be no reason to notice that he never wrote it
in just these words unless there were the need, as
now, to understand it in Real Time. Real Time is
where "Live" once was as the claim to what was
other than prerecorded. As such, Live could only
plausibly be asserted so long as there was enough
reality remaining to life credibly to issue its coun-
terfeit. To say that Live helped exhaust the life that
was all that sustained it would be more like a pun
than a joke, but it is also true. It even helps set in
relief the absolute advantage of Real Time over the
now-defunct Live, that respiration has no part in it.
In promoting the source that it depletes, its factual
breathlessness would be unable to fog a mirror.
Real Time is the digital synchronized to a handheld

The South Atlantic Quarterly 117:4, October 2018
DOI 10.1215/00382876-7165830 © 2018 Duke University Press

clock, ourselves as observers. It is the contemporary metric of rebarbarization. At any hour, as things are now set, the collapse of arctic ice, the launch-
ing of a nuclear weapon, cannot possibly occur except in Real Time. To read
in its news feed—for instance—that "intelligence officers looked on in *real
time* as Russian government hackers searched computers around the world
for the code names of American intelligence programs" leaves no alternative
than to be clocking real time with one's own eyes, looking on at an even more
distant remove (Perlroth and Shane 2017; my emphasis).

Metric of Rebarbarization

The metric of rebarbarization calibrates the force of the Synchronized Now
that has snapped the thread of human history. In reflection on this caesura,
Real Time would lay claim to the level of cognition its syllables potentially
assert—that horror is no longer exceptional—rather than to the dogmatic
element in the timing mechanism that the thinking ear now hears echo in
the idiom as pronounced (Adorno 2006: 19). Dogmatic, here, is not meant in
the sense of the doctrinaire as we generally think of it, but as Hegel might
have used it. In his age, the dogmatic was the refusal to acknowledge the
contrary implied in a concept, as if up and down, for instance, might be
understandable without the reflection of each on the other. In spite of the
productive discernment of this critique, it was limited by the claimed trans-
parency of language to the logic of the contraries developed. This was effectively Cartesian in subserving the rationalist prohibition on the association
of word to word as the locus of error. The prohibition is a function of method,
the principle of organization per se that ascertains truth only in the achievement of the separation of knowledge from its object. The dualism of mind
and body—that of the human and animal as of the internal and external—is
an implication of this need, for method as method, not its premise. Hegel, in
whatever many ways its critic, was all the same located in this tradition in
that he was no more prepared to follow the threading impulses in the texture
of language or those that cleave through that texture than he would have
been ready to understand history as the domination of nature. He would not
have discerned, as we must, any clue to the blindsidedness of Real Time in
the juxtaposition, on one hand, of the self-confirming alacrity with which it
is spokenly affirmed—as if nothing might be more real or alive than that—
and, on the other hand, the deflecting, principled refusal that would meet
any asserted, perceived sense of "the primitive" in Real Time. It is as if, of all
words, the primitive may only be stated legitimately when skeptically classed
as a prejudice, as in the "primitive." The scare quotes that mean to quaran-

tine this thought from cognition, however, are the function not of a Cartesian but of a social block. If instead, however, the primitive were heard in each and any statement of Real Time, the feeling of that block as we now have it, the sense of being unable to know what we know perfectly well, the occluding rain in the storms we now experience, of rain coming straight down, as if thrown, the unprecedented temperatures, the months in which no two days are of one recognizable season, the absence of any preparation for what we are in the midst of, would shatter that block.

Studies in Prejudice

The perspective of the primitive is inimical to the given idea of a perspective modeled on the telescope. It neither establishes an angle of observation selected from innumerable possible others or implies the interposition of an optic; it is as averse to any instrument of method as it might be inclined toward a musical instrument. It developed in the realization that subjectivity is not possibly able at the far end of its labors to transmute sensation into judgment in the achievement of objectivity; it would never arrive at the world it insists is there directly in front of its eyes but would instead be trapped at every step of the way in unrecognizable proliferations of its own self-reflection. In the recognition of this dead end, when this philosophical tradition faltered, the whole of perception became a level of judgment at every degree of feeling rather than being remaindered in the act of intellection. Geist became Erdgeist in an uttermost transformation of any logically sedimented extraction of the directions of up and down. Erich Kahler acutely named this development, which occurred somewhere around 1900 in a centuries-long development, the *spiritualization of the senses*. The ear, for instance, would need to be recognized as a "thinking ear" rather than as a strangely pressed device for the reception of sensa for transmission to the brain (Adorno 1983: 19). In this same realization every word would necessarily be understood as being as listening as it is speaking. These are implications of the critique of representation that the whole of modern thought, philosophy, and the arts continue to contend with— implications without which neither Freud's technique of free association in the relation of one word to the next or Adorno's paratactical style, the philosophical correlative of free association, would ever have become possible. In Adorno's work the critique of representation is summarized in the unsummarizable thesis of the primacy of the object. He writes, "What I most have in mind is a kind of restitution of experience against its empiricist deformation" (Adorno 1998: 242).

Primordial Restitution

In Adorno's early writings, the intention of this restitution of experience developed in figures such as the much-studied essay on natural history (Adorno 2008a) and was later elucidated as a negative dialectics that directs concepts, by developing their nonidentity with their object, to their dependency on it. This form of criticism fulfills cognitively the mimetic impulse that precedes and breaches the diremption of subject and object. As Rolf Tiedemann has written, mimesis is generally synonymous in Adorno's writings with the idea of nature. Concepts are themselves transformations of the mimetic impulse as elements of natural history. In these terms, Adorno did not need to reject the tradition of the representational mind as mistaken, but recognized its hall of mirrors as objective. Its thinking provides the only keys that correctly fit the locks of its own manufacture. In alliance with Hegel's immanent critique of dogmatism—the thesis that *the only way out is through*—Adorno internalized that tradition within the perspective of the primitive where its antinomies, every point at which the concepts of the representational mind are blocked and apparently impede themselves, could be translated out of the language of self-preservation and interpreted back into what these concepts had set themselves against as historical expressions of what life suffers under. In *Dialectic of Enlightenment* Horkheimer and Adorno call this critique of domination—in its most well-known formulation—the recollecting awareness of nature in the subject [das Eingedenken der Natur im Subjekt] (Horkheimer and Adorno 2007: 32). What this fully means remains to be understood. But, in any context that is also a consideration of psychoanalysis—as is this discussion of authoritarianism and especially of *The Authoritarian Personality*, an entirely psychoanalytical study—any number of cognate psychoanalytic formulations immediately come to mind, such as, for instance, on the economic level of the psyche, the transformation of drive defense into drive impulse. But even Adorno's idea of the *block*, though always presented in a presumed Kantian reference, could be a translation of Freud's model of trauma, fixation, symptom formation, and so on. And there are reasons to speculate that even *Negative Dialectics*, ostensibly Adorno's work least concerned with psychoanalysis, is most closely built in parallel with it. Likewise, in considering *Aesthetic Theory*, if one knew of the work only that it presents the idea that art is the unconscious transcription of the history of human suffering, one might guess that *Aesthetic Theory* is somehow altogether a psychoanalytical aesthetics, unless, that is, one had studied the first pages of this aesthetics at all. Even while citing it at length, Adorno urgently distinguishes his thinking and any group of his ideas from being confused with psychoanalytical thought, however homologous they often are. Likewise, in his own day he sought to elude any entanglement of his work with the archaicizing and neopagan doctrines that urged a return to a primordial world. In the engulfing of Germany in the Third Reich, Adorno witnessed the factual return of that primordial world as if in utter fulfillment of the most profound wish, as if that primordial world had never been left behind in the first place. Had Adorno not needed to differentiate his own efforts from psychoanalysis, on one hand, and the archaicizing social development he witnessed, on the other, he might conceivably have called the form of interpretation he developed—that memory of nature—the recollection of the primitive in the subject.[1]

Interpretation neither Stringent nor Arbitrary

The contemporary concept of perspective is method itself, a set of procedures contracted to a mobile, subjective point and applied from that vantage. It officiates over an epistemological truce sustained only on the condition of a pursuit of happiness that is presumed indeterminate in its constitutive concept of liberty. The standard of knowledge it establishes is as proleptically concessive as it is authoritative, as all-seeing as it is blinkered; its certitude is voiced as resignation: "That's my perspective, anyway." By contrast, a critique of the primitive from the perspective of the primitive, while nothing like a telescope, all the same remains a perspective in the recognition that truth as interpretation is neither stringent nor arbitrary. Without a given compass it lays claim to knowing the object itself. Its focal point converges binocularly beyond any pursuit of happiness restricted exclusively to its pursuit. If it is more on the order of untying a knot than of tying one tight, truth is only true when it is binding. If it must be struggled for, it can only be found. For each of these reasons it is never a match for the motivated lie.

Savage Beating

America is in many ways divided like it's never been before. . . . We're living in a time, an age that we never thought possible before. The vicious barbarism we read about in history books, but never thought we'd see it in our so-called modern-day world. Who would have thought we would be witnessing what we're witnessing today. . . . Thank you very much, God bless you and God bless America.
—Donald Trump, speech at the Alfred E. Smith Foundation Dinner, 2016

If truth were sought in the swaggering figure straight out of Petronius's *Satyricon* who at the Al Smith dinner on October 20, 2016, addressed the nation along with the competing presidential candidate, Hillary Clinton, it would be necessary to consider the perspective of the primitive that is an attack on it. The candidate rose to the occasion to deplore a nation divided against itself and a world that had relapsed into "vicious barbarism." Throughout the speech as in the few lines exampled here from his closing remarks, anaphora conceals anacolutha in parody of the grand style. There is no thinking, only the promulgated self-evidence of its own primacy and a feigned humility momentarily postponing attack. The speaker is as selfless as only a suburban yogi might someday dream of being. In florid self-reference, he is unable to recognize himself. Repeatedly shifting his stance at the podium to back up the taunting provocation on the pugilist's face, the candidate who was that evening deploring rancor and barbarism had, throughout a year's campaign, ceaselessly labored to inspire *bellum omnium contra omnes.* He had advocated the legitimacy of torture, threatened the life of the competing candidate, sworn to deny the laws governing elections should he lose and, just prior to his closing remarks that night, subjected his own wife to general humiliation by directing her to stand and bow for plagiarizing the words of the then First Lady. So when the candidate proceeded to insist of his audience, "Who would have thought we would be witnessing what we're witnessing today," the affirmation he demanded was not the terrified "Exactly!" that was written across many of the faces of those seated around Trump's podium on stage who were either staring fixedly at him or avoiding looking at him altogether. And although the audience would not likely have concluded conceptually that they were witnessing a barbaric attack on the barbaric, it was apparent to all that the speaker himself was unable to distinguish one side from the other. Audible in the self-pitying tone ensconced in vituperation was a candidate half in reverie addressing, as if face to face in the hall of mirrors he solely occupies—no matter how many homes he owns—the loser who has spent a lifetime failing at every turn finally to get even. As he has put it, "we must beat the savages" (Risen and Fink 2017). Ruthless hardly begins to describe the tenor of the effort of a man who never smiles willingly, only willfully.

Get Even for What?

But, why would the man who has everything, and everything again times billions, need to get even? Get even for what? How is he the loser? On the eve of the election, the political commentator Edward Luce remarked on Trump's continuing insistence that the election was "rigged" against him. Luce (2016) noted the puzzle. Since "a Trump victory could still happen," it is "so odd that he plays the sore loser before actually losing." Add to this only, first, that Trump is incapable of play. No matter the number of golf courses possessed, his only experience is of life versus death. Add second that Trump knew himself the loser not only prior to the election but well before, during, and after: "Look at the way I've been treated lately . . . No politician in history—and I say this *with great surety*—has ever been treated worse or more unfairly" (Haberman and Thrush 2017a; my emphasis). The parenthetical statement begins to present the dynamic of what stands in place of a self, its surrogate. For the self, as self, is the capacity for self-transcendence, ultimately as self-relinquishment. Trump, by contrast, demonstrates exclusively a capacity for tactical delusion when he lays claim to how he had been treated *"with great surety."* The assertion is a demand for raw belief in opposition to the whole of reality whose pressing weight is exclusively the contrary of his statement. Under the threat of fragmentation, the partially psychotic president produces his own phenomena and inflicts it on himself as on anyone around him, now including much of the world. It is the only truth the fragile president can tolerate. His need for delusive reprieve is ceaseless and makes chaos of the rest of his thinking. It deprives the man the nation has charged with making its gravest executive decisions of capable judgment. The single lesson he has grasped, to which he spontaneously makes all other thought and evidence subordinate, is that he is the object of the greatest injustice in the whole of history. He states this pathologically, as fact. He could never shake himself free of this perception because whatever he has acquired in a lifetime of relentless and often hateful acquisition and attained in stupendous magnitude goads him with an abysmal sense of having nothing—except for the chance it offers of producing envy in others and humiliating them: at the inaugural dinner "he was still *reliving his campaign fights* with relish. 'I will say, the other side is going absolutely crazy,' he told supporters" (Poniewozik 2017; my emphasis). The impulse to humiliate in a moment of triumph is not an expression of joy in success, but it does comment on what extends considerably beyond reliving his campaign fights. For under any circumstance, no matter the winnings, he always comes away empty-handed. Except for the gloating, every victory encompasses a bitter taste. Whatever he possesses or next desires seems as if it is being stolen directly out from under him. To his own bewilderment, even in winning the presidency and virtually the same day, the man who has aimed to cheat most everyone he has ever come in contact with immediately felt that he himself was being cheated out of the electoral triumph (Haberman and Thrush 2017b). In the certitudes of the claim's stridency, it was as if the supposed theft was what he had been elected to prove in the first place.

It was indeed what he was elected to prove by the resentfully embittered who determined the nation's electoral decision. Candidate and constituency never once met, and would not have tolerated each other for as much as a photo op. But on this condition and without ever once coming in contact, Trump and his electorate found themselves locked together in the devoted embrace of omnipotent fantasy. Each became flesh of the other's flesh; each dreamed the other's dream in outraged dispossession. While the audiences dependably worked themselves into a state of exhilaration in making the defeated Croesus in front of their eyes swell with power, he assured the palpably diminished that they were the only people he truly felt comfortable with and could care about. With tantalizing largesse and in widely dispersed interviews and campaign rallies, often with his plane parked in the digital background, he assured his audiences that he needed nothing of what he had amassed around himself. He was, as it were, offering on a vote to begin unloading their bequest from the plane's deep belly, airlifted to them from what they could only envision as an unsurveyable expanse of riches and luxury. In this, the campaign was a successfully manipulated cargo cult. It had been long in the making, constructed not of mud runways and control towers lashed together out of straw, but from tarmac, concrete, steel, glass, and storage tanks of jet fuel. The always arriving executive plane, the seats of the golden interior stamped with monarchical crowns, swept back and forth across the country with the heavily lettered fuselage bearing the name of one of the lost ancestors, one of the Big Men.[2] He was returning not to Melanesia or Vanuatu, but to lead a disoriented white population of a widely dispersed Rust Belt who knew themselves severed from their own people and leaders. How and when the electorate had been cut adrift from their own kind, they were not sure, but they were precise on who had done it: it was the immigrants, the elites, the blacks, the terrorists, a criminally uncontrollable woman, the Jews, the media, and perhaps all of them, and anything at all they had heard or ever set eyes on. The electorate had waited a long time for the man who debarked from the side of the vessel and descended the mobile jet gangplank to the tarmac to announce, "I will give you everything. I will give you what you've been looking for, for 50 years. I'm the *only one*" (Stokols 2016; my emphasis). The candidate's disinterest in distinguishing truth from lie, amounting to an inability for that distinction, was by no means antipathetic to his audience. After all, what was there not to believe when he swore to bring the booty on shore again, to "take back everything that has ever been taken from us"—the disappeared factories, the jobs, the purloined riches, prestige, real estate towers, libidinal and destructive privilege to fill the treasure house of revenge. In exchange for the vision of this upended cornucopia, the best deal his audiences had ever been offered, the single request the candidate made of them was that they elect him as the *only one.*

But, whatever the promises to give beyond giving, and however unfeigned Trump's remoteness to all that he has, a figure who in the most profound sense is incapable of having anything himself could have nothing to give. He would never make a bestowal of any smallest part of his holdings without seeking to rip away something more for himself, preferably the whole of it. In offering to help the economically and socially foundering get back their own, he could only mean that they would serve him in recovering all that has been stolen from him. The plane that in their eyes functioned in a hypnotically induced promise of inexhaustible cargo was never to him anything but the exact same thing they knew it to be: a device of omnipotently proud and exclusive expropriation. The primitive dynamic recurrently transpiring for Trump, and, as evidenced in his election, not only for him, is a self-provoking vengeance—*primitive* meaning what remains incapable of escaping its own origin with which it is unreconciled. The motive force of the dynamic is a manic effort whose hold on the world is as tenuous as fingertips against a sheer cliff. In the struggle for revanchist conquest pitched in opposition to shattering humiliation, moments of ascent are indistinct from moments of tumbling. The need to catch at any oblique grip justifies whatever impulse he has for corrupt dealing, tyrannical scorn, compulsive deceit, sexual aggression, and imperious torture. Since the world itself has been stolen from him, nothing less would fulfill the quitclaim he carries on his face, often convulsed—not heartbroken, but with hatred. To say that his face convulses with the primacy of the death instinct is not allegorical. The mandate he presents is antithetic to wish; achieved it would be without gratification. We are feeling the initial months of that achievement now. Thus, the president of the United States.

The Use of Humankind

From the moment of Trump's election, one has assumed that the vice president would replace Trump in a nation that is not likely ever to overtake, let alone draw even with, the increasing velocity of disaster that has now been engaged, worldwide, and for which the United States bears a heavily increasing responsibility. But however long the Trump presidency lasts, it will be the first in American history rightly to be characterized as a regime. Though legally elected, it seeks to conduct itself as an imposition from above, not by rule of law. And if Adorno is correct that one only begins to understand history when one has become its target, the United States, which to date has counted itself an exception among nations specifically as an exception from history, may now be getting a sense of what it is all about. For authoritarian regimes first and foremost turn their aggression inward; this is axiomatic and, at least provisionally, amounts to a definition of authoritarianism. The intention of an assault on society so prevails in an authoritarian regime that even to save its own command it is unable to support or come to the aid of the population that brings it to power. While this seems to be an extraordinarily irrational implication of authoritarianism—and it is—it reveals what is normatively irrational in any form of coercion. For all coercion is so necessarily implicated in what it dominates that from its first moment its command sets itself fully and blindly under its own assault (Adorno 2006: 19). The splintered allegiances, the inextricably locked suspicions and paranoia, sometimes murderous, that destroy them, are the only remaining routes they have to discern what it is about themselves from which they are otherwise fully shuttered by their own methodology—the destruction of what they depend on.

It is characteristic that the Trump campaign "sent the message that norms and institutions were made to be smashed" (Poniewozik 2017). And at no point in the campaign would Trump have lost track of his intention, if once in power, to teach his lesson of success—the principle of dispossession as the fiercest form of possession—to the millions who rallied for him. For even if few figures more decisively than Trump factually embody the force that tore apart the lives of his electorate, he is already long in the midst of inflicting on them and the world as a whole incalculably more harm in destroying the nation's limited institutional protections and transforming these agencies into powerfully efficient vehicles of plunder, all that might have stood between now and utter calamity.[3] It would be simplistic to claim that it is a relation of macro- to microcosm, but there must be more than an analogy between, on one hand, the richest nation in the history of the world—which all the same to itself feels swindled and where indeed whole populations are violently deprived—and, on the other hand, a president who has stocked up more fortune than most anyone would ever bother to imagine, who all the same effectively has nothing beyond an impulse for more plunder and the desire to preside over a long table of cabinet ministers, each hoisting a pickax on one shoulder. If there were a way to say that without the good, which the United States is now without, there is nothing at all to have, not in any quantity and not by anyone, one would say that.

Alexis de Tocqueville did find a way to say it when he wrote in the 1830s, with the exacting pith of a reality seen for the first time, that Americans "clutch at everything but hold nothing fast" (Tocqueville 2003: 536). His work is increasingly true, not as an act of prescience but because it discerns a societal mechanism that integrally reproduces its own inability to escape its own origin. Tocqueville did not need to wait for Trump to come along to know him cold, nor did he need to hesitate in the recognition of the primitive. He captures an entire civilization of pioneering entrepreneurship in what would someday be a president's faux Louis XVIII dining room sets, the isolated, egoless ego shaped only by competition, the strangely juxtaposed wife and the uncannily undifferentiated look in the eyes of the progeny: "To obtain a comfortable life, he has braved exile, solitude, and the countless disasters of the primitive life. . . . Focused upon this single aim of making his fortune . . . [he] . . . has finally created a totally individual existence for himself; family feelings have fused into a bottomless egoism and it is doubtful whether he sees in his wife and children anything other than a detached part of himself" (Tocqueville 2003: 887).

In *Democracy in America*, Tocqueville describes this figure as one among "the hardest that have appeared on earth." He was stunned by its sudden existence "which we see rising before our eyes." Its "object is not to rule" as did rulers of the past. That rulership felt "obliged by law, or thought of itself obliged by custom, to come to the help of its servants and relieve their distress." By contrast, the only aim these figures have for the population is "to make use of it." And "when it has impoverished and brutalized the men it uses," it "abandons them in time of crisis." At the moment Tocqueville was writing these words, he thought that what was then a disorganized cohort—which he refers to as an "aristocracy created by industry"—had little impulse or resource to act as a concerted force and would restrain itself. But he feared this restraint might be temporary: "The friends of democracy should keep their eyes anxiously fixed in that direction. For if ever again permanent inequality of conditions and aristocracy make their way into the world, it will have been by that door that they entered" (Tocqueville 2006: 557–58).

"The Authoritarian Personality"

Tocqueville did not know what to call the situation he saw developing: "The *thing* is new," he wrote, and "I cannot find a word for it" (Toqueville 2006:

691; my emphasis). The words he had were inevitably those of his own day and none other, but Tocqueville was sharply aware that his words had come to speak for another day, no longer his: "Such old words as 'despotism' and 'tyranny' do not fit" (691). "Aristocracy"—as in an "aristocracy . . . created by industry" (555)—would be another old word that did not fit. A century later when Adorno was working on *The Authoritarian Personality*, the "thing" was no longer new and there were more than enough words for many of its aspects, necessarily neologisms. Most of these words had only become familiar in recent decades, among them *authoritarianism*—a prewar term of opprobrium; *fascism* and *totalitarianism*—initially terms to describe Italian fascism; and *ethnocentrism*; *eugenics, racist,* and *racism*—a group of concepts that arose inseparably from the terror experienced on many levels in the developing discovery of homo sapiens as a species, that is, of ourselves as essentially primitive selves. *Anti-Semitism* was another relatively recent word of characteristically German origin, a language that for a complexity of reasons, including the constructed modernity of many of its terms, alongside words of considerable antiquity, builds a broad expanse of its thinking out of ideas of force, strictly for and against, negative and positive, as is the case in German philosophy from Leibniz to the will to power, to a *Negative Dialectics*. In its style it can just as suddenly become a language of deepest endearment and the most acute longing. In Adorno's style, especially, what can be abrasively austere, abrupt, and domineering in its reasoning and rhetoric— "*No happiness without fetishism*"—can become a body of language that is immediately pleading, suffering, verging on the hallucinatorily lyrical, acutely torn by modern realities and an imponderable number of bodies (Adorno 1974: 121). *The Authoritarian Personality* is a German title of modernity in extremis written in English. To the thinking ear it carries an archaic resonance, as if there might never have been anything more to life than force. To an American ear in particular and until recently, it has been this aspect of Adorno's writing that has seemed an extreme and even bizarre distortion of what a nation could possibly imagine that considers itself to have had almost as much good fortune historically as Germany has not.

It does not need to be said that a work is known by its title. But in the case of *The Authoritarian Personality*, the title is generally all that is known of its nearly one thousand rarely read pages. Even those prepared for the long haul, perhaps wanting to situate rumors of Adorno's F-scale in the whole of it, find the work taxingly difficult to sustain, and without close study the work's composite research models remain obscure. Still, the election of a president devoted exclusively to force and the study's evocative title, the very words often enough said to characterize the new president, have raised expectations that *The Authoritarian Personality* might reveal the long-buried Rosetta Stone of political science. Fully unearthed, we might read the lingua franca across its surface in which the current rise of authoritarian figures and governments in the West could be understood. There are good reasons for these expectations. For the project of *The Authoritarian Personality*, as Horkheimer writes in the preface in an often quoted remark, was to study "the rise of an 'anthropological' species we call the authoritarian type of man" (Adorno et al. 1950: ix). *Authoritarianism*, then, was not to be understood in the vernacular sense of a political program in which rulers arise who act to wipe out the freedom of the populous in favor of the imposition of enforced obedience. On the contrary, in the postwar years when it was feared that, even having been defeated, fascism might still spread worldwide, the study posited a dreaded societal tautology: an emergingly authoritarian society—a totalitarian society—was asymptotically producing an authoritarian individual.

In their research the Berkeley scientists effectively put this posited tautology to a test. Their work parallels that of an entire generation of anthropologists, now recognized as the culture and personality movement—Géza Róheim, Abram Kardiner, Geoffrey Gorer, and Margaret Mead—who were using psychoanalysis to comprehend national character and broadly societal behavioral patterns. They likewise sought to use psychoanalysis to comprehend societal dimensions of psychodynamic structure. What those anthropologists meant by "culture and personality" is approximately what Adorno in *The Authoritarian Personality* meant by "ideology and personality" (Adorno et al. 1950: 603), though one important distinction is that the Berkeley scientists were considering a *new* anthropological type that was hypothesized as emerging society-wide, all-inclusively. This is why there are no *Doge di Venezia*, Caesars of antiquity, despots, or autocrats anywhere to be found in *The Authoritarian Personality*. However hard-fisted fascist leaders characteristically are, they would be of the same new type of human being as those who would assemble as their willing followers; the leaders too would be impeded functionaries of a macrosocial dynamic and subject to the same dependencies, fragility, and aggression.[4] To carry out this project, the scientists used questionnaires and interviews, not with the intention of collecting a distribution of political opinions, but to prompt and assemble nonintentional material, a kind of free association, as the manifest content out of which the latent reality of this personality structure could be analyzed. The psychometric devices identifying this structure would allow the small subject population they studied to be differentiated as "high" and "low" scorers, as eagerly available or not at all eager to join the ethnocentric persecution that is the focal point of authoritarian mobilization.

Even in brief synopsis it is evident why the ingenious psychosocial collaboration stands among the several most commented on studies in the history of the discipline's literature. When it was published in 1950, the preeminent social and personality psychologist, Gardner Murphy, recognized the work as a *monumental* achievement: "There is no other study known to me which deals so systematically, maturely, and competently with the problem of ethnic prejudice and its relations to socioeconomic, political, and other attitude dimensions" (Frenkel-Brunswik 1974: 19).[5] The deserved accolade, however, does not touch on what to this day remains the study's most controversial and urgently revolutionary contribution: its research of the primitive in the human. It was only on the basis of Freud's seminal discovery of unconscious drives that *The Authoritarian Personality* could possibly seek to comprehend the psychodynamic personality structure of the authoritarian personality through the differentiation and interpretation of the manifest and latent content of their research population. Freud's discovery was and remains so—primordially—antagonizing, even when it is casually presumed, that it is possible not to recognize that the motive of the development of psychoanalysis was not to disturb us with all that is below that no less defines what is above, but to comprehend why it is that we are—individually and socially—unable to escape the repetition of our own calamitously reinflicted origins and, to some degree, free ourselves from it. It is the decisive development of the insight of modernism as radical modernism, the most profoundly developed critique of the primitive from the perspective of the primitive. In recognizing the primitive in us and in the world around us, it neither deplores the primitive to castigate it triumphantly from the stance of a higher civilization; or, in concealed identity with its castigation, prescinds from the acknowledgment of the *primitive* as if the word itself were a crime against nature; or seeks to return to the primitive as the solution to the depredations of civilization.

In this psychoanalytic conceptualization of the primitive, which comprehends psychic suffering as originating in transformations of the repression of primitive impulses and made possible an entirely new form of interpretation built on the recognition of those impulses, we recognize ideas not only shared by all of the anthropologists of the character and personality movement, but the central thought of Adorno's philosophy. And even though Adorno only ever fully acknowledged Hegel as his preeminent teacher—and would never have accepted Freud in his place—it is this inextricable entwinement of Adorno with Freud that is resonant in the final sentence of *The*

Authoritarian Personality. It reads: "If fear and destructiveness are the *major* emotional sources of fascism, *Eros* belongs *mainly* to democracy" (Adorno et al. 1950: 976; emphasis added, with the exception of "Eros"). The apothegm hoists an American flag in what must have seemed a heartening postwar gesture. But, in its "majors" and "mainlys" and partly in spite of itself, the statement is somber. The caveats are more than expressive of the researchers' own hesitations in the work's concluding statement. For had they in fact supposed that destruction, the unnamed Thanatos in that concluding phrase, pertains as exclusively to fascism as would Eros to democracy, they never would have undertaken a six-year project to understand the danger of the rise of fascism in a democracy in the first place. The pronouncement's idealizing cadence falteringly seeks belief just as we, reading it now, might only wish to find it true, as if we might be directly inspired by it. Then, the United States, which at this moment remains a democracy, could consult *The Authoritarian Personality* and know better what it is now experiencing in its recent presidential election; it could be equally confident in its own democratic resources in confronting what there might be to fear in the nation's putative confrontation with a well-recognized enemy—fascism—a power America has already once proudly defeated in battles that legitimated its now-lapsed postwar hegemony. And if the apothegm were true in every single regard, including the identity it construes between the political and the psychological—the tautology the researchers presumed—then the close labor demanded of ourselves at this moment as researchers to unearth every last detail of the insights and techniques of the remarkable collaboration of *The Authoritarian Personality* would in fact reveal that much-sought-after psychosocial Rosetta Stone. It would come nodding to us out of the unearthed depth of its own proximally terrifying past into our own proximally terrifying present bearing lucid avowals of what this world has long been, accompanied by charts for sorting out high-scorers on anti-Semitism from low-scorers on ethnocentrism.

Is It Fascism?

In the war years the enemy successfully named itself, immemorially. And for the Berkeley researchers, several of whom had only escaped its reality with their lives, the meaning of that name was as resonant in its self-understood synonyms: *authoritarianism, totalitarianism,* and *anti-Semitism*. The terms were used entirely interchangeably throughout the study. It is understandable that it would only with difficulty have occurred to them to think of differentiating, for instance, fascism from authoritarianism. But, had it occurred to them, the construction of the research program left little potential for developing such distinctions. The tautological presupposition of the research obviated any consideration of comparative political analysis. When Adorno writes in *The Authoritarian Personality*, for instance, that "the extremely prejudiced person tends toward 'psychological totalitarianism,' something that seems to be almost a microcosmic image of the totalitarian state at which he aims," there could be no doubt what the study was looking for (Adorno et al. 1950: 633). This sealed the work off in itself, exclusive of historical or political reflection. The insularity of the research, on one hand, provided the power of Adorno's rhetoric in such statements of micro- and macrocosm in which micro might as well be macro as the other way around. But, on the other hand, there are reasons to consider that while this insularity made the research possible—and, indeed, made it possible in the first place for Adorno to collaborate in the psychoanalytic study—this came at a heavy price. For at the end of the six-year investigation, the results achieved were unexpectedly contradictory and self-refuting. A proportion of high-scorers on several scales designed to measure an ethnocentric characterology turned out instead to demonstrate liberal dispositions, while low-scorers on these same scales, those relatively free of a tendency toward prejudice, could all the same demonstrate narrowly conventional psychological dispositions. These results stood as a challenge to the study's claim to have discerned the psychodynamic reality of the ethnocentric, authoritarian personality. Adorno speculated interestingly on how these results might all the same be reconciled with each other. Yet, one obvious implication of the study's self-contradictory results, though not one that Adorno was ever prepared to consider—and it is hard to see how he ever might have—is that the results demonstrated that there must be considerably more to be differentiated in the relation of the psychological and social reality of individuals than the structure of the study could permit. But if Adorno himself did not investigate this possibility, the project as a whole acknowledged that a great deal must be missing from its work. For even when the results presented consistently high- and low-scoring subjects across the scales and interviews, the researchers noted that overall "we are pretty much in the dark" (972). Although the study was able to discern in its subject population differential tendencies toward violence, it had no ability at all to say who in the population they studied was actually ready to capitulate to fascism, to support it, or do whatever it might ask of them.

The acknowledgment of the work's limitation was responsibly candid and helped open the study to decades of serious and productive criticism. That material has since accumulated in such vast proportions that no one reader could possibly review the whole of it except schematically. It can be assumed though that it has already been remarked, perhaps innumerable times, that of all the reasons the study was "pretty much in the dark" is that the psychoanalytic researchers could not distinguish those attitudes that are symbolic and those that are pragmatic, a distinction entirely familiar to social psychology. Symbolic attitudes "have almost no conceivable personal relevance to the individual, but have to do with . . . [the individual's] . . . moral code or sense of how society should be organized" (Nisbett and Cohen 1996: 70–72). They have limited concrete implications or goal directedness, by self-evident contrast with "pragmatic" attitudes. It is, in other words, one thing to dress up in a Nazi uniform for a website photograph, eyes fixed hypnotically on an unwaveringly distant land of racial superiority, and essentially another to have an ideal of racial supremacy with the intention of founding society on racial violence that comprises—as did National Socialism—the readiness to commit murder to achieve that aim. But even had the researchers had this distinction available to themselves, they would have been unable to make use of it. For to begin to research the distinction between symbolic and pragmatic attitudes, pragmatic sociopolitical reflection is required, of which, as said, there is next to none in *The Authoritarian Personality*. In noting its limitation, the urgent social psychology question that was left untreated by its authors can be recognized as remaining no less urgent in our own moment in wanting to comprehend the conditions in which a transition—one that the United States may well be in the midst of— from proud photograph to real pitchfork, from symbolic to pragmatic attitudes, can and does or does not occur.

Though it was his responsibility most of all, Adorno, the prominent sociologist in the group, did not help the project in this regard. This distinction, in just these terms, is not what his thinking was most developed to understand. Its absence is one sense in which the accusation—otherwise false—that his work is bereft of praxis, is true. And while the psychoanalysts acknowledged the puzzle of this distinction as it became evident in their results, their own work could not reflect on it in lieu of another form of psychosocial collaboration that Adorno could have helped them achieve. These limitations, which result from an absence of sociopolitical reflection, are diffused through the project in many directions and continue to hamper what *The Authoritarian Personality* can contribute now to any contemporary understanding of American political realities. For if comprehending the American situation today were restricted to the Berkeley study's own terms, in its synonymization of fascism and authoritarianism—in its absence of actual sociopolitical reflection—it could only agree with the distinguished *Washington Post* columnist Robert Kagan (2016) when he claimed in alarmed expectation of the authoritarian candidate more than a year before he was elected that "this is how fascism comes to America." Since that alert, the rhythmically pulsed assertion of Trump—*the fascist*—as if the self-evidence of the accusation itself were enough to bring the enemy down, has only increased. *The Authoritarian Personality* would itself be helplessly mute in understanding why the accusation leaves its target untouched. Distinctions are needed. And it is only for starters to point out that German fascism was a counterrevolutionary critique of capitalism that wanted to reconstruct a society that had in every major institution collapsed after the economic crash of 1929. This reconstruction was not to be based on a restored capitalism, such as occurred in the United States under FDR, but literally by seeking to establish a *new* society of *new men* and *new women*—truly a new type of human being whose personality structure the Nazi state directly sought to inculcate and manipulate—who would be capable of direct violence and immediate domination in every dimension of a society reestablished on a world-encompassing racial hierarchy (Fritzsche and Hellbeck 2008: 302–48). German society so fundamentally disintegrated that social institutions could survive only on the basis of seeking to establish their own utter autonomy from each other and the rest of society. What emerged were mutually avoidant autonomous islands of command, in some instances so severely isolated as to require for their survival independent supply lines of natural resources (Geyer 1987). Adorno's extraordinarily hypertrophied—almost fluorescent—idea of autonomy, as if its achievement alone might be what could be done, even helplessly done—if it makes any sense to speak in such terms—to save the day, may have aspects of its origins in that particular situation.

There is, then, reason to consider whether the research of a new anthropological type in the United States did not more closely pertain to the nation the researchers dreaded than the nation they were studying. At one point in the work where it breaches its own ahistorical sanctum, Adorno provided the thesis—often asserted in his writings including his history of music—that this new type of human being resulted from the displacement of the competitive structures of a liberal economy by monopoly powers. The result was a psychodynamic failure to internalize the father imago and—in reasoning that will not be traced here—a faltering of what had formerly been the identity structure of the autonomous individual. There may be something, even a great deal, to the transformation of the figure of the father, especially as it pertains to the fateful transformation of the historically liberal Frankfurt in which Adorno was raised. But even without examining the thesis in detail, the idea that it was the lapsing of a liberal economy and competitive markets in the United States that accounts in some all-purpose way for what might have been occurring psychodynamically is not possibly correct. For it was not only the primordial enterprise of the new president of the United States that Tocqueville was able to recognize in Jacksonian America. One hundred years prior to Adorno's work—and in a liberal economy—Tocqueville himself already wanted to understand the characteristic transformation of individuality that was emerging in a society ruled by the principle of equality. While this society itself tended toward what he faute de mieux termed *tyranny*, he showed, as one of the first modern sociologists, that this transformation not only incapacitates resistance to it but that this incapacitation occurs from *within* the individual. As Tocqueville writes, the dynamic of equality in America—an idea cognate with Adorno's development of the principle of identity—destroys "those individual powers which were . . . [formerly] . . . able singlehanded to cope with tyranny" and produced a "weakness of all" (Tocqueville 2006: 15). This imbrication of authority and submission occurs in a way that so obviates possible opposition that it struck Tocqueville, who wanted to defend the possibility of democracy against the very agent of its emergence, with "a kind of religious dread." In a single sentence and with the poignant lucidity of a thinker who like Adorno was a critic of enlightenment, though by contrast, certainly a conservative in the tradition of Guizot, Tocqueville had already more than begun to recognize what would become the broad thesis of *The Authoritarian Personality* when he wrote: "Who can say where the exigencies of authority and the yielding of weakness will stop?" (313).

Recognizing the limitations of *The Authoritarian Personality* provides the impulse to consider that apostrophizing the new administration as fascist—whatever that administration and fascism may have in common that is real and urgently needing of comprehension—may be delusive. Involuntarily, if also self-servingly, the conflation veils the harder part of the contemporary situation to acknowledge that the entrepreneurial ideal that the new administration represents may be all that is remaindered of the idea of freedom. It is the private government of corporate order, whose form of command is both authoritarian and common to enterprise, that has in the recent election been established as a kind of national proprietary government (Anderson 2017: xix–xxiii). The thesis asserted by the new administration that "norms and institutions were made to be smashed" is the spirit of enterprise itself (Poniewozik 2017).[6] Taking this stance, the new administration has adopted the role of a vindictive straggler nation that has been cheated of hegemony and unfairly left behind by the rest of the world. The stance has consolidated the aggression needed to seek to invalidate the laws, treaties, rules, and conditions previously regulating internal affairs and international contests. Other nations have pursued this strategy, fascist and otherwise; Sweden, for example, had already done so in the seventeenth century (Kopstein and Lichbach 2000: 120). All failed calamitously in what is now becoming a spontaneous tactic worldwide, nation by nation. For—if we are not there already in increasingly seasonless years—we are soon to live in a world of which the whole of humanity, one by one, will feel deprived and cheated as by opaque forces whose many names will still not be enough for anyone to be able to name them all.

Rebarbarization indicates why *The Authoritarian Personality*, however hobbled by its lack of sociohistorical understanding, was invaluably worth undertaking. For even if Tocqueville, in sounding the alarm at the danger to democracy in the rise of possibly unprecedented inequalities at the hands of an "aristocracy of industry" was often able to describe American society more accurately than could Adorno, bringing Tocqueville's reflections to bear on *The Authoritarian Personality* does not discredit it in the name of perspicacious sociohistorical insight and the more familiar labors of historians. What the Berkeley scientists had to consider was considerably more difficult than what Tocqueville had to comprehend; it represented an advance and required turning away, as if sometimes obliviously, from the level of sociohistorical reality that Tocqueville was still able to observe. This is evident when we realize that the dialectic of equality that Tocqueville (2006: 705) feared with "a kind of religious dread" would—as he writes in the last sentence of *his* massive study—lead either "to servitude or freedom, knowledge or barbarism." For Tocqueville conceived this dynamic of rebarbarization as a *return* to barbarism in a collapse of civilization conceived as the exact antithesis to barbarism. He had not yet been compelled to or had the possibility of considering the insight that Adorno was struggling to comprehend and make good on throughout the entirety of his works and that remains the most difficult, urgent, and often intolerable insight of radical modernism: the psychoanalytic insight that the recurrence of the primitive in our lives is not a regression to what was left behind in the development of European society after its barbarian disintegration, but an archaic reality that is reproduced moment by moment.[7] In "Freudian Theory and the Pattern of Fascist Propaganda," an essay written immediately after the conclusion of *The Authoritarian Personality*, for instance, Adorno cites Freud's *Civilization and*

Its Discontents as if Freud himself were speaking directly for Adorno's (1982: 127) own macrosocial thesis of the origins of fascism: "As a rebellion against civilization fascism is not simply the recurrence to an archaic past but its reproduction in and by civilization itself." This not only states that civilization produces barbarism, but that civilization itself is the reproduction of barbarism in the form of fascism. Adorno was fully aware that, whatever purpose to which he had turned Freud's thinking in support of his own, this is not a thesis that Freud would have accepted. For Adorno's thesis even comprises the implication that, insofar as Freud's work is civilizatory, it too is a dynamic of fascism.

Transcendental Deduction of Psychoanalysis

The Authoritarian Personality is a psychoanalytic study, shaped throughout by psychoanalytic concerns, but the place of psychoanalysis in the research is not simple or to be presumed. Of the four major researchers, Else Frenkel-Brunswick's chapters demonstrate the one outstandingly developed psychoanalytic capacity, though the others were impressively capable. Adorno himself was no doubt broadly prepared for the project; he apparently knew the entire corpus of Freud's writings viscerally and sometimes page by page. He was one of the earliest philosophers of the twentieth century to develop a body of thought that is inextricably entwined with psychoanalytic reflection—its interpretive style, insights, and conceptual models. On emigrating to the United States where he would join Paul Lazarsfeld's radio research project, Adorno even claimed on his curriculum vitae to be a "psychoanalytical researcher." Yet Adorno had no psychoanalytical training whatsoever and would never have accepted supervised training in the field. Neither did he have any experience of psychoanalysis himself, which he also would have vehemently refused unless it were a chance to pretend to be the analyst. There is only counterevidence in his oeuvre to any psychoanalytic interest in his own psychical life. Apart from the epitomization of the profundity of childhood, he rarely reflects on the reality of his earliest years except to note the disturbance to that kingdom by bullies and the velocity of his precocity. And whereas the whole of Freud's psychological discoveries was developed on the basis of the interpretation of dreams, the collection of dreams that Adorno self-consciously prepared for posthumous publication uses dreams for anything but psychological reflection. His dream depositions, said to have been transcribed spontaneously on awakening, are masterpieces of spontaneous secondary elaboration in which the author severs his visions from possible psychological inquiry. The one remark, for instance, that Adorno attaches to a dream—in which Jürgen Habermas warns him that cancer could result from his seeking to "surrender inwardly to whatever moved" him—is that Habermas's inhibitedness may have been the result of psychoanalytic treatment. So much for latent and manifest content. If every dream contains its own interpretation, only the dreamer holds the key, which Adorno stringently withholds. This is not possibly the thinking of a psychoanalytically trained researcher. In *Minima Moralia*, Adorno raises the ante considerably on his characterization of the inhibiting aspect of psychoanalytic treatment, which he considered invidious to human autonomy, and associates it with the authoritarianism of the fascist imagination as a regnum of nosological pronouncement.[8]

Though Adorno nevertheless made considerable use of it, and his work is densely replete with psychological observation, often acute, he considered psychoanalysis something properly done unto others, not unto oneself—though without that there is no psychoanalysis. When he questions in "On Popular Music" whether the "whole psychoanalytic distinction between the conscious and the unconscious is still justified" (Adorno 2008b: 307), one wonders whether he had ever had any experience at all of the realities he speculates on cavalierly. He is so emphatic in his criticism of psychoanalysis in passages in *Minima Moralia* that were written in the context of the years while he was working with the Berkeley scientists that one no less wonders how he was able to participate in the psychoanalytic project of *The Authoritarian Personality*. The answer is that when Adorno did psychoanalysis unto others, it was not always that psychoanalytical. The essay Adorno wrote in the same years as the Berkeley project, "Stravinsky or Reaction"—the counterfigure to the "Schoenberg or Progress" essay in the *Philosophy of New Music*—is condensedly illuminating. In this work, Adorno develops a diagnostic psychoanalytic typology of severe mental illness—hebephrenia, catatonia, psychosis, and depersonalization—that is largely homologous with the use of "paranoia" in "Elements of Anti-Semitism." In this latter instance, Adorno wants to use the psychoanalytic model of paranoia to show how the anti-Semite is prohibited from any possible cognition of the object itself and instead develops a destructive hatred of the object that is projected in its stead, a phantasm of the denied development of the mimetic impulse for the object. In the Stravinsky essay, the blunt nosology of severe mental disturbance becomes, correlatively, an analysis of techniques of bad composition. Here Adorno's study means to analyze motivic and technical elements in Stravinsky's music that delineate its failure to achieve the autonomous compositional work of Schoenberg at its most successful. Aesthetic success or failure—a capacity for the object itself that Adorno characterizes as political progress or reaction—hinges, in Stravinsky's instance, on psychological debilitation. The analysis, however, does not concern the empirical Stravinsky, either psychologically or politically. Adorno makes the distinction explicit. The idea of psychoanalyzing Stravinsky himself, or considering his political stance as if it defined his aesthetic labor, would to Adorno have been a travesty of aesthetics. On the contrary, in this instance and characteristically, he uses psychoanalytic concepts to comprehend what is interposed between subject and object in their differentiation that objectively incapacitates autonomous composition. It is the block, not the individual, that Adorno wants to interpret. While bearing the closest resemblance to psychoanalysis, it is as if psychological defense mechanisms have become elements of objective spirit in an objectless world.

Psychoanalytic concepts allow Adorno to speculate on how these mechanisms, functions of the block—of a society built on the principle of exchange—result in objectively motivated pathic projections that all the same seem to be those of an omnipotent subjectivity (Cavalleto 2016: 261). Adorno might have used Freud to naturalize Kant, but the intention is the other way around. Freud is being translated, sometimes broadly, sometimes in detail, into epistemological elements with meta-epistemological intention. In part 3 of *The Authoritarian Personality*, "Qualitative Studies in Ideology," which he calls a phenomenology, Adorno begins by carrying out what is effectively a transcendental analysis of the constitution of the ethnocentric object. Just as Adorno had some years earlier analyzed the techniques of popular music for presenting stereotypical objects as if they were singular occurrences (Adorno 2008b: 468), here he presents the subjective conditions for the existence of what is a kind of stereotypically hallucinated object as if it were an individual: "The Jew must be tangible, but not too tangible; he must be historically plausible and defined in rigid and well known stereotypes; he must have features that harmonize with destructive tendencies, including clannishness, weakness and masochism" (Adorno et al. 1950: 608). The object is constituted whole cloth and without any relation to the Jew per se. Adorno presents confirmation for the constituted nature of the object in explaining that it has only a "functional" existence: it provides a beacon of orientation "in a cold, alienated and largely ununderstandable world" (608–11). The thesis, at this point, has become a hybrid of pragmatic psychology and Marxist existentialism; it is not at all psychoanalytic. Then Adorno appends the thesis to psychoanalysis almost as an afterthought:

When the prejudiced person experiences the inevitable conflict between the stereotypy of the constituted object and real experience, the conflict is resolved in favor of the anti-Semite's unconscious wishes and destructiveness (608–11).

This helps explain how Adorno was able to consider himself a psychoanalytic researcher and participate in a psychoanalytic study while working in substantially different terms in *The Authoritarian Personality* to translate psychological realities into epistemological structures that can be criticized as elements of the representational mind. The thinking is brilliant and illuminatingly profound and some part of this world. But while employing psychoanalytic concepts with facility, though with limited psychoanalytic experience of the concepts, Adorno excludes much of what psychoanalysis recognizes as psychical life. The complexity of the problem of tolerating reality and taking it in, of being able to use one's capacity to think, is endlessly more intricate than Adorno was wanting to suppose. There are schematic statements about childhood, but not much understanding of it. In the name of psychoanalysis—and in claims in *The Authoritarian Personality* such as that psychological compulsivity is what sociologists call reification (Adorno et al. 1950: 487)—he explores in order to encapsulate and in a sense extract a dimension of life that it was psychoanalysis's revolutionary achievement to have discerned. Adorno even means to draw psychology itself, as any kind of human reality, and psychoanalysis altogether into the form of his metacritique of epistemology and with startling implications. In "Freudian Theory and the Pattern of Fascist Propaganda," Adorno writes at one point that it is *"not an overstatement"* to say that Freud's *Group Psychology and the Analysis of the Ego "clearly foresaw"* on a theoretical level the rise of fascism, as by a kind of psychoanalytical second sight (1982: 120; my emphasis). The surprising thesis, on which Adorno builds his entire essay, demands a duplicitous rhetoric: the only reason the author has for saying that the statement is "not an overstatement" is that it so obviously is just that, and the recognition must be closely parried and normalized. That is the role of the *"clearly"* in the *"clearly foresaw"* as if every doubt has already been dismissed. Adorno goes on to potentiate the enchantment and invokes with apparent esteem Freud's *"clairvoyance"* in having foreseen the rise of fascism. But, as may be sensed, this is not altogether a compliment to the magisterial psychologist. For as Adorno develops his thesis, Freud's unconscious second sight serves to identify his *Group Psychology* whole cloth and summarily with the emergence of fascism. This places Freud, the seer, in the grip of a much greater sorcerer, the one who knows the magic, who at the same time is seeking to envelop

Freud's theory of dreams and the unconscious itself into the cunning of history. The compliment to the psychologist thus turns out to be drastically backhanded. After admiring Freud in *Group Psychology* for "restricting himself to the field of individual psychology," this restriction turns out to be fatal to psychoanalysis itself. For, as Adorno continues, shifting the terrain entirely to a rationalistic philosophical reason, the "so-called psychology of fascism is itself largely engendered by manipulation," by rational fascist devices, and this can only be understood by "an explicit theory of society, by far transcending the range of psychology." Any claim that fascism is a psychological reality is itself "essentially fascistic." For fascism "is *not* a psychological issue and any attempt to understand its roots and its historical role in psychological terms still remains on the level of ideologies such as the one of 'irrational forces' promoted by fascism itself" (135).

Adorno would have discredited himself fundamentally had he developed these thoughts to claim that Freud and psychical life itself—a phrase Adorno never uses—are by this same measure fascist. And Adorno succeeds at not drawing the conclusions he has implied. Instead, he finishes the essay by once again appropriating the force of psychoanalysis for his own thesis. Freud, we learn, now vanquished, did not consider psychology—which in psychoanalysis means psychical life—an inherent aspect of humanity. We know this of Freud because, Adorno claims, Freud held that *id should become ego*. If something seems to have gone wrong with the byword, something has, and it must be fully read, fully to be disbelieved: "For Freud the concept of psychology is essentially a negative one. He defines the realm of psychology by the supremacy of the unconscious and postulates that what is id should become ego. The emancipation of man from the heteronomous rule of his unconscious would be tantamount to the abolition of his 'psychology'" (Adorno 1982, 136).[9] The inversion is exciting, perhaps, but one might not want to try it out any too soon; that would be Timothy Leary avant la lettre, even if this is not at all what Adorno intended. Adorno's understanding of Freud, at this point, seems either undiscerningly faulty or intellectually opportunistic. For, in his well-known image, Freud conceived of the ego as "riding" the id, an image and concept of the ego that Adorno's thesis makes senseless. It is hard to believe that even Adorno could believe what he was developing in this essay—there must be more to it—and it plainly weighs on him when he himself is motivated to wonder in the name of the reader: "One may ask: why is the applied group psychology [Freud's] discussed here peculiar to fascism rather than to most other movements that seek mass support?" He lets that same prying reader—who happens to be an aspect of himself held at a distance—know in the very next phrase that the question is naive: "Even the most casual comparison of fascist propaganda with that of liberal [propaganda] . . . will show this to be so" (136). And if, as said, there must be more to this reasoning than appears, it can be recognized that the idea of life without psychology emancipated for the object itself coheres with all of Adorno's unbelievables, the thesis of life uninterrupted, the thesis of life without suffering, and the cornucopia of nature reborn out of the messianic landscape, as a kind of philosophical civil religion, as objects of devotion in the austerities of a strictly negative philosophy dug in, heels first, in desperate opposition to a fascist nation sworn to murder and death equally surpassing belief (Ziemer 1941).

It would be possible to mock the sacraments of this civil religion if in Real Time it did not make one catch one's own breath reading Adorno's thesis, in which he effectively summarized the experience of National Socialism, that "we have forgotten how to wish" (Adorno 2007: 7). For the temporality of Real Time is marked out most of all by the vanishment of any envisionable posterity, within some thirty years, even of flying insects.[10] And if there is no posterity, there is nothing at all to wish for, which is the felt desperation in the velocity without movement that is Real Time. As Senator Bob Corker wrote in an uncannily unidiomatic phrase of the unprecedented despoilation of the future that is now being planned between Congress and the executive branch in negotiations over tax reform, "It's party like there's no tomorrow time in Washington" (Kaplan 2017). It may soon be another victory in the Capital of the enraged. The self-invited have been so humiliatingly cheated out of what they never really had in the first place, that—were foresight any part of their calculations—it would seem that the single pleasure they might claim in their triumph is in at least making sure that there will be no others. Senator Corker's "no tomorrow time" is writ large in crooked letters, as if in a language already being forgotten.

The Uninterpretation of Dreams

In *Minima Moralia*, Adorno writes that "horror is beyond the reach of psychology" (Adorno 1974: 164). Adorno may be correct in this; in a sense, and urgently, I think he is. The apothegm defines in the negative a capacity of his work that is distinct from psychology and the import that it bears. But in whatever regard Adorno is correct in his thesis, in whatever way Real Time is not in psychology's purview—not as such—Adorno would be pitifully wrong, and he was, in imagining that his own capacity for self-relinquishing

experience was more capable than that of psychoanalysts to relinquish themselves to reality, to that of their patients and their struggle for autonomy and
what certainly can be the horror of their lives. This is part of every psycho-
analyst's practice, not to mention in continuing to work with generations of
holocaust survivors and their progeny, but in what is a degree of horror in
every childhood, however fortunate. If horror were beyond 'psychology,'
Freud's (1950: 187) thesis that psychoanalysis has "no other end in view than
to throw light on things by tracing what is manifest back to what is hidden"
would be a fraud. It turns out—and it is a considerable puzzle—that a listening acuity for music and literature, such as Adorno demonstrates at the high-
est degree and that is the motivic impulse for the whole of his work and his
philosophical labor's capacity for historical perception—gives little indication of an individual's capacity to listen to someone else or know what is
being said. The former capacity—for art—and what may well be its over-
whelming intensities can develop in opposition to the latter, and with great
success occlude it entirely, along with any chance of ever knowing what has
been missed.

In the thesis that "horror is beyond the reach of psychology," it could
not occur to Adorno, a mind otherwise alert to every potential inversion—
even of ego and id—to consider the implication that psychology may, by that
same measure, be beyond the reach of critical philosophy. This inference
was not a detail that Adorno somehow overlooked amid much else. His philosophy in its entirety, its language of suffering, depends on this omission,
which Hegel might have termed *dogmatic* except for that it itself—this specific lack of reflection—is a dogmatic aspect of Hegel's own philosophy. As
Dieter Henrich (2008, 291) has noted, absolute idealism means an idealism
not founded on the mental. It is as a function of this aspect of absolute idealism that Adorno's work develops as a voice of history. His philosophy poten-
tiates the incapacity of the Hegelian dialectic for mental activity, which is
necessarily inclusive of the psychical life that is the object of psychoanalytic
thought. Hegel had no other way to solve the question of the representational
mind, the diremption of subject and object, the thing-in-itself, than to make
subjectivity the movement of the *concept* as the direct inheritance of Kant's
unity of apperception, which became *Geist* itself—though not as any individual's mind. That individual mind, in the psychoanalytic sense, does not
and cannot exist in Hegel's thinking. On no other basis than the radical
reduction of the individual's mental activity, with some amendment for subjective reason, could Hegel have posited that the "whole is the true."
Adorno—in propounding this same thesis in the form of the statement that

the "whole is the untrue," that the unifying power of mind itself is the
process of the domination of nature—effectively mobilized the philosophy
of mediation as the dynamic of what befalls the individual as well as the
whole of nature. It is complex, to say the least: the philosophy could not more
emphatically seek subjective emancipation as a capacity for unreduced experience. It is contrary to Hegel, in alliance with him, that Adorno develops
Hegel's thought as a *via negativa*, as a possibility for the actual spontaneity of
subjectivity, and developed a critique of psychoanalysis that wanted to sup-
plement and perhaps supplant libido theory with mimetic behavior. This
is why the austerity of his philosophical voice is so unmistakably his voice.
In a phrase that could be psychoanalytic—and is and then again is not—
Adorno's form of interpretation is an attention to "what falls mute" as memory of nature in a subject that has been excluded from history by the only
movement that history is capable of: the telos of its own autonomy as the labor
of those whose mental activity, here a synonym for life, is remaindered by it.

Hegel's historically affirmative dialectic was thus transformed into an
allegorical, a gutting dialectic. The transformation made it an instrument
for immanently assessing the weight of history. In Walter Benjamin's (1998:
166) terms, in which this dialectic also originates, it became a potential for
expressing the *facies hippocratica* of history—the Hippocratic visage, the
mortally suffering face—as the *trend* of history. The demands of this allegorical stance, however, are inimical to the psychoanalytic development of
symbolic interpretation and the actual psychodynamical contents of mental
life, at considerable interpretive loss. In his many volumes Adorno's work
may be difficult and challenging and studded at every turn with invocations
of the primordia of spells, taboos, and fetishes. But there is nothing whatever
in it, not on any single page, no single line, that is as taboo and fraught as are
the contents of any single psychoanalytic hour which, to exist, requires so
extraordinary a degree of confidentiality for that to be said which a patient
would never even dare, or be able to tell himself, not in a lifetime. As Lou
Andreas-Salomé (1994: 97) summarizes, "this is why Freud was so thoroughly disliked when he pointed out the significance of the infantile stages
of our entire spiritual life. . . . As a result of which it becomes necessary to
return to these beginnings in therapy; the most *primitive* state in individual
spiritual experience . . . the *primal* level which always remains within us."

Thus for its discoveries psychoanalysis became the object of prejudice—even, as Freud well knew, as the science of prejudice, the necessary
object and straw man in waiting of any possible prejudice[11]—and for just this
reason it is an unparalleled resource for understanding the nature of ethno-

centric prejudice itself, still to be developed in a way that might be tolerably known. To date, however, it remains "the old joke about the psychoanalyst who wonders what his doorman really meant when he said 'Good morning'" (Rose 2010: 8). An old joke. The tomato aimed at the analyst hits the doorman. The purpose of his reassuringly perfunctory life is reduced to a ditty: he must not have one more thought of his own than the speaker of the witticism wants to disown. There is exactly as much fun here as in having a partially psychotic president that the nation is terrified of removing from office, since this would require recognizing as real the psychological as the primal in us. It is in this sense that "America now exists primarily in order not to know what it is thinking." Better to stand directly in the path of catastrophe than acknowledge what everyone on some level knows perfectly well anyway.

Though fundamentally distinct, Adorno's participation in this prejudice in his failure to reflect on what critical philosophy cannot reach in 'psychology' was of a part with his thinking as it developed into a jargon of suffering. In spite of itself, "horror" and "suffering" at moments in his writings acquire a luxurious aspect, as if these emphatic statements have something else on their mind that they enjoy not quite saying. However mobile the dialectic, it is too pat in its own conception, by its own concept. What it finds needs to be found, but of all that it finds, which is magnitudes more than considerable, it finally always finds the same thing. In another of Adorno's dream depositions, a psychotherapist is giving a grotesquely off-key lecture on Schubert. Adorno is "overcome by an insensate fury." He harangues the listening audience around him with "the argument that this performance was so barbaric that it turned anyone who tolerated it into a barbarian as well. My eloquence did not go unheeded." The audience clubs together with Adorno, and they beat the psychotherapist to death. At that moment, Adorno writes, as if to prove the intolerance of his dream censor with bad aesthetics, "I became so agitated that I awoke" (Adorno 2007: 68–69). This dream is itself a kind of witticism, immune as dreams often are to their own humor. It will not occur to this dreamer, who treats his visions as nocturnal Lares and Penates, that the grotesque lecturer and the lecture as well are aspects of his very own self; not any more than he is prepared to reflect on the self-admiring eloquence of his outcry; let alone on what critical philosophy may be unable to reach in psychology. Dimensions to the known world extraneous to Adorno's philosophy appear when the American poet, Mark Strand, commented on Adorno's dictum—no writing poetry after Auschwitz—that "you can't even eat lunch." One result of the exclusion of these dimensions from Adorno's work is the rigidification that befell critical theory after Adorno, as if to this day he can still only be quoted. The meta-epistemological reduction of psychoanalysis to 'psychology' separated the critique of domination from the many contemporary developments in psychoanalysis, which are internationally exponential and vital compared to the ongoing efforts in critical theory to sort through what Adorno really meant and, often enough, historicize it. But this reduction likewise deprived Adorno's concept of domination from layers of perception that would contribute to its further articulation.

Primitive Thread of Human History

The thread of human history is neither thread nor history. Not a thread, because even though it can be severed, it cannot be stretched from point to point, say, from Rome to Charlemagne. Not history for the same reason in that even when it can be sensed, it is something else than knowledge of the Carthaginians or the seventeenth-century birthdate of Claude Poullart des Places. In calculating all that the thread of human history is not, it must be taken into account that it is not even exactly human. For human must mean all kinds of kidding around, but no angry pushing, no shoving; not to disappoint the United States of America, but it has no need of violence. And, if so, then even in better moments in time—than in Real Time—of which there have been endlessly many, the thread of human history has never been disentwined from the trend of history and thus it has never once been of the human simpliciter. When sensed in its complexity, it is a tracery of impulses suspended between memory and expectation. It is a longing, as if in the perception of these impulses one might know what to do in seeking "to do with something that which most of all can be done with it by its own measure"— as opposed to the contrary, doing what cannot be done with it, by some other measure, as an infliction. In Adorno's idea of composition, as a model, what the composer has to follow is where the notes by their own direction want to go as that which can most of all be done with them. On the part of the composer this requires all possible resistance to where, caught in the trend of history, these impulses would otherwise irretrievably go; that, no less, is what playing an instrument may amount to.

And although psychoanalytic practice is not art in the making, it has—as does Adorno's own "essay as form" (Adorno 1984), which also rejects any claim to being art—an aesthetic element in this same principle of doing with something what most of all can be done with it, by its own measure. When Bernard Bosanquet in *A History of Aesthetic* named this as the central principle of idealism, "that nothing can be made into what it is not capable of being," he touched on an origin common to psychoanalysis as well as to Adorno's philosophy (Bosanquet 2005: 290). Both recognize that only the truth can reconcile, that to be found it must be struggled for and that in doing so what is sought must at every point be inseparable from where its own course leads. It is not method. In the recognition of the primitive in us, the critique of domination that is implicit in this principle became the critique of the primitive from the perspective of the primitive. It traces the manifest back to the latent as to what is archaic and unable to escape its own origin without the interpretation of what falls mute as the intolerable object of what is itself archaic. In this particular context, it may be productively termed *prejudice*. The interpretation is oriented not to the pursuit of happiness but to the gratification of that pursuit in recognizing ourselves in the primitive, not by condescending to it. As understood in both Adorno's and Freud's thinking, this is the single possibility of what might be other than primitive. It is anything but a view of the world as through a telescope. In its immanence, it is not any kind of perspective at all. In the many regards in which this form of insight is ineluctably modern, since its insight is the origin of radical modernism itself, the *primitive* "was the first word in which our modern historical sense finds expression . . . as applied by the Reformers to the early Church" (Pearsall Smith 1912: 227). As the development of the sixteenth-century perception of the depth of history and the desire to recover what has not yet been despoiled, however transformed the concept now is, the primitive is the element of the thread of human history that cannot be calculated out of it any more than out of the trend of history. In this regard, the thread of human history and its trend are indistinguishable.

Historical Trend: Real Time

Adorno and Freud are of a mind in wanting to rescue wish from its barbaric self-destruction. But what unites them here no less serves to divide them as what 'psychology' truly cannot reach. Thus, in the same essay on fascist propaganda that has already been much discussed, Adorno holds fascism most culpable in what he calls "the secret itself of fascist propaganda." The secret amounts to nothing more than what Adorno discerns as the worst, the intention to leave men and women as they are, "largely robbed of autonomy and spontaneity, instead of setting goals the realization of which would transcend the psychological *status quo* no less than the social one" (Adorno 1982: 134). They are abandoned to rage, as Adorno goes on to explain in a phrase from the précis of *The Authoritarian Personality* he sent to Horkheimer at about the same time. "Each is stimulated to boundless outbreaks of wrath because the power that oppresses the barbarian in him is itself barbarism" (20). A variant of this phrase, which would someday appear in one of Adorno's manifestly conceptual dreams, where the thesis would bring psychological reflection to a halt, serves the same purpose here. The rhetoric's negation of negativity, which is itself negation, is considerably more powerful than its reasoning. Whatever may or may not be true in the claim, its compact *force de frappe*, which amounts to its self-evidence, freezes the ability to think at just the point where the complex questions of the reality of psychical life would need to be considered. But where Adorno leaves the psychological behind—as would, he supposes, a better world—is also the point at which the urgent importance of his philosophical labors becomes distinct. As Adorno continues, the individual is provoked to destroy "the very idea of the good," which has been polluted by civilization. His "fury against his oppressors becomes an energy to hate the good" (20). The psychological observation goes beyond psychology in the intention of comprehending the barbarism that Adorno witnessed as the societal destruction of the possibility of the good—the developing incapacity of society to wish the good for itself. Adorno conceives of this developing incapacity as the trend of history.

In *History and Freedom*, one of Adorno's last and most important lecture series, he presents the trend of history as the constantly increasing capacity of rationality, the means-ends power of humanity to preserve itself. It veers toward disaster because it fails to recognize that domination is necessarily bound up with what it dominates and in destroying it, necessarily destroys itself. But why is the heteronomous control of nature unable to reflect on the toll it takes? As often in Adorno's lectures, as in *History and Freedom*, he presents his thesis if not casually, all the same with a degree of informality: "Nowadays, there really is something like a perversion of consciousness, a reversing of what is primary and what is secondary" (18). Because rationality is always expressed in the form of particular interests, the trend of history comes to appear secondary to the apparently spontaneous individual phenomena. We are dragged after the trend of history as what is most acutely felt, while each and all, certain of nothing but of oneself, only function as the particular interests that mask it—as if we will get to the problem of catastrophe once the really important matters have been taken care of. Even the contemporary retort to the election of the new president that "he is not my president" only again serves to mask what this presidency most of all is. That mask is now shattering. In Real Time, the president, in sequentially and immediately destroying what he rules as what we see he plainly depends on, and which at any moment may happen to engulf ourselves and the world as a whole as well, is carrying out in deed the reflection that would otherwise be needed to keep this from happening. Real Time retransforms what was veiled by the particular, the spuriously primary, back into what has every appearance of being the anonymous force of destruction itself. In the words of the National Security Administration operative who railed bitterly that the computer machinery the agency had only recently developed for invading other nations had already been seized and is now being turned back on this nation, "The agency doesn't know how to stop it—or even what 'it' is" (Shane, Perlroth, and Sanger 2017). If there were a way to say, if only to repeat, that without the good, which the United States is now without, there is nothing at all to have, not in any quantity and not of any two people of each other, one would say that. In Real Time, as the wind comes straight and flat across every sea and the birds fall dead out of the sky, authoritarianism now means domination as immediate self-destruction.

Notes

1   In German, Adorno uses the primitive and the archaic frequently throughout his writings and as correlative concepts, more often the former than the latter, with slight degrees of distinction. English usage differs. More to the point here, however, is that during walks in casual conversation with Rolf Tiedemann, Adorno would remark, "See how primitive it is."

2   See Harris 1989; Lindstrom 1990; and Worsely 1987.

3   See Kormann 2018.

4   See Adorno (1982: 125): "The modern leader image sometimes seems to be the enlargement of the subject's own personality."

5   See also *Psychological Issues* 8, no. 3 (1996), monograph 31.

6   See *Psychological Issues*, 9.

7   See Hullot-Kentor 2008 and 2010.

8   While positivists among the Vienna Circle, Adorno's arch contraries, sought to develop a philosophical defense of psychoanalysis, many of Adorno's own attacks on psychoanalysis—even in the context of what may be an ultimate antagonism of philosophy and psychology—might fairly be classed as borderline crackpot. Here he comments on the fate of its patients: "Alienating himself totally from himself, denouncing his autonomy with his unity, psycho-analysis subjugates him totally to the mechanism of rationalization, of adaptation." The ego must "capitulate. The psycho-analyst's wisdom finally becomes what the Fascist unconscious of the horror magazines takes it for: a technique by which one particular racket among others binds suffering and helpless people irrevocably to itself, in order to command and exploit them. . . . What was formerly help through greater knowledge has become the humiliation of others by dogmatic privilege." "Psychology" is "the bottomless fraud of mere inwardness" (see Adorno 1974, 64).

9   Adorno continued to develop this idea into his formulation in *Negative Dialectics* as the "additional—or, needed—impulse"; the thought closely parallels aspects of Freud's model of the drives. Adorno uses 'psychology' as such, in single quotation marks, in "Freudian Psychology and the Pattern of Fascist Propaganda" to denote psychoanalysis though with a somewhat wider range than that. This practice is maintained here whenever *psychology* is being used as Adorno meant it.

10   See McCarthy 2017: "Even the most successful organisms that have ever existed on earth are now being overwhelmed by the titanic scale of the human enterprise."

11   See, characteristically, Crews 2017.

References

Adorno, Theodor W. 1948. "Remarks on The Authoritarian Personality." Page 20. Max Horkheimer Archive at the Universitätsbibliothek, Goethe University, Frankfurt.

Adorno, Theodor W. 1974. *Minima Moralia*. Translated by E. F. N. Jephcott. London: Verso.

Adorno, Theodor W. 1982. "Freudian Theory and the Pattern of Fascist Propaganda." In *The Essential Frankfurt School Reader*, edited by Andrew Arato and Eike Gephardt, 118–37. London: Bloomsbury.

Adorno, Theodor W. 1983. "Cultural Criticism and Society." *Prisms*. Translated by Shierry Weber Nicholsen and Samuel Weber. Cambridge, MA: MIT Press.

Adorno, Theodor W. 1984. "The Essay as Form." Translated by Robert Hullot-Kentor and Frederic Will. *New German Critique* no. 32: 151–71.

Adorno, Theodor W. 1998. *Critical Models*. Translated by Henry W. Pickford. New York: Columbia University Press.

Adorno, Theodor W. 2006. *History and Freedom*. Translated by Rodney Livingstone. Cambridge: Polity Press.

Adorno, Theodor W. 2007. *Dream Notes*. Cambridge: Polity Press.

Adorno, Theodor W. 2008a. "The Idea of Natural-History." In *Things beyond Resemblance*, translated by Robert Hullot-Kentor, 252–69. New York: Columbia University Press.

Adorno, Theodor W. 2008b. "On Popular Music." In *Current of Music*, edited by Robert Hullot-Kentor, 307. Cambridge: Polity Press.

Adorno, Theodor W., Else Frenkel-Brunswik, Daniel J. Levinson, and R. Nevitt Sanford. 1950. *The Authoritarian Personality*. New York: Harper and Row.

Anderson, Elizabeth S. 2017. *Private Government: How Employers Rule Our Lives*. Princeton, NJ: Princeton University Press.

Andreas-Salomé, Lou. 1994. *Looking Back: Memoirs*. Cambridge, MA: Da Capo Press.

Benjamin, Walter. 1998. *The Origin of German Tragic Drama*. London: Verso.

Bosanquet, Bernard. 2005. *A History of Aesthetic*. New York: Cosimo Classics.

Cavalleto, George. 2016. *Crossing the Psychosocial Divide: Freud, Weber, Adorno, and Elias*. Abingdon, UK: Routledge.

Crews, Frederick. 2017. *Freud: The Making of an Illusion*. New York: Metropolitan Books.

Frenkel-Brunswik, Else. 1974. *Selected Papers*. Edited by Nanette Heiman and Joan Grant. Madison, CT: International Universities Press.

Freud, Sigmund. 1950. "On the Universal Tendency to Debasement in the Sphere of Love." In Vol. 18 of *The Complete Psychological Works of Sigmund Freud*, translated by James Strachey. London: Hogarth Press.

Fritzsche, Peter, and Jochen Hellbeck. 2008. *Beyond Totalitarianism: Stalinism and Nazism Compared*. Edited by Michael Geyer and Sheilah Fitzpatrick, 302–44. Cambridge: Cambridge University Press.

Geyer, Michael. 1987. "The Nazi State Reconsidered." In *Life in the Third Reich*, edited by Richard Bessel, 57–67. Oxford: Oxford University Press.

Haberman, Maggie, and Glenn Thrush. 2017a. "Trump, Saying He Is Treated 'Unfairly,' Signals a Fight." *New York Times*, May 17.

Haberman, Maggie, and Glenn Thrush. 2017b. "Trump Called National Park Chief over Twitter Post on Inaugural Crowd." *New York Times*, January 26.

Harris, Marvin. 1989. *Cows, Pigs, Wars, and Witches: The Riddles of Culture*. New York: Vintage.

Henrich, Dieter. 2008. *Between Kant and Hegel: Lectures on German Idealism*. Cambridge, MA: Harvard University Press.

Horkheimer, Max, and Theodor W. Adorno. 2007. *Dialectic of Enlightenment*. Translated by Edmund Jephcott, edited by Gunzelin Schmid Noerr. Stanford, CA: Stanford University Press.

Hullot-Kentor, Robert. 2008. "A New Type of Human Being and Who We Really Are." *Brooklyn Rail*, November 10.

Hullot-Kentor, Robert. 2010. "What Barbarism Is?" *Brooklyn Rail*, February 3.

Kagan, Robert. 2016. "This Is How Fascism Comes to America." *Washington Post*, May 18.

Kaplan, Thomas. 2017. "White House Requests More Disaster Aid but Also Seeks Cuts as Deficits Rise." *New York Times*, November 17.

Kopstein, Jeffrey, and Mark Lichbach. 2000. *Comparative Politics*. Cambridge: Cambridge University Press.

Kormann, Carolyn. 2018. "Climate Change and the Giant Iceberg off Greenland's Shore." *New Yorker*, July 20.

Lindstrom, Lamont. 1990. "Big Men as Ancestors: Inspiration and Copyrights on Tanna (Vanuatu)." *Ethnology* 29, no. 4: 313–26.

Luce, Edward. 2016. "American Democracy's Gravest Trial." *Financial Times*, November 7.

McCarthy, Michael. 2017. "A Giant Insect Ecosystem Is Collapsing due to Humans. It's a Catastrophe. *Guardian*, October 21.

Nisbett, Richard E., and Dov Cohen. 1996. *Culture of Honor: The Psychology of Violence in the South*. Boulder, CO: Westview Press.

Pearsall Smith, Logan. 1912. *The English Language*. New York: Henry Holt.

Perlroth, Nicole, and Scott Shane. 2017. "How Israel Caught Russian Hackers Scouring the World for U.S. Secrets." *New York Times*, October 10.

Poniewozik, James. 2017. "Mr. Reality TV Goes to Washington." *New York Times*, January 20.

Risen, James, and Sheri Fink. 2017. "Trump Said 'Torture Works.' An Echo Is Feared Worldwide." *New York Times*, January 5.

Rose, Jonathan. 2010. *The Intellectual Life of the British Working Classes*. New Haven, CT: Yale University Press.

Shane, Scott, Nicole Perlroth, and David E. Sanger. 2017. "Security Breach and Spilled Secrets Have Shaken the N.S.A. to Its Core." *New York Times*, November 12.

Shear, Michael D., and Maggie Haberman. 2017. "Trump Called National Park Chief over Twitter Post on Inaugural Crowd." *New York Times*, January 26.

Stokols, Eli. 2016. "Unapologetic, Trump Promises to Make America Rich." *Politico*, May 26.

Tocqueville, Alexis de. 2003. "Two Weeks in the Wilderness." In *Democracy in America—and Two Essays on America*, translated by Gerald E. Bevan. London: Penguin.

Tocqueville, Alexis de. 2006. *Democracy in America*. Translated by George Lawrence. New York: Harper Perennial.

Trump, Donald. 2016. "Read the Transcript of Donald Trump's Speech at the Al Smith Dinner." *Time*, October 21.

Worsely, Peter. 1987. *The Trumpet Shall Sound: A Study of "Cargo" Cults in Melanesia*. New York: Schocken.

Ziemer, Gregor. 1941. *Education for Death*. Oxford: Oxford University Press.

Benjamin Y. Fong

The Psychic Makeup of
the New Anthropological Type

In what seems now to be something of a prelude to the present special issue, Peter Gordon revisited *The Authoritarian Personality* in an important work of clarification in the summer of 2016, just as Americans began pinching themselves in the hope that the Trump phenomenon was indeed a dream and not a new political reality. Gordon's (2017) primary contribution lay in illuminating a basic tension between Theodor Adorno and his collaborators on the project, R. Nevitt Sanford, Else Frenkel-Brunswik, and Daniel Levinson: while the other authors aimed to delineate a distinctively authoritarian type—a social product, no doubt, but a pathological one—Adorno, having "identified stereotypical thinking and authoritarianism with general features of the modern social order itself," understood the high-scoring individual on the F-scale (measuring fascist tendencies) as an "emergent social norm."[1] At stake here is the difference between seeing "Trumpism" as "the fascism of a personality type" and viewing it rather as "the political consequence of a mediatized public sphere in which politics in the substantive sense is giving way to the commodification of politics" (Gordon 2017). Gordon is undoubtedly right that the latter view is the more accurate one, and

The South Atlantic Quarterly 117:4, October 2018
DOI 10.1215/00382876-7165845 © 2018 Duke University Press

thus that references to the "authoritarian personality," the "new anthropological type," and the "new type of human being" in the works of the Frankfurt
School are best understood as attempts to delimit an emergent norm rather
than a psychological type, but he enters troubling territory when he wonders
aloud "whether the 'mind' remains a useful category of political analysis,"
and thus if psychoanalytic categories are still of any help in making sense of
the new types of human being that we all, in theory, at least partially are.

As this essay is a critique and extension of the Frankfurt School's use
of *the mind* as a category of political analysis, I want first to address Gordon's
skepticism about the continued relevance of psychoanalysis, one that is quite
common today. I will admit from the outset to being someone who finds in
psychoanalysis something I am not able to find elsewhere, ways of making
sense of and living in capitalist modernity that are not just relevant but
essential, but for my present purposes, I do not believe I need any external
justification for the relevance of psychoanalysis here, and for two reasons.
First, while the thinkers of the Frankfurt School certainly understood the
emergence of the "new anthropological type" and the "Obsolescence of the
Freudian Concept of Man" (the title of an essay by Marcuse) as a major turn
in Western capitalism, they did not conceive of this shift as a total epistemic
break, as if the coordinates of subjectivity were thrown in the air and rear-
ranged in bizarre and totally new ways. They rather saw the old anthropological type—let's say, the repressed bourgeois subject of the nineteenth century, the kind that would end up on Freud's couch—and the new
anthropological type—the less repressed and less reflective subject born of
the Fordist-Keynesian era—as possessing many common features, none
more important than the fact that they are both capitalist subjects.[2] For making it seem as if returning to the psychoanalytic mind today is like trying to
revive phlogiston theories after Antoine-Laurent Lavoisier, Adorno would
accuse Gordon of obscuring the important continuity between the old and
new anthropological types.

Second, I follow Gillian Rose (1976: 74) in thinking that any claims to
"completeness" in Adorno—and these include those pertaining to an "end
of the individual," an "end of subjectivity," and a "total reification"—must be
understood as attempting to "induce in his reader the development of the
latent capacity for non-identity thought." If society and individual subjectivity were both "totally reified," Rose argues, there would be no critical consciousness capable of understanding the thesis of total reification. One
might say that until Adorno becomes not just partly but completely unintel-
ligible, there is still hope "to prevent the complete reification which is immi-

nent" (74). Applied to the present case, this means that the crisis of subjectivity theorized by the Frankfurt School is an unstable moment of transition between types, not the wholesale replacement of the old by the new. In some of his recent work, Adorno translator and interpreter Robert Hullot-Kentor (2008) has suggested we give up the old project of cultivating critical individuals and embrace "who we really are": that is, new anthropological types, brutally instrumental and unthinking, but nonetheless capable of blunt and primitive resistance. Usefully provocative as this statement is, it assumes that we are already the kind of people who can only misunderstand Adorno (and perhaps this is, in the end, Hullot-Kentor's point). If we are going to continue on in good faith, however, I believe it makes sense to understand both ourselves and the new kinds of capitalist subjects theorized by the Frankfurt School as somewhere *between* the old and new anthropological types, in transition like Nietzsche's tightrope walker but headed in a direction no more salutary than its opposite.

In brief, not only do the worlds of the old and new anthropological types share important features, but we have not passed definitively from one to the other. It is for both of these reasons that the Frankfurters thought it necessary not to do away with psychoanalysis but to show how the psyche has changed in psychoanalytic terms, how the dynamics of the psyche as theorized by Freud had come undone using Freud's theories. In short, the idea that psychoanalysis has become obsolete is a reflection of an inadequate understanding of the historical transition that the critical theorists were attempting to articulate. For the Frankfurt School, but certainly not them alone, Freud's is a death that keeps on giving (Schechter 2014: 21).

Ego Weakness

Although the authoritarian personality is described in multiple ways, *ego weakness* is the central psychoanalytic term that characterizes the type as a whole. Adorno and his collaborators (1950: 234) find ego weakness "in such phenomena as opposition to introspection, in superstition and stereotypy, and in overemphasis upon the ego and its supposed strength." It is "expressed in the inability to build up a consistent and enduring set of moral values within the personality," which they take to be responsible for the three primary characteristics of the authoritarian personality, "conventionalism, authoritarian submission, and authoritarian aggression" (234, 233). At one time or another, they link all nine characteristics of the authoritarian personality to ego weakness, and thus it is reasonable to assume that the new anthropological type was defined in their minds as the kind of person with a weak ego.[3]

The designation *ego weakness* was an established term in psychoanalytic theory by the time Adorno and company latched onto it as a synonym for authoritarianism. In a short paper from 1938, "Ego Strength and Ego Weakness," Otto Fenichel (1954) defines a weak ego as one that is anxious, defensive, and generally unable to undergo psychoanalysis. A strong ego, by contrast, is one that is able to tolerate exposure to vulnerability and injurability, one that is reflective and emotionally capable. As Eli Zaretsky (2015: 147) argues forcefully in his recent *Political Freud*, this is a lesson that ought to be remembered today to combat the caricatured version of the psychoanalytic ego that is too often trotted out by postmodern critics as evidence of psychoanalysis's supposed normative preference for rigid autonomy and obsessive mastery. Ego strength, in other words, is primarily about analyzability, the capacity to be vulnerable and reflective enough to profit from psychoanalytic interpretations.

That being said, the criterion of analyzability bore a sordid history in American ego psychology, the dominant form of psychoanalysis in America at the time of the publication of *The Authoritarian Personality*. As the ego psychologist Kurt Eissler (1953: 121–22) explains in an infamous paper from 1953, "The Effect of the Structure of the Ego on Psychoanalytic Technique," a normal, strong ego is one that "would guarantee unswerving loyalty to the analytic compact"; "it surrenders, so to speak, to the voice of reason." The weak-egoed patient, by contrast, who needs "more warmth, reassurance, or direction from the doctor," "behaves like someone who has in his grasp all the riches of the world but who refused to take them and must be forced to do so"; that is, forced to do so outside of the psychoanalytic setting, with more forceful and directive means (Schechter 2014: 43; Eissler 1953: 116). To translate these claims into practical terms: patients who do not treat their psychiatrist as a beneficent voice of reason have weak egos, are "regressed in their real-life functioning," and, on account of their inability to submit to a "therapeutic alliance," should be seen by lesser mental health professionals such as psychologists, social workers, and counselors (Schechter 2014: 43–44). Though ego strength in the broadest sense always signified openness and relatability, in 1950 it was an openness and relatability *to* and *as defined by* a narrow-minded psychiatric elite.

The problem here, in other words, is that Adorno and company's primary characterization of the authoritarian personality was defined by a psychoanalytic establishment that was itself authoritarian. It is safe to presume that the patient who was "unswervingly loyal" to a doctor considered to possess "all the riches of the world" would have been a high-scorer on the F-scale, and yet this is precisely the kind of person that Eissler describes as having a strong ego. Of course, one could always argue that Adorno was wresting a perfectly good term away from its corruptors—and his generally dire assessment of the American psychoanalytic scene would support this reading—but my suspicion is that he was unwittingly colluding with an ego psychology regime that was already beginning to crumble for its arrogance. In any event, the primary reason to reconsider this term *ego weakness* is not its history but rather its being descriptively off the mark—at worst wholly misleading, and at best too general to capture the specific idiosyncracies of the new anthropological type. This history is only briefly mentioned here as a spur in that direction.

The Problem with Overgrown Children

In the ego psychologist's view, the weak-egoed are to be understood as regressed in their personality, having avoided the difficult transition from the pleasure principle to the reality principle, and thus enslaved to their own wild fantasies. The high-scorer on the F-scale is also described as regressed, caught in what Melanie Klein would call the paranoid-schizoid position and prey to simple, stereotypical thinking and childish superstition, and perhaps with the Left's stereotyped Trump supporter in mind,[4] one might think that Adorno did indeed have the right psychoanalytic term for the authoritarian personality. I will call this understanding of the new anthropological type the *overgrown child* model, according to which the new emergent type of human being is simply a child in an adult's body. This model offers an initially plausible and attractive interpretation of the hypothesis of the new anthropological type. As cultural theorist Shane Gunster (2004: 53) presents it, the culture industry encourages its subjects to give in to "the ever-present temptation of regressing to a state where the basic desires for libidinal gratification—which are never eliminated, only disciplined—once again take control," and it is this socially organized regression that is responsible for the emergence of the new anthropological type. If the Trump supporter does not satisfy, one might also turn to the example of those unthinking millennials immersed in entertainment and social media, "split between the prescribed fun which is supplied to them by the culture industry and a not particularly well-hidden doubt about its blessings. . . . Without admitting it they sense that their lives would be completely intolerable as soon as they no longer clung to satisfactions which are none at all" (Adorno 1991: 103). These last lines were written by Adorno about American consumers in the 1960s, but they are no less apt today. In this view, the culture industry traps us in a web of childish satisfaction, unconscious self-hatred, and a general fear about losing the very fantasies that debilitate us.

The overgrown child model finds great support in Adorno's call for an "education to maturity," which is described in disarmingly straightforward terms in a conversation with Hellmut Becker. Adorno and Becker (1983: 109) envision

> attending commercial films in high school (but in the grammar schools, too) and quite simply showing to the students what a fraud they are, how full of lies, etc., or in the same way immunizing them against certain Sunday morning radio programs that play happy and carefree music, as if we were still living in a "healthy world" (a term that gives true cause for alarm); or reading a magazine with them and showing them how they are being taken for a ride by an exploitation of their own instinctual needs. . . . Thus, one simply tries first of all to arouse the awareness that men and women are constantly being deceived, for the idea that "the world wants to be deceived," applied globally, has become the mechanism of immaturity today.

If the emerging types of human beings are overgrown children, it is because they are not educated to insulate themselves properly from the mechanisms that insist upon their immaturity; thus the need for historically specific pedagogical countermeasures that would allow us to grow up and "glimpse a chance of maturity" (Adorno 1991: 197).

The obverse of the claim that new anthropological types have weak egos is thus that they have developmentally inappropriate id strength, a primary process that has not given way to a secondary process, a pleasure principle that has not ceded to a reality principle. Although there is much that is appealing and applicable about this overgrown child—which we might now call an *overgrown id*—model of the new anthropological type, it fails to capture many particularities that are central to Adorno's understanding of the reified thinking of pseudoculture. For one, Adorno and colleagues (1950: 232) make it clear that the authoritarian personality is a product of a repressive culture, having "been forced to give up basic pleasures and to live under a system of rigid restraints." Indeed, it is an overriding concern of the Frankfurt School as a whole to demonstrate that the pleasures allowed by the culture industry are gratifications of "false needs," those whose "satisfaction provide[s] momentary pleasure [and which] perpetuate a system whose continuation impedes the fulfillment of individual and social needs and potentials" (Kellner 1984: 244). As Adorno (1994: 459) puts it, with his characteristic concision, happiness today is "to actual happiness what unemployment is to the abolition of work."

One does not need to stomach the strong version of the culture industry thesis—that the pleasures it offers are wholly "false," unreal in some way—to accept the basic idea these pleasures serve to ameliorate the alienation of living in capitalist society, and thus to wonder about the adequacy of the overgrown id model. In a way, it is an insult to children to compare their pleasures to the poor imitations of the new types of human beings, who are not in blind pursuit of pleasure but rather immunizing themselves against an alienating world with small doses of prepackaged pleasure.

That the pleasure of the culture industry is a calculated pleasure, and one that should not interfere with wage labor, touches upon a point that is of even more concern for the overgrown id model: as prone as they are to wild fantasy and superstition, new anthropological types are also remarkably efficient executors of instrumental reason. If, as Freud says in many places, the ego's primary function is "reality-testing," the making of the existing world into something navigable, calculable, useful, a place within which it is possible to pursue pleasure in modified form, then the egos of new anthropological types cannot be characterized as "weak." Indeed, the problem seems to be rather that they are too *strong*, that they are *too in touch with reality, this* reality, at the cost of being able to think beyond its confines.

There is a great deal in Adorno's work to suggest that this problem, that capitalist subjects today are "rigid" in their thinking, only able to see things in one way, is the primary one he was trying to capture in the figure of the new anthropological type. In the brief "Notes toward a New Anthropology," for instance, Adorno characterizes the late capitalist subject as "Vor-Sich-Hinleben," or "living straight ahead," an expression related to *vor sich hinschauen*, or "looking straight ahead" (468). This "living straight ahead," living without taking the time to "live around," as it were, to experience without direction, is, Adorno explains, ingrained in children from an early age, when they are taught "ceaselessly to follow goals, stubbornly live for them, their eyes consumed by the gain one is always trying to snatch up, without looking left or right" (471). In the even shorter "Problem of the New Type of Human Being," he claims that these unidirectional types are "without illusions. They finally see the world as it is, but pay the price of no longer seeing how it could be" (Adorno 2009: 466). Adorno insists that this illusionless connection to a static reality can be made sense of in terms of weak or degraded egos, but the fit is clearly inexact: Freud, for one, would certainly question the idea that the desire to change existing reality has anything to do with having a strong ego.

Perhaps Adorno is right to insist that "reality-testing" should include the ability to see present reality as in need of supersession, but how then to characterize the cold instrumentality of the new anthropological type? Is *ego weakness* a category broad enough to accommodate both "hardened" rigidity and superstitious fantasy? We are here pressing up against the limits of the term *ego weakness*: there may be some good in thinking of the quasi-religious zealot and the cold, task-oriented engineer as suffering the *same* psychic debility, but it might be better to find a new way of characterizing the often conflicting tendencies of the new anthropological type. For the moment, I will give in to the suggestion already made that instrumental thinking and an attendant adherence to present reality ought to be understood as evincing an excessive development of the ego, which Freud often describes as a cortical "shell" of the id. The ego, in this view, is strong, able to insulate a more fragile psychic core, but rigid and unpliable in its strength.

Strange as it may sound to characterize a psychic pathology in terms of ego strength, there is a good deal of precedence for the view that the calculating obsessive is suffering from an excess of "I"-ness. Jacques Lacan (2002: 265), for one, warned against "trying to strengthen the ego in many neuroses that are caused by its overly strong structure," for him the primary fault of the ego psychologists. His student and later detractor Jean Laplanche (1987: 146) contended that while "there is surely a death of the psyche by disintegration," a death that results from an insufficiency of ego strength, "there is also a kind of psychic death by rigidification and excessive synthesis, psychic death by the ego." In similar fashion, Donald Winnicott (1992: 246) often spoke of "the overgrowth of mental function reactive to erratic mothering." In his view, the cortical layer of the id is prematurely hardened in an unstable and hostile environment in early life. Even a member of the ego psychology ranks, Hans Loewald (1980: 23), cautioned against seeing ego strength as an unquestionable good, pointing out how a "discrepancy between the individual needs and the support of the environment" often leads to an excessive rigidification of the ego that deadens the psyche as a whole. The idea that ego strength is itself a kind of psychic debility thus has a long history in psychoanalysis. To be clear, the aim here is less to malign the category of ego strength than it is to define ego maturity as lying between fragility and excessive strength, "between polymorphism and rigidity," consisting of a material which is neither "too 'hard' [n]or too 'soft'" (Malabou 2002: 175).

From this new viewpoint, the problem with new anthropological types is that they somehow have both overgrown ids *and* overgrown egos, raging drives and fantasies managed carefully and craftily by the culture industry and a cold, precise control over a reality that they cannot imagine differently. What is particularly appealing about this model of the late capitalist subject is that it makes sense of its schizoid reality, its bizarrely regular alternation between an exacting rationality, efficiency, and technical skill in certain parts of life and a blinding stupidity in others, between a state where the ego is fully in control and one where there appears to be no ego whatsoever. Adorno himself points to the example of successful professionals who "adjust relatively easily" to new tasks, are therefore presumed to have a certain disposition of "maturity and independence," but who "prove immature by then losing their heads at the sports arena on Sunday" (Adorno and Becker 1983: 108). To return again to the inspiration for this special issue, if we accept this schizoid model of the new anthropological type, then its paradigm case would be not just the enraged Trump supporter caught in a web of fantasies but that same person who very efficiently and willingly undertakes alienated labor.

Superego Weakness

In what, then, does the particular weakness of the new anthropological type lie? Perhaps schizoid existence is difficult enough, but it also makes sense to attribute weakness to that third agency in the so-called "structural" model of the psyche: the superego. Adorno and colleagues (1950: 234) give us reason to believe that this is indeed the case in claiming that the authoritarian personality's "conscience or superego is incompletely integrated with the self or ego," resulting in "the inability to build up a consistent and enduring set of moral values within the personality." Like many psychoanalytically minded thinkers of the time, Adorno relied upon an integration-based understanding of superego health: the superego, a "grade in the ego," is considered healthy in virtue of its integration into the life of the ego. Without proper integration, without in effect becoming one with the ego, the superego becomes excessively punitive and fickle, driving the ego to uncertainty and fear rather than stability and morality.

Despite his adoption of the integration model in *The Authoritarian Personality*, there is a great deal in Adorno's work to suggest that his thinking chafed under any model of psychic streamlining, any model that encouraged an adaptive synergy of psychic parts. As he claims in "Sociology and Psychology," the goal of the "well-integrated personality" is objectionable because it expects the individual to establish an equilibrium between conflicting forces which does not obtain in existing society—nor should it, because those forces are not of equal moral merit. . . . [The] integration [of the well-balanced individual] would be a false reconciliation with an unreconciled world, and would presumably amount in the last analysis to an "identification with the aggressor," a mere character-mask of subordination. (Adorno 1968: 83)

The ideal of integration thus not so secretly encouraged the very tendencies that Adorno was delimiting in *The Authoritarian Personality*; it is, to say the least, curious to see it validated there.

How instead ought we to think about the superego? Throughout Adorno's (1991: 118) work, he laments a "loss of inner tension" in the individual, a loss of "whatever raises from within itself a claim to being autonomous, critical and antithetical." Through the "predetermined resolution in the 'happy ending' of every tension whose purely apparent character is revealed by the ritual conclusion" (69), the culture industry produces a "slackening of intellectual tension" (Adorno 2005: 87), a slackening of anything that might oppose the seamless alternation between "sport on the Sunday day off and the wretchedness of the working week" (Adorno 1991: 90–91). In place of the integration model, it thus makes sense to affirm what we can call a *tension* model of superego functioning: the superego is there not to be integrated with the ego but rather to provide a counterpoint to the ego's claims, to be *in tension with* the ego, to struggle with it if necessary. The problem with new anthropological types, from this vantage point, is that their egos have no worthy conversational adversary, no other agency there to challenge, when necessary, the legitimacy of instrumental rationality. The strength of their id causes them to "lose their heads" at regular intervals in domesticated escape, but there is no agency there when the ego returns to itself to cause it to wonder about the administered loss of itself.

Although superego weakness seems like the right term for this condition, one might object right away that Adorno (1973: 272) himself rejected the idea that the superego could actually be a good agency, agreeing with Freud that the superego is nothing but "blindly, unconsciously internalized social coercion." What Adorno criticizes in attempts to mark off some good part of the superego, however, is the desire to separate good forms of social coercion from bad ones, and given the state of ego psychology at the time, he certainly had reason to worry. What is being suggested here, by contrast, is that we might think of the superego as an agency that both serves that coercion in its weak form but provides the resources to resist that coercion in a strong form. A weak superego, in this view, is something like a motivational coach, cheering the ego on to live according to preestablished norms, to follow goals and stubbornly live up to them, to live "straight ahead."[5] A strong superego, by contrast, is one that "disrupt[s] our lives in somewhat unpleasant and unfamiliar ways," to borrow from Jonathan Lear's (2012) description of irony. It engages the ego in a difficult dialogue that creates an inner tension in the individual.[6]

This conception of superego weakness, in addition to being more generally convincing and consonant with Adorno's other work than the integration model (Adorno et al. 1950: 234), helps us address a potential weakness in *The Authoritarian Personality*: that the claim that this type of human being is not capable of building up "a consistent and enduring set of moral values within the personality" does not make sense of the so-called "values voter," precisely the kind of personality we would like to be addressed. On this point, the traditional Republican base does indeed seem quite different than the aforementioned driftless millennial, though the emergent tendencies of the new anthropological type are supposed to apply to both. If we understand the weakness of the superego to lie not in its incomplete integration but rather in its inability to be in *tension* with the ego, then we can say that the new anthropological type suffers not from a lack of enduring values but rather from the incapacity to assess those values reflectively. It is this inability to submit one's own tasks, goals, and values to searching and uncomfortable criticism, an inability to really dialogue with oneself and with others in a way that might lead to unexpected conclusions, that defines the new anthropological type.

Conclusion

In this essay, I have attempted to come to a more convincing understanding of the new anthropological type than one finds in *The Authoritarian Personality*, one rooted in Adorno's work but never articulated by Adorno himself. The first move was to have challenged Adorno's use of the term *ego weakness*, for the primary reason that so much of his writing is devoted to describing an incipient rigidity and instrumentality in thinking that is most aptly characterized as a form of ego *strength*. This is not to say that the kind of regression captured in the term *ego weakness* is not present, only that the regression is but one piece of the puzzle. If the new anthropological type is not in fact a psychological type but an emergent tendency in anyone who can be called a subject of late capitalism, then it is a tendency that pulls us in two directions simultaneously: one toward an exacting but prescribed rationality and the other toward a wild and unthinking irrationality. The new anthropological type can and does serve two masters but at the expense of the superego, in theory the developmental heir to id energy and moral adversary of the ego. The superego, in this view, is what creates the kind of inner psychic tension of which Adorno was constantly bemoaning the loss.

Raymond Geuss (2005: 113) says of the Frankfurt School that for them, modern society "generates illusions and distortions, presenting a façade that is actively misleading." Adorno (2005: 43) himself directly refutes such a conception of his work in *Minima Moralia* in a section titled "Baby with the bath-water":

> Among the motifs of cultural criticism one of the most long-established and central is that of the lie: that culture creates the illusion of a society worthy of man which does not exist; that it conceals the material conditions upon which all human works rise, and that, comforting and lulling, it serves to keep alive the bad economic determination of existence. This is the common notion of culture as ideology, which appears at first sight common to both the bourgeois doctrine of violence and its adversary, both to Nietzsche and to Marx. But precisely this notion, like all expostulation about lies, has a suspicious tendency to become itself ideology. . . . To identify culture solely with lies is more fateful than ever, now that the former is really becoming totally absorbed by the latter, and eagerly invites such identification in order to compromise every opposing thought. If material reality is called the world of exchange value, and culture whatever refuses to accept the domination of that world, then it is true that such refusal is illusory so long as the existent exists. Since, however, free and honest exchange is itself a lie, to deny it is at the same time to speak for truth: in face of the lie of the commodity world, even the lie that denounces it becomes a corrective.

One of Adorno's points here, almost tailored to our recent election, is that we are invited to call out products of the culture industry for their phoniness and bluster, to denounce them as unbearable lies, without acknowledging that they represent, in however perverted a form, some refusal of domination. For my present purposes, this means that the conception of the new anthropological type qua overgrown child participates in the equation of culture and ideology that is itself ideology. In the view presented here, new anthropological types do indeed lean on socially managed fantasies, but their more prominent and problematic feature is an unreflective adherence to a reality, a stubborn, blinkered, one-way kind of thinking and living. From a psychoanalytic perspective, one might say that what is lost in late capitalism is not reality, not ego strength, but rather the kind of inner psychic tension that makes possible the pliability of reality. It is the lack of this tension, which I attribute to super-ego weakness, that defines the new anthropological type.

Notes

I am grateful to the participants of "The Authoritarian Personality Revisited," and especially the conference's organizer, Robyn Marasco, for their comments on a shorter version of this essay. I would like also to thank the Analytic Social Psychology group of the Society for Psychoanalytic Inquiry and its organizer, Jeremy Cohan, as well as the Works in Progress group of Barrett, the Honors College at Arizona State University and its organizer, Laurie Stoff, for their feedback on longer drafts.

1   The F-scale measured the susceptibility of individuals to fascistic propaganda, as demonstrated by nine traits: conventionalism, submission, aggression, anti-intraception, superstition/stereotypy, power/"toughness," destructiveness/cynicism, projectivity, and an obsession with sex. To reiterate, these nine characteristics are intended to describe someone with a *susceptibility* to fascism, not the personality traits of a fascist leader, though the two are obviously connected.

2   As Moishe Postone (1993: 31, 159) has persuasively argued, Marx's theory of alienation is best understood not as referring "to the estrangement of what had previously existed as a property of the workers" but rather as involving an *"abstract impersonal domination . . .* not grounded in any person, class, or institution." In his view, "even the labor of an independent commodity producer is alienated . . . because social compulsion is effected abstractly, as a result of the social relations objectified by labor when it functions as a socially mediating activity. The abstract domination and the exploitation of labor characteristic of capitalism are grounded, ultimately, not in the appropriation of the surplus by the nonlaboring classes, but in the form of labor in capitalism" (160–61). For Postone (2004: 68, 59), everyone who lives under capitalism confronts "the existence of 'species capacities' that are constituted historically in alienated form" and is affected by the "form of social relations that is unique inasmuch as it is mediated by labour." Thus, though capitalism may be "lived" very differently by different people, anyone who lives in capitalist society will be *alienated* in the sense of being subject to an impersonal form of social domination (alienation, in this specific sense, must be distinguished from material exploitation and immiseration). To be clear: to say that capitalism produces certain kinds of subjects is not to say that subjectivity today is determined wholly by capitalism. No doubt many ingredients—family background, race, gender, class, etc.—go into the formation of psyches, but those psyches will always have certain quasi-universal features so long as they are formed in capitalist social conditions. And it is these conditions that are responsible for the specific features of the new anthropological type.

3   Since, however, the very act of thinking "in such terms as strong versus weak" is asserted to be characteristic of the authoritarian type, it is immediately curious that Adorno et al. (1950, 238) would choose this binary to distinguish between the old and

new anthropological types. The authors do note that ego weakness typically finds outward manifestation in "power and 'toughness,'" but this casual reversal of the outwardly strong and narcissistic into its opposite is troubling (237). Excessive, unbending, and unthinking strength may be a weakness, but it is a particular kind of weakness, and my hunch is that we can better understand the new anthropological type by avoiding the overly tidy reduction of outward strength to inner weakness.

4   As I agree with Gordon that the hypothesis of the new anthropological type ought to be understood as attempting to describe an emergent tendency in thinking rather than a distinct psychological type, one might wonder why it is still useful to think in terms of types like the *Trump supporter* or the *unthinking millennial*. Adorno himself addresses this point in *The Authoritarian Personality* (747): "There is reason to look for psychological types because the world in which we live is typed and 'produces' different 'types' of persons. Only by identifying stereotypical traits in modern humans, and not by denying their existence, can the pernicious tendency toward all-pervasive classification and subsumption be challenged." I hope that my use of these two types will be proved useful by the point made in clarifying the tendencies of the new anthropological type later in the paper.

5   A longer discussion of this point can be found in Fong 2016: 98–101.

6   The idea that superego strength might be a sign of maturity will undoubtedly strike many as being as counterintuitive as the idea that ego strength can be a form of pathology, but once again, there is a long tradition of psychoanalytic theory that supports this line of thought. Freud himself wondered about the positive functions of the superego in the late paper "Humour," and many after him have found it necessary to distinguish "good" and "bad" sides of the superego, or to separate the "ego-ideal" from the superego, in recognition that some part of what Freud described under the name *superego* was a positive influence on the psyche as a whole. See Freud 1966, Schafer 1960, and Sandler, Holder, and Meers 1963.

References

Adorno, Theodor W. 1968. "Sociology and Psychology, Part II." *New Left Review* 1, no. 47: 79–97.

Adorno, Theodor W. 1973. *Negative Dialectics*. Translated by E. B. Ashton. London: Routledge.

Adorno, Theodor W. 1991. *The Culture Industry: Selected Essays on Mass Culture*. Edited by J. M. Bernstein. London: Routledge.

Adorno, Theodor W. 1994. *Notizen zur neuen Anthropologie* (*Notes toward a New Anthropology*). Vol. 4.2 of *Briefe und Briefwechsel* (*Letters and Correspondence*). Frankfurt: Suhrkamp.

Adorno, Theodor W. 2005. *Minima Moralia: Reflections on a Damaged Life*. Translated by E. F. N. Jephcott. London: Verso.

Adorno, Theodor W. 2009. "The Problem of the New Type of Human Being." In *Current of Music*, edited by Robert Hullot-Kentor, 461–68. Cambridge: Polity.

Adorno, Theodor W., and Hellmut Becker. 1983. "Education for Autonomy." *Telos* no. 56: 103–10.

Adorno, Theodor W., Else Frenkel-Brunswik, Daniel J. Levinson, and R. Nevitt Sanford. 1950. *The Authoritarian Personality*. New York: Harper and Row.

Eissler, Kurt. 1953. "The Effect of the Structure of the Ego on Psychoanalytic Technique." *Journal of the American Psychoanalytic Association* 1, no. 1: 104–43.

Fenichel, Otto. 1954. "Ego Strength and Ego Weakness." In *The Collected Papers of Otto Fenichel*, 70–80. New York: Norton.

Fong, Benjamin Y. 2016. *Death and Mastery: Psychoanalytic Drive Theory and the Subject of Late Capitalism*. New York: Columbia University Press.

Freud, Sigmund. 1966. "Humour." In Vol. 21 of *The Standard Edition of the Complete Psychological Works of Sigmund Freud*, edited and translated by James Strachey. London: Hogarth Press and the Institute of Psycho-Analysis.

Geuss, Raymond. 2005. *Outside Ethics*. Princeton, NJ: Princeton University Press.

Gordon, Peter E. 2017. "The Authoritarian Personality Revisited: Reading Adorno in the Age of Trump." *boundary 2* 44, no. 2: 31–56.

Gunster, Shane. 2004. *Capitalizing on Culture: Critical Theory for Cultural Studies*. Toronto: University of Toronto Press.

Hullot-Kentor, Robert. 2008. "A New Type of Human Being and Who We Really Are." *Brooklyn Rail*. www.brooklynrail.org/2008/11 /art/a-new-type-of-human-being-and-who -we-really-are.

Kellner, Douglas. 1984. *Herbert Marcuse and the Crisis of Marxism*. Berkeley: University of California Press.

Lacan, Jacques. 2002. *Écrits*. Translated by Bruce Fink. New York: Norton.

Laplanche, Jean. 1987. *Nouveaux Fondements pour la psychanalyse* (*New Foundations for Psychoanalysis*). Paris: Presse Universitaires de France.

Lear, Jonathan. 2012. "A Lost Conception of Irony." *Berfrois*. www.berfrois.com/2012/01 /jonathan-lear-lost-conception-irony/.

Loewald, Hans. 1980. *Papers on Psychoanalysis*. New Haven, CT: Yale University Press.

Malabou, Catherine. 2002. *The New Wounded: From Neurosis to Brain Damage*. Translated by Steven Miller. New York: Fordham University Press.

Postone, Moishe. 1993. *Time, Labor, and Social Domination: A Reinterpretation of Marx's Critical Theory*. Cambridge: Cambridge University Press.

Postone, Moishe. 2004. "Critique and Historical Transformation." *Historical Materialism* 12, no. 3: 53–72.

Rose, Gillian. 1976. "How Is Critical Theory Possible? Theodor W. Adorno and Concept Formation in Sociology." *Political Studies* 24, no. 1: 69–85.

Sandler, Joseph, Alex Holder, and Dale Meers. 1963. "The Ego Ideal and the Ideal Self." *Psychoanalytic Study of the Child* no. 18: 139–58.

Schafer, Roy. 1960. "The Loving and Beloved Superego in Freud's Structural Theory." *Psychoanalytic Study of the Child* no. 15: 163–88.

Schechter, Kate. 2014. *Illusions of a Future: Psychoanalysis and the Biopolitics of Desire*. Durham, NC: Duke University Press.

Winnicott, Donald W. 1992. "Mind and Its Relation to the Psyche-Soma." In *Through Paediatrics to Psycho-Analysis: Collected Papers*. New York: Brunner-Routledge.

Zaretsky, Eli. 2015. *Political Freud: A History*. New York: Columbia University Press.

Fadi A. Bardawil

Césaire with Adorno:
Critical Theory and the Colonial Problem

Decolonizing Critical Theory

During the Second World War, C. L. R. James and Theodor Adorno met for a lunch arranged by Herbert Marcuse, their common friend, near the New School of Social Research in New York (Traverso 2017: 167). "There is no doubt," Enzo Traverso surmises, "that it was a failed encounter, and we can legitimately suppose that they met only to acknowledge their mutual dislike and incomprehension" (167). Traverso relates the story of this failed lunch between these two distinguished thinkers to highlight the missed encounter between critical theory and the black Marxist tradition and ask what could have been brought into the world should that encounter have taken place. The Frankfurt School's silence on questions of colonialism led Traverso to deduce that the missed dialogue was symptomatic of critical theory's "colonial unconscious" (175). Efforts to bring together anticolonial and postcolonial thinkers with intellectuals associated with the Frankfurt School, as well as calls to decolonize critical theory, are gaining more traction today as political theorists realize that the glaring omissions of colonialism, race, and religion from critical theory

The South Atlantic Quarterly 117:4, October 2018
DOI 10.1215/00382876-7165857 © 2018 Duke University Press

render their own understanding of an increasingly interconnected world parochial, if not complicit with imperial powers.

Susan Buck-Morss initiated such a dialogue in the wake of the proliferation of watertight distinctions between *Islam* and *the West* that followed the attacks of September 11, 2001. Buck-Morss's courageous intervention countered civilizational trenches by calling for translation between different intellectual traditions as she thought through the possibility of a global leftist politics in the present. She made a forceful case for the necessity of translating Islamist thinkers such as the mid-twentieth-century Iranian Ali Shariati and the Egyptian Sayyid Qutb into the space of critical theory and to rescue the critical kernels of their works. This project of translation sought both to disrupt the self-referentiality of Western critical thought, which reinscribes its authoritative status by assuming its conceptual arsenal sufficient to interpret the world, and "to rediscover one's own commitments in a foreign political language, and to ask not only what is lost in translation but also what might be gained" (Buck-Morss [2003] 2006: ix).[1]

Today, as we witness the proliferation of neofascist formations, the rise of populist right-wing movements, and the rabid nationalisms that drive their racist, antirefugee, and anti-Muslim politics, the long-forgotten *Authoritarian Personality* (1950) is being revisited and put into circulation again in the hopes of providing analytical tools through which we can critically assess the bleak contours of our global present. I revisit *The Authoritarian Personality* in light of Buck-Morss's challenge to the politics of critical theory and her call to disrupt its self-referentiality. I do so however by taking a different route. Buck-Morss's translational move brings Muslim thinkers into the pantheon of critical theory underlining in the process the rediscovery of one's own critical commitments in a foreign idiom. It seeks to render the unfamiliar familiar. This is a generous move that brings into the fold of critical theory thinkers who were either neglected or banished altogether from theoretical conversations in the West on the basis of their religious politics. However, it also risks underplaying those aspects of these thinkers' thought that may potentially trouble some of the fundamental theoretical premises and commitments of critical theory. My worry is that this translation project may end up bolstering critical theory's authority instead of interrogating its politics and its omissions by underscoring its capacity to recognize and grant membership to non-Western thinkers in its private metropolitan club.

In the remainder of this essay, I read three texts that were published in 1950: Aimé Césaire's *Discourse on Colonialism*, Adorno et al.'s *The Authoritarian Personality*, and Octave Mannoni's *Prospero and Caliban: The Psychol-*

ogy of Colonization. In the first part of the paper, I head in the opposite direction of Buck-Morss not by arguing for the inclusion of Césaire into the pantheon of critical theory but rather by asking how his *Discourse* challenges Adorno's historiographical narratives, civilizational units of analysis, conceptual building blocks, and modality of critique in *The Authoritarian Personality*. I then engage Césaire's critique of Mannoni's usage of psychoanalysis to account for the dependency of the colonized on the colonizer. I conclude the essay by highlighting how both Adorno's notions of the liquidation of the individual by an increasingly standardized society and colonial notions of weak individuality (Mannoni) mobilize a psychoanalytic notion of *ego weakness*. These critical diagnoses, which lament the deficit of individuals, who are either standardized by society in the metropoles (Adorno) or still entangled in culture in the peripheries (Mannoni), foreclose the possibility of emancipatory political practice and internationalist solidarity by excising revolutionary subjects and their practices from the domain of the political.

Adorno's and Césaire's Genealogies of Fascism

A few years after the end of the Second World War, the authors of *The Authoritarian Personality* affirm that "no socio-political trend imposes a graver threat to our traditional values and institutions than does fascism" (Adorno et al. 1950: 1). In order to help fight fascism, and understand what makes the phenomenon gain so much traction, they propose to examine "the personality forces that favor its acceptance" (1). The concept of personality, which cannot be isolated from the social totality, is what they put forward to account for the coherence of an individual's political, economic, and social beliefs. The coherent pattern these beliefs form is an expression of deep trends lying in an individual's personality. Accessing these deeper trends, the authors argue, is what enables the detection of the potential for antidemocratic thought and action among individuals. Personality structure is the hinge concept that is deployed to explain the relative consistency and permanence of human behavior against both those who ground fixity in the biological or racial categories of the Nazis and those who posit an "infinite human flexibility" (6). Basing their research in the United States as the Second World War was coming to an end, the multidisciplinary authors write about the "potentially fascistic" (1) individual since none of their research subjects openly identified themselves with fascism. By isolating the deep trends of an individual's personality structure for analyzing the predispositions to fascism, *The Authoritarian Personality* broadened the semantic range of fascism beyond the conscious adherence to a clearly articulated ideology and the distinct practices of political regime. In a nutshell, you could be a leftist living in a liberal democratic regime while displaying deep authoritarian personality traits.

Anti-Semitism constituted the starting, and focal, point of the book's inquiry into the nature of the potentially fascistic individual. The symptoms of anti-Semitism, Adorno writes, can "hardly be explained by the mechanism of neurosis; and at the same time, the Anti-Semitic individual as such, the potential fascist individual, is certainly not a psychotic (Adorno et al. 1950: 618). One of *The Authoritarian Personality*'s major insights is that anti-Semitism has a functional character. It is relatively independent of its object. This account of the workings of anti-Semitism displays a parallel move to the one performed by the concept of personality, which avoided oscillating between the two extreme positions of either grounding fixity of behavior in biology or positing infinite flexibility. In this case, Adorno dissolves another false binary, by carving out a path of analysis that dodges grounding prejudice in the characteristics inherent in the object, say the Jew or the Muslim, and what he dubs the scapegoat position, where any object can become the target of socially diverted "unconscious destructiveness" (608). The object in Adorno's account must be tangible, have appropriate historical backing, be defined in stereotypes, and "possess features, which harmonize with the destructive tendencies of the prejudiced subject" (608). "The ultimate theoretical explanation of an entirely irrational symptom which nevertheless does not appear to affect the 'normality' of those who show the symptom," Adorno writes, "is beyond the scope of the present research" (618). Having said that, he attempts to answer the cui bono question What does the anti-Semitic subject gain from adhering to these views? His answer is that the complexity of modern society, which is the result of the "objectification of social processes, their obedience to intrinsic supra-individual laws, seems to result in an intellectual alienation of the individual from society" (618). This alienation is experienced as a disorientation accompanied with fear and uncertainty by increasingly ignorant and confused individuals who cannot grasp the abstract and complex processes that are constitutive of their world. "Political stereotypy and personalization," Adorno writes, "can be understood as devices for overcoming this uncomfortable state of affairs" (618).

The standardized society results in what Max Horkheimer (Adorno et al. 1950: ix), in his preface to the series in which the book was published, dubs "the rise of an 'anthropological' species we call the authoritarian type of man," which combines "ideas and skills . . . typical of a highly industrialized society with irrational or antirational beliefs. The ultimate goal of the book, continues Horkheimer, is "to develop and promote an understanding of social-psychological factors which have made it possible for the authoritarian type of man to threaten to replace the individualistic and democratic type prevalent in the past century and a half of our civilization, and of the factors by which this threat may be contained" (x).

Adorno, who is very much aware of how the construction of typologies is part and parcel of how fascists work and is indexical of their stereotypical modalities of thought defuses the argument against his own construction of types in two moves. First, he distinguishes between the elaboration of biological and static typologies and historical and dynamic ones. And second, and more importantly, he reflexively relates the condition of possibility of construction of psychological types to the increasingly standardized society that liquidates individuality. "Individualism," Adorno notes, "opposed to inhuman pigeonholing, may ultimately become a mere ideological veil in a society which actually is inhuman and whose intrinsic tendency towards the 'subsumption' of everything shows itself by the classification of people themselves. In other words the critique of typology should not neglect the fact that large numbers of people are no longer, or rather never were, 'individuals' in the sense of traditional 19th-century philosophy" (747).

The Authoritarian Personality was published in the same year as the *Discourse on Colonialism* by Aimé Césaire, another thinker working with and through the conceptual tools of the Marxian tradition. Césaire opens his landmark book by lambasting the so-called European civilization by affirming that it is decadent, stricken, dying, and morally and spiritually indefensible for having failed to solve the two problems it gave rise to: the problem of the proletariat and the problem of colonialism. Whereas Adorno and Horkheimer in their inquiry into fascism map a break and a regression from the democratic individual of the nineteenth century to the authoritarian type of the twentieth, Césaire sees a continuity between the colonialism of the nineteenth century and the fascism and Nazism of the twentieth. He writes:

> First we must study how colonization works to *decivilize* the colonizer, to *brutalize* him in the true sense of the word, to degrade him, to awaken him to buried instincts, to covetousness, violence, race hatred, and moral relativism.
>
> And then one fine day the bourgeoisie is awakened by a terrific boomerang effect: the gestapos are busy, the prisons fill up, the torturers standing around the racks invent, refine, discuss.
>
> People are surprised, they become indignant. They say: "How strange! But never mind—it's Nazism, it will pass!" And they wait, and they hope; and

they hide the truth from themselves, that it is barbarism, the supreme barbarism, the crowning barbarism that sums up all the daily barbarisms; that it is
Nazism, yes, but that before they were its victims, they were its accomplices;
that they tolerated that Nazism before it was inflicted on them, that they
absolved it, shut their eyes to it, legitimized it, because, until then, it had been
applied only to non-European peoples; that they have cultivated that Nazism,
that they are responsible for it, and that before engulfing the whole edifice of
Western, Christian civilization in its reddened waters, it oozes, seeps, and
trickles from every crack. (Césaire [1972] 2000: 36)

The new "authoritarian" species, Césaire seems to be saying, is not new at
all. It is the offspring of the "colonist" species—to draw on the opening sen-
tences of Frantz Fanon's *The Wretched of the Earth*, where he defines decolonization as "quite simply the substitution of one 'species' of mankind by
another" (Fanon [1963] 2004: 1). As Robin Kelley notes in his introduction to
the *Discourse*, Césaire locates the origins of fascism within colonialism and
"within the very traditions of humanism, critics believed fascism threatened" (Césaire [1972] 2000: 10).

In reading *The Authoritarian Personality* alongside *The Discourse on
Colonialism*, which were both published in 1950, I am not after a presentist
dismissal of this magisterial work, say by unmasking indigenous European
assumptions parading as universals. Neither am I interested in highlighting
the difference between the West and its Others, which then highlights the
inadequacy of the conceptual tools of critical theory to capture the historical
and political processes working through colonial and postcolonial societies.
Rather, I would like to gauge the challenge the incorporation of the colonial
problem, to borrow Césaire's words, poses to the theoretical backbone of *The
Authoritarian Personality*, and how it throws fresh light on the assumptions
undergirding Adorno's analysis. In doing so, what I am also after is a rethinking of the politics of critical theory in and for our present. "The colonizer,"
Césaire ([1972] 2000: 42) writes, "who in order to ease his conscience gets into
the habit of seeing the other man as an *animal*, accustoms himself to treating
him like an animal, and tends objectively to transform *himself* into an animal."
"No human contact, but relations of domination and submission," he continues, "which turn colonizing man into a classroom monitor, an army sergeant,
a prison guard, a slave driver, and the indigenous man into an instrument of
production. My turn to state an equation: colonization = 'thingification.'"

Césaire points to an earlier moment of inhumanity and violence: stereotypy and pigeonholing. Césaire though is not only calling attention to a

historical precedent. He is underscoring how this historical precedent was constitutive of European modernity. Adorno's democratic nineteenth-century individuals, by being either direct participants in or accomplices of colonial barbarism, were in the process of "cultivating that Nazism" that will boomerang on them a few decades later. If the nineteenth century cannot be separated from colonial and imperial conquests and their impact on both the colonizers and the colonized, the metropoles and peripheries, can we still talk about "the rise of a new anthropological species" and lean on the explanatory purchase of Adorno's theories regarding the liquidation of individuality and overall regression in an increasingly standardized society to make sense of fascism?

Reading Césaire with Adorno raises cardinal questions about the latter's historiographic periodization, whether fascism is an aberration or in continuity with nineteenth-century colonial practices, and his civilizational unit of analysis (the West). For instance, Adorno writes,

> The very fact that our social system is on the defense, as it were, that capitalism, instead of expanding the old way and opening up innumerable opportunities to the people, has to maintain itself somewhat precariously and to block critical insights which were regarded as "progressive" one hundred years ago but are viewed as potentially dangerous today, makes for a one-sided presentation of the facts, for manipulated information, and for certain shifts of emphasis which tend to check the universal enlightenment otherwise furthered by the technological development of communications. (Adorno et al. 1950: 661–62)

What are the boundaries of "our social system"? Of course, Adorno and Horkheimer were very much aware of the global imperial nature of nineteenth-century capitalism, but its effects were still articulated on civilizational and territorial assumptions inhabited by an unmarked individual/society dialectic that is internal to Western civilization. How does capitalism expand? Where are the processes of primitive accumulation taking place and how? And who are the people for whom it opens innumerable opportunities?

There is more to Césaire's challenge than the rearticulation of the temporal and spatial coordinates of Adorno's account that undoes its discontinuity and underscores its Western exceptionalism. As important as these things are, I don't want to be read as only arguing that Adorno, by being blind to the impact of colonialism, got his coordinates wrong and believed that the history of the West could be written as an internal story of regression. To do so would be to argue that by reading Césaire with Adorno we discover that the latter's nineteenth-century democratic individual was actually either a racist colonizer or his accomplice; and therefore, his reverse historicism, which takes the form of highlighting a general regression from the democratic and individualistic type to the authoritarian species, is complicated to say the least by the practices and ideologies of the colonist species.

Césaire's challenge lies not only in providing us with an alternative account of European fascism by underscoring how the practices of colonial barbarism are intimately tied to those undertaken later on in the metropoles. More importantly, he offers us a different modality of practicing critical theory, a different form of critical theory if you will. In lieu of the grand account that focuses on how the trials and tribulations of the unmarked individual/society dialectic under late capitalism produces a general liquidation of individuality and the rise of a new authoritarian species, Césaire offers us a theory of subject-formation premised on the primacy of practice. Adorno's process-driven regression narrative begins with a nineteenth-century democratic individual who exits the stage after the increasingly standardized capitalist societies bring about an authoritarian personality type. Césaire, on the other hand, emphasizes that it is through his material practices that treat the colonized as an animal that the colonizer "tends objectively to transform *himself* into an animal" (Césaire [1972] 2000: 41). He offers us a critical theory that reveals how the colonizer's subjectivity is fashioned out of his material practices of domination and submission of the colonized. In seeking to dehumanize the colonized and turn him into an instrument and a thing—*chosification* in French—the colonizer ends up decivilizing himself and becoming the instrument of his own reification. The boomerang effect that Césaire describes is only possible because he posits a modality of explanation that ties the metropoles to the colonies through positing the primacy of political, material practices and ideological processes. By emphasizing that the act of colonization works to decivilize the colonizer, Césaire preempts any severing of the intimate ties between the metropoles and their colonies along the usual demarcation line: democratic at home, imperial abroad.

The Authoritarian Personality's explanation in terms of a grand regressive narrative, risks, I fear, obliterating the thickness and complexities of political, economic, religious, and military entanglements, which in this particular case take the form of cordoning off, and sanitizing, the metropole from its colonial practices and their effects. In light of this cordoning off, Adorno's cornerstone notion of the nineteenth-century democratic individual who is then liquidated in the twentieth comes close to a posited notion that is hardly impacted by the different practices it engages in. Moreover, the notion of the liquidation of individuality in an increasingly standardized society is marshaled by Adorno not only to account for fascist tendencies and anti-Semitic prejudice but also, for instance, to explain, in his critical engagement with Walter Benjamin's essay "The Work of Art in the Age of Mechanical Reproduction" (1969), how the concept of musical taste itself became outmoded. "The very existence of the subject who could verify such taste," Adorno writes, "has become as questionable as has, at the opposite pole, the right to a freedom of choice, which empirically in any case, no one any longer exercises" (Adorno 1992: 271). Contemporary listening, adds Adorno, "has regressed, arrested at the infantile stage" (286). Whether he is accounting for the fetish character in music in the age of the culture industry or the coming into being of "authoritarian man," Adorno's admirable theoretical elaborations are undergirded by a common regressive schema that not only comes close to positing the nineteenth-century individual by evacuating how practice shapes the subject but in so doing risks erasing the capacity for analytical differentiation between the different forms the liquidation of individuality could take, say between jazz lovers and anti-Semite fascists.

My second worry cuts to the heart of *The Authoritarian Personality*'s project. It has to do with how Adorno's explanatory account articulates the standardization of individuals on particular psychoanalytic concepts to understand fascism's appeal in terms of the coming into being of a new *psychological* species. The recourse to political stereotypy and personalization to orient oneself in, and as an attempt to 'master,' an increasingly estranged world is one of Adorno's main insights in *The Authoritarian Personality*. Both, in his view, are "inadequate to reality. . . . Their interpretation may therefore be regarded as a first step in the direction of understanding the complex of 'psychotic' thinking which appears to be a crucial characteristic of the fascist character," one which is not predicated mainly on his psychological dynamics, but is in part related "to the relationship or lack of relationship between this reality and the individual" (Adorno et al. 1950: 665). Adorno writes,

> Stereotypy misses reality in so far as it dodges the concrete and contents itself with the preconceived, rigid, and overgeneralized ideas to which the individual attributes a kind of magical omnipotence. Conversely, personalization dodges the real abstractness, that is to say, the "reification" of a social reality, which is determined by property relations and in which the human beings themselves are, as it were, mere appendages. Stereotypy and Personalisation are two divergent parts of an actually non experienced world, parts which are not only irreconcilable with each other, but which also do not allow for any addition which would reconstruct the picture of the real. (665–66)

As I read those lines, I was struck by how the complex of "psychotic" thinking that Adorno associates with an oscillation between empty generalizations and a mire of concreteness and which in both cases evades the experience of the world has been a feature of disciplines inquiring into the non-Western world. In the introduction to *Orientalism*, Edward Said, in a similar vein to Adorno's discussion of anti-Semitism's independence from its object, notes how "Orientalism responded more to the culture that produced it than to its putative object, which was also produced by the West. Thus the history of Orientalism has both an internal consistency and a highly articulated set of relationships to the dominant culture surrounding it" (Said [1978] 1994: 22). In the opening pages of the book, Said asks a methodological question about how to best approach the Orientalist archive. He writes,

> In a sense the two alternatives, general and particular, are really two perspectives on the same material: in both instances one would have to deal with pioneers in the field like William Jones, with great artists like Nerval or Flaubert. And why would it not be possible to employ both perspectives together, or one after the other? Isn't there an obvious danger of distortion (of precisely the kind that academic Orientalism has always been prone to) if either too general or too specific a level of description is maintained systematically?
>
> My two fears are distortion and inaccuracy, or rather the kind of inaccuracy by too dogmatic a generality and too positivistic a localized focus. (8)

If Said was keen on not reproducing in his own critique the traps of Orientalist scholarship that engendered the Orientals by either fixing them in dogmatic generalizations or positivistic particularities, Claude Lévi-Strauss criticized a similar ideological contraption in the opening paragraph of *The Savage Mind* ([1962] 1966). Anthropologists, he observed, argued for the "intellectual poverty of the Savages" (1), either because they don't have words to express concepts such as *tree*, while having words for the varieties of species or by going in the opposite direction for having such general concepts but not having specific names for the different species. In Said's case, it was the Orientalist's knowledges that oscillated between the general and the particular, while in Lévi-Strauss's the mental inferiority of non-Western people was inferred by anthropologists from the degree of abstraction or particularity of their concepts. If Césaire's boomerang effect tied metropolitan fascism to colonialism, Said brought *Orientalism*'s introduction to a close by writing, "In addition, and by an almost inescapable logic, I have found myself writing the history of a strange, secret sharer of Western anti-Semitism. That anti-Semitism and, as I have discussed it in its Islamic branch, Orientalism resemble each other very closely is a historical, cultural and political truth that needs only to be mentioned to an Arab Palestinian for its irony to be perfectly understood" ([1978] 1994: 27–28).

In bringing Said and Lévi-Strauss into the conversation, I want to underscore how they have both analyzed the production of the non-Western "Oriental" and "savage" via a power-knowledge colonial contraption, which highlights their inferiority by oscillating between locking them in the general or the particular. Like Césaire, Said and Lévi-Strauss provide us with an alternative racialized colonial genealogy regarding the processes of stereotypy and personalization that Adorno explains as the result of the increasing standardization of modern society and ignorance and confusion of its members. By underscoring how the ideological construction of "The Oriental" and "The Savage" was a product of Western hegemony, they steer us away from grounding the workings of this colonial contraption in psychologizing terms that generate personality types. Adorno's "psychotic thinking," an attribute of the standardized individual, who evades experience by oscillating between stereotypy and personalization, was displayed by and constituted a cornerstone of modern Western disciplines trying to make sense of non-Western alterity in the colonial era.

The Missing Individual and the Conundrum of Political Practice

In addition to the publication of *The Authoritarian Personality* and *Discourse on Colonialism*, 1950 witnessed the publication of a third book that also caused quite a stir: Octave Mannoni's *La Psychologie de La Colonisation*, which appeared in English under the title *Prospero and Caliban: The Psychology of Colonization* in 1956. The book, which is premised on a theory of psychological dependence of the Malagasy which Mannoni ([1956] 1964: 39–40) extends toward other "non-civilized peoples," was very critically received in anticolonial circles. Césaire's *Discourse* engages it, as does chapter 4 of Fanon's *Black Skin, White Masks*, "The So-Called Dependency Complex of the Colonized" (Fanon [1952] 2008). Here is what Césaire ([1972] 2000: 59) has to say about it:

> Follow him . . . and he will prove to you . . . that there are in this world groups of men who, for unknown reasons, suffer from what must be called a dependency complex, that these groups are psychologically made for dependence; that they need dependence, that they crave it, ask for it, demand it; that this is the case with most of the colonized peoples and with the Madagscans in particular. Away with racism! Away with colonialism! They smack too much of barbarism. M. Mannoni has something better: psychoanalysis.

Psychoanalysis was diverted from its emancipatory potential to become in Césaire's reading of Mannoni a tool justifying colonial power in the peripheries. In discussing the complex of dependence among the Malagasies, Mannoni argues that they and colonized peoples in general are characterized by a weak ego. He writes, "All this would seem to suggest that the ego is wanting in strength, and that is borne out by the fact that hallucinatory disturbances and panic appear the moment the feeling of security is threatened. The individual is held together by his collective shell, his social mask, much more than by his moral skeleton. And this, with but slight modifications, must be true of many other 'primitive' societies" (Mannoni [1956] 1964: 41).

In fact, Mannoni's take on the weakness of the individual in the colonies is neither new nor unique to him. The distinguished anthropologist Stefania Pandolfo (2008: 335) has underscored the "century-long colonial narrative [in Morocco] characterizing the indigenous culture and family structures as obstacles to the development of individual responsibility and European style citizenship." "Leaving little room for uncertainty, discontinuities, experiential discrepancies, and for the recognition of historically different ways of being a subject," she adds, "this narrative stresses the fundamental role of the patriarchal family in Islam, the overarching weight of the group, the force of a collective imaginary that makes it impossible for individual to exist qua individual, and the weight of a religious law where the sacred is the voice of the group" (335). This narrative is still very prevalent in liberal circles that affirm that progress hinges on the development of an individual free of her multiple religious, ethnic, sectarian, regional, and familial attachments.

But why am I mentioning Mannoni's argument and Césaire's response? Because I would like to draw some parallels between the colonial narrative's culturalist diagnosis of the colonized in the peripheries and Adorno's societal one of standardized men and women in the metropoles of the world. Mannoni and Adorno ground their accounts in a theory of ego weakness. Both the "pre-individual" of the colonies enmeshed in culture and the "post-individual" of the metropole living in an increasingly standardized society fail to develop an internal authority, a conscience. Mannoni talks of a social mask that holds the individual together instead of a "moral skeleton," while Adorno notes, "Weakness in the ego is expressed in the inability to build up a consistent and enduring set of moral values within the personality; and it is this state of affairs, apparently that makes it necessary for the individual to seek some organizing and coordinating agency outside of himself. Where such agencies are depended upon for moral decisions one may say that the conscience is externalized" (Adorno et al. 1950: 234).

The individual, whose ego is wanting in strength, is held together by heteronomous forces. These could be religion, the family, the sacred law—in brief, culture—for the pre-individual and fascist propaganda for the liquidated post-individual. The individual is either not yet to be found or no longer to be found. The historicist logic of the "not yet" reigns in the colonies, while Adorno's narrative of regression diagnoses the "no longer to be found" that is substituted by the new anthropological authoritarian species.

Both these diagnoses in terms of ego weakness entail consequences for the possibility of political practice and the conditions of its intelligibility. There is a tension in *The Authoritarian Personality* between the overarching claim that authoritarianism, which cuts through the ideological spectrum of Left and Right, is the outcome of an increasingly standardized society on the one hand, and, on the other, what Adorno dubs its pragmatic aim: "the necessity that science provide weapons against the potential threat of the fascist mentality" (Adorno et al. 1950: 748). Both Horkheimer and Adorno draw on the language of cancer and malignancy in describing prejudice. "One cannot 'correct' stereotypy by experience," Adorno writes; "he has to reconstitute the capacity for *having* experiences in order to prevent the growth of ideas which are malignant in the most literal, clinical sense" (617). As for Horkheimer, he asks in his preface, "What tissues of life of our modern society remain cancerous, and despite our assumed enlightenment show the incongruous atavism of ancient peoples?" (v). The answer is eradication, which "means re-education, scientifically planned on the basis of understanding scientifically arrived at" (vii). The collective introduction to the volume states the following:

> The present writers believe that it is up to the people to decide whether or not this country goes fascist. It is assumed that knowledge of the nature and extent of antidemocratic potentials will indicate programs for democratic action. These programs should not be limited to devices for manipulating people in such a way that they will behave more democratically, but they should be devoted to increasing the kind of self-awareness and self-determination that makes any kind of manipulation impossible. (10)

But who are the political agents—the people—who will undertake this task? How will they be able to escape societal standardization? And what form will this political practice take? It seems to me to enable a liberal reformist paternalism premised on the efficacy of science in fighting prejudice that seeks to reconstitute the individual, to strengthen his ego, one that is very close to the narrative of a colonial liberalism that seeks to fashion individuals out of communitarian subjects.

Herbert Marcuse attempted to resolve the conundrum of emancipatory politics and its subjects in an increasingly one-dimensional world that integrates the working class into the system, by positing an outside to it. He writes, "Underneath the conservative popular base is the substratum of the outcasts and outsiders, the exploited and persecuted of other races and other colors, the unemployed and unemployable. They exist outside the democratic process; their life is the most immediate and the most real need for ending intolerable conditions and institutions. Thus their opposition is revolutionary even if their consciousness is not" (Marcuse [1964] 1991: 257). Adorno's increasingly standardized society engulfs both the minorities and the prejudiced majority that threaten them. Marcuse, on the other hand, posits an outside to the system. This outside enables him to reconfigure revolutionary opposition, at the same time as he notes the severance of mediation between revolutionary theory and practice. The opposition of outsiders and outcasts "is an elementary force, which violates the rules of the game and, in doing so, reveals it as a rigged game" (257). The status of minorities is not developed in Adorno's text. What place do the minorities who are prejudiced against occupy in society? Are they as prone to the same processes of standardization as the majority? Adorno, who focuses on the functional character of anti-Semitism for the prejudiced subjects, does not spend much time on the characteristics of the different prejudiced objects. He notes in passing the anti-Semitism of certain other minority groups and of certain Jews themselves, as well as the "strong 'conformist' tendencies" among them (Adorno et al. 1950: 611). Adorno writes, "Hardly any traces of solidarity among the different out groups could be found" (611). Unlike Marcuse's outsiders who threaten the system from without, the minorities in Adorno's text don't enjoy a privileged political status, leaving unanswered the question of who will undertake the tasks of eradicating prejudice, reeducation, and democratic self-awareness.

Coda

The diagnosis in terms of ego-weakness that both the standardized individual in the metropoles (individual/society) and the culturally marked preindividual in the peripheries share (individual/culture) severs the process of mediation between critical theory and revolutionary political practice without positing Marcuse's way out (integrated/outsider). To think contemporary nationalist politics by mobilizing a notion of ego-weakness in an increasingly standardized society fails to account for the complexities of our increasingly interconnected world and leaves us with the quasi-impossible mission of looking for the nonstandardized individuals who will carry out the fight against fascism. In the US context, for instance, it fails to account for the manner in which both the metropole and the periphery are transformed by colonial and imperial ventures, say for example by assessing the domestic repercussions of the war on terror and the invasion of Iraq.

In the peripheries of the world, on the other hand, theories of ego weakness excise emancipatory practice from the domain of the political by either pathologizing it or relocating it via different strategies to the domain of the prepolitical. "If you point out to M. Mannoni," Césaire ([1956] 1964: 61) writes, "that the Madagascans have nevertheless revolted several times since the French occupation and again recently in 1947, M. Mannoni, faithful to his premises, will explain to you that that is a purely neurotic behavior, a collective madness, a running amok." Moving closer to our present, it is not difficult to see how the Syrian citizens, who rose in March 2011 against the brutal Assad regime that had been ruling them since 1971, had their uprisings banished from the domain of the political. If the Madagscans' revolts had been portrayed as a collective neurosis, the Syrian revolutionaries have been framed by politicians and commentators both on the Left and the Right through the culturalist language of sectarianism, the statist-security lingo of terrorism, and the humanitarian discourse of refugees. These three types—the vengeful sectarian, the radical terrorist, and the victimized refugee—excise the political dimension of a struggle for emancipation by the citizens of a mass murder regime. In categorizing the Syrian revolutionaries as victims to be saved by a humanitarian intervention or as madmen of religion and identity to be bombed, the negation of the political renders emancipatory practice illegible and forecloses the possibility of internationalist solidarity.[2]

To sum up, in reading Césaire, I showed how his genealogy of fascism and his discussion of colonial thingification calls into question Adorno's tightly sealed theories about the increasing reification of social processes in the West and the ensuing regression from democratic man to authoritarian species. In a second moment, I read Adorno's diagnosis of the standardized individual characterized by a weak ego alongside culturalist colonial narratives that share a similar diagnosis to account for a supposed deficit in individuality in non-Western societies. In doing so, I underlined how both of these diagnoses in terms of egoweakness enable top-down paternalistic forms of politics and foreclose the legibility of emancipatory politics in the ex-colonies, undercutting in the process the potential for internationalist political solidarity.

Like the humanist traditions of the past that Césaire criticized, critical theory's omissions may entangle it in colonial and imperial webs. To heed Césaire's call is not only to call for the decolonization of critical theory as if this were a one-time task performed and ticked off on one's schedule. It is also to remain attentive to the question of what counts as critical theory in different political conjunctures and to how its travels, as Césaire's critique of Mannoni's use of psychoanalysis shows us, may at times transform it from the name of a desire to liberate human beings to an ideological tool.

Notes

I would like to thank David Kazanjian, Sina Kramer, Joan Scott, Massimiliano Tomba, and Linda Zerilli for their generous comments and suggestions on earlier versions of this paper.

1   This project is resumed in Buck-Morss 2010. I engage both texts in more detail in Bardawil 2016.

2   I develop these points in Oz 2016.

References

Adorno, Theodor W. 1992. "On the Fetish-Character in Music and the Regression of Listening." In *The Essential Frankfurt School Reader*, edited by Andrew Arato and Eicke Gebhardt, 270–99. New York: Continuum.

Adorno, Theodor W., Else Frenkel-Brunswick, Daniel J. Levinson, and R. Nevitt Sanford. 1950. *The Authoritarian Personality.* New York: Harper and Row.

Bardawil, Fadi. 2016. "Dreams of a Dual Birth: Socialist Lebanon's World and Ours." *boundary 2* 43, no. 3: 313–35.

Benjamin, Walter. 1969. "The Work of Art in the Age of Mechanical Reproduction." In *Illuminations*, edited by Hannah Arendt, 217–52. New York: Schocken Books.

Buck-Morss, Susan. (2003) 2006. *Thinking Past Terror: Islamism and Critical Theory on the Left.* London: Verso.

Buck-Morss, Susan. 2010. "The Second Time as Farce . . . Historical Pragmatics and the Untimely Present." In *The Idea of Communism*, edited by Costas Douzinas and Slavoj Žižek, 67–80. London: Verso.

Césaire, Aimé. (1972) 2000. *Discourse on Colonialism.* Translated by Joan Pinkham. New York: Monthly Review Press.

Fanon, Frantz. (1952) 2008. *Black Skin, White Masks.* Translated by Richard Philcox. New York: Grove.

Fanon, Frantz. (1963) 2004. *The Wretched of the Earth.* Translated by Richard Philcox. New York: Grove Press.

Kelley, Robin D. G. 2000. "Introduction: A Poetics of Anticolonialism." In *Discourse on Colonialism*, translated by Joan Pinkham, 7–28. New York: Monthly Review Press.

Lévi-Strauss, Claude. (1962) 1966. *The Savage Mind*. Chicago: University of Chicago Press.

Mannoni, Octave. (1956) 1964. *Prospero and Caliban: The Psychology of Colonization*. Translated by Pamela Powesland. New York: Praeger.

Marcuse, Herbert. (1964) 1991. *One-Dimensional Man: Studies in the Ideology of Advanced Industrial Society*. Boston: Beacon Press.

Oz, Zeynep. 2016. "Revisiting Internationalists: Fadi Bardawil in Conversation with Zeynep Oz." *IBRAAZ*, July 10. www.ibraaz.org/interviews/197/.

Pandolfo, Stefania. 2008. "The Knot of the Soul." In *Postcolonial Disorders*, edited by Mary-Jo DelVecchio Good, Sandra Teresa Hyde, and Sarah Pinto, 329–58. Berkeley: University of California Press.

Said, Edward. (1978) 1994. *Orientalism*. New York: Vintage Books.

Traverso, Enzo. 2017. *Left-Wing Melancholia: Marxism, History, and Memory*. New York: Columbia University Press.

Robyn Marasco

There's a Fascist in the Family:
Critical Theory and Antiauthoritarianism

I consider the survival of National Socialism *within*
democracy to be potentially more menacing than
the survival of fascist tendencies *against* democracy.
—Theodor W. Adorno, "The Meaning of Working
through the Past"

This essay aims to clarify the uses of psychoanalysis for critical theory. It also aims at a reassessment of *The Authoritarian Personality*, in light of
the genesis of the project, its connection to other
studies conducted by the Institute for Social
Research in the 1930s and 1940s, and its complex
coauthorship. These aims are related: *The Authoritarian Personality* is widely recognized as a classic
in the social sciences, but its influence on contemporary critical theory is limited, and its application
of psychoanalytic concepts has been controversial.
It is hailed as a landmark study of the prevalence
of ethnocentric prejudice and authoritarianism in
postwar America, but has not had the impact of
the more theoretical works from the early Frankfurt School. It offers a systematic investigation
into the menacing survival of fascism *within* liberal democracy—a liberal democracy that had just
been fighting fascism abroad. But it also seems to
shrink from the full implications of its findings,

The South Atlantic Quarterly 117:4, October 2018
DOI 10.1215/00382876-7165871 © 2018 Duke University Press

especially as it pertains to the critique of liberalism and the analysis of late capitalism. It spawned the discipline of political psychology and innovated the use of empirical methods in the social sciences. And for many political scientists and sociologists and academic psychologists, it will be the only encounter with the name Adorno. But despite all this—or maybe because of it—*The Authoritarian Personality* goes mostly unmentioned in recent work on the politics of critical theory.

The book has been criticized for "psychologizing" political problems and mistaking social conditions for individual symptoms (Hyman and Sheatsley 1954). This charge addresses, in the most basic terms, the title itself: authoritarianism is mistaken for a personality disorder, not a political development. Fascism becomes a matter of weak egos and unresolved Oedipal issues as opposed to social, economic, or political forces, geography, social class, ideology, militarization, or national culture. Fighting fascism becomes a question of collective therapy—as if this were possible—as opposed to political struggle. There are other criticisms.[1] For some, its methods are faulty and its logic circular (Martin 2001). It presumes the personality type it purports to discover. It stereotypes an "authoritarian personality" but says that stereotypical thinking is the very trademark of this type. For others, its conclusions are either too pessimistic or too sanguine, its definitions too ideological or its real political commitments too muted (Shils 1954). Some say it is compromised by a positivist conceit, a reliance on dubious data, or a misguided determination to study fascism as a behavioral problem, as opposed to a sociohistorical development (Samelson 1993). Others say the problem lies in the unscientific discourse of psychoanalysis (Smith 1997). Either it adheres too much to the norms of scientific positivism or it abandons them in pursuit of an unfalsifiable pseudoscience. Even the most extensive and generous handling of the book in recent years—Peter Gordon's (2016) reassessment of *The Authoritarian Personality* in the age of Trump—is a bit embarrassed by it. Gordon tends to pin the blame on Adorno's coauthors.

Whatever the merits of substantive criticisms of *The Authoritarian Personality*, this approach—which absolves Adorno for bad arguments because his admirers don't want to believe he actually made them—seems misguided. First, it must be acknowledged that Adorno was a principal architect of the book's main theoretical construct—the so-called F-scale—and not a minor influence on its overall presentation. Far from disavowing or distancing himself from the project, Adorno invoked the idea of the authoritarian personality on several occasions after the book's publication in 1950, even if correspondence during the project reveals tensions and disagreements with his collaborators. Besides, his collaborators *agreed* on the primacy of social forces and also rejected any simplistically psychological explanation for fascism. Furthermore, the concept of the authoritarian personality, as well as the prospects of an empirically oriented interdisciplinary social science, had been at the core of Max Horkheimer's vision for the Institute for Social Research in the decades prior (see Jay 1973: 113–42). In other words, *The Authoritarian Personality* is the continuation of a critique of fascism that the Institute developed in the 1930s and 1940s, not a departure. There are, of course, some significant revisions. In the 1930s, it was the "revolutionary" who stood opposed to the authoritarian type; by 1950, it was the "democratic character" or even the "genuine liberal" (Adorno et al. 1950: 383–85; Jay 1973: 131, 227). In the 1930s, the problem of authoritarianism was a crisis in the theory and practice of political authority itself. By the 1950s, a rational political authority appeared to be the only protection against the pervasive pathos of authoritarianism, as faint as this appearance of rationality was. Still, there is a consistent argument that connects the early studies of authority with the later work on authoritarianism, and it is this argument that animates the whole of *The Authoritarian Personality*: that fascism begins in the family.

Reading *The Authoritarian Personality* in terms of a basic argument about the family puts us in a position to appreciate the distinctive way that the early Frankfurt School—Horkheimer and Adorno, for the purposes of this essay, but Herbert Marcuse too—draws from psychoanalysis in its critique of fascism (see Marcuse 1970). For them, fascism was not chiefly a problem of mass psychology or the so-called Hitler psychosis, this notwithstanding their recognition of the complex forces that bind a crowd of followers to their leader (Reich 1970: 17). So the Freudian treatment of group psychology, building on the dubious theories of Gustave LeBon, is rather marginal to their work (Freud 1959). Fascism was not about the decline of the sacred, as Georges Bataille—following Durkheimian sociology and cultural anthropology, but also in a psychoanalytic vein—argued (Bataille 1985). And it could not be explained by orthodox historical materialism. If fascism was an economic problem, it was not simply that. Instead, it was a problem arising from the interaction between economic developments, social conditions, cultural practices, and psychological patterns. In more basic terms, fascism reflected a crisis in authority, which was not moral or metaphysical, but social and historical. Fascism flourished where the social, political, and economic foundations of authority fell into contradiction, where the foundations of authority in one domain conflicted with its basis in another or were absent altogether. Capitalism had created these conditions, where male supremacy inside the home fell into conflict with the worker's exploitation outside the home, but the rise of mass culture meant that the whole social order could be seized by the profit imperative—and, with it, routinized violence, imperial bloodlust, ethnocentric and racial domination, and misogynist fantasy. Fascist authoritarianism was the irrational rationalization of the absence of a rational authority. It was a reaction-formation all the way down: a political reaction to communist and socialist movements, but also a psychic reaction to the collapse of authority. And it was *this* argument about authority and its political effects that pushed Horkheimer and his associates into the family and toward the basic lessons of psychoanalysis.

I consider the 1936 *Studien über Autorität und Familie* (*Studies on Authority and the Family*), especially Horkheimer's introductory essay, in the following section. This early research is key to making sense of what I take to be the principal discovery of later work, namely, that the "authoritarian personality" indicates a pathology in the bourgeois family and that the survival of authoritarianism within the family poses a real threat to democratic principles and practices. Far from psychologizing political problems, this strand of critical theory politicizes psychological problems, showing how they reflect and express social structures and relations. What seems individual and isolated is shown to be social and historical. What seems private is shown to be collective, not only in its effects but also in its origins and expression. What looks like individual disorder reflects and expresses a pervasive social sickness. Political psychology offers a refracted view of society.

In his preface to *The Authoritarian Personality*, Horkheimer says that the book reveals "the rise of an 'anthropological' species we call the authoritarian type of man" (Adorno et al. 1950: xi). What he might have said, additionally, is that this man was not born, but *made*—and made in a certain type of family pattern, which has its own social context and historical development. Defining and detailing that family pattern, attending to its variations across time and space, mapping the social positions and power relations within the household and beyond it, explaining how the authoritarian family forms in relation to capitalism and the state, accounting for the productive and reproductive labor done in the family and by whom, depicting the "democratic" or even the "revolutionary" family—these efforts seem, to me, as vital as identifying the personality variables on Adorno's famous F-scale. But this was not the direction taken in *The Authoritarian Personality* or in the Institute's later research. And the family has since receded from view in Frankfurt, with a few exceptions.[2] Even where psychoanalytic insights or political commitments remain, these seem not to warrant considerations of the family as the site of early psychological development and primary politicization—or, early socialization into a basic relationship with authority. Early critical theory offers resources for treating the family, not simply as a site of biological and social reproduction, but also as the "first creator of the authoritarian relationship" (Marshall 1937: 6).

Second-, third-, and now fourth-generation Frankfurt School critical theory has little to say about the family. It might be that this can be explained by social conditions and historical forces, for it was also the view of the first generation that the bourgeois family was being supplanted in its functions by mass culture and that the authoritarian leader was a symptom of these developments. They saw the family radically diminished in its status and significance from the nineteenth century to the twentieth. And they saw the decline of patriarchal authority as a mostly regrettable development. In some troubling ways, their arguments anticipate the infamous "report" by Daniel Patrick Moynihan published fifteen years after *The Authoritarian Personality*, which describes a "tangle of pathology" that plagues the black family in America (Moynihan 1965). For Moynihan, too, the pathology springs from a crisis in patriarchal authority. Moynihan believed the crisis was caused by cultural factors more than economic conditions, "ghetto culture" more than poverty and joblessness. The early Frankfurt School posits that culture and economy cannot be separated and, moreover, that the Culture Industry has done more to destroy the patriarchal family than any other cultural factor. Moynihan believed the pathology to be limited to the black underclass and imagined it in the image of the all-powerful black matriarch. The early Frankfurt School thinkers saw the deterioration of the patriarchal family as a more general historical development and conceived of it in the image of a weak authoritarian without real authority. But they share the conceit that fathers are the foundation of the family and of the social order more broadly.

Horkheimer and his associates believed in the primacy of the Oedipal drama and, therefore, in the supreme importance of fathers (or father figures) in ego formation. Another strand of psychoanalytic theory, which gives primacy to the pre-Oedipal phase of early infancy and emphasizes the mother's role in psychological development, might lend itself to a very different view of the family (see Benjamin 1988)—as would a non-Oedipal Freudian theory of autoeroticism and polymorphous perversity (see Marcuse 1964). But even from the perspective of their very modest revisions to Freudian theory, emphasizing the historical character of the ego and the mediated role of the family in social reproduction, their defensive attachment to strong fathers and patriarchal authority is odd. Against the idealization of fathers a very different lesson could—and should—be drawn from early critical theory: that antifascism begins with a real equality in the family, not only between men and women but between parents and children.

That *The Authoritarian Personality* is a book about the authoritarian family—and that antifascism might hang on the prospects of discovering an antiauthoritarian family structure—becomes even more apparent when its other authors are permitted to have a greater say in how we read it, especially Else Frenkel-Brunswik, a trained psychologist who had been researching the psychology of racism for several years before working with Adorno. Another aim of this essay is to amplify the voice of Frenkel-Brunswik, not only because she wrote a large part of the final manuscript, gathered and prepared much of the empirical data, responded extensively to criticisms of the work, and revised key claims in light of new evidence and argument. Not only because she was the only woman among the principal authors or because the project is probably her brainchild, though Adorno and Sanford were named project codirectors (Jay 1973: 239).[3] Not only because of her extraordinary life and work or her tragic death, an intentional overdose by barbiturate when she was just fifty years old, months after she lost her husband to sickness and suicide. My interest in Frenkel-Brunswik is theoretical more than biographical.[4] It stems from how she perceives the primacy of the family in the study of fascism, how she understands psychoanalysis and the basic contributions of Freud, and how she relates these contributions to fundamental problems in the social sciences.

Admittedly, her approach to the family is limited to only some of its dimensions, especially parenting practices and mating behavior. She does not consider the division of labor, care relations, or the external social forces that mediate and are mediated by the family. She does not deal with the family as a historical institution, which the early Frankfurt School theorists aspired to do, even when they idealized it. She does not discuss sex and sexuality or those family patterns conducive to antiauthoritarianism or to the defense of democratic principles. She does not deal with the specific historical forces that shape the different family patterns in America, for instance, how the violence of chattel slavery got passed through generations or how structural oppression has affected domestic life.[5] Still, Frenkel-Brunswik's research pivots on the family as the place where sociology, psychology, and political science meet. She too sees the authoritarian personality in terms of an irrational power structure in the household. For Frenkel-Brunswik, the problem is social and historical, but also personal and biographical: the authoritarian personality is a disordered reaction to an arbitrarily and unexpectedly violent authority figure in the household, often fathers but not always.[6] "Our material shows the family of the ethno-centric person to be more often father-dominated," she writes, "whereas that of the unprejudiced is more frequently mother-centered" (Frenkel-Brunswik 1952: 53). So her attitude toward patriarchal authority is substantially more ambivalent than what is found in the early Frankfurt School. Though trained in a somewhat different theoretical tradition from Horkheimer and Adorno, more liberal than Marxist, and closer to Vienna School positivism than either dared to step, Frenkel-Brunswik shows why critical theory needs Freud, why the psychoanalytic strand in critical theory is not bad psychology but good social science, and why a social science that opposes fascism starts at home.

Family Matters

It is a commonplace criticism that the early Frankfurt School has no political theory.[7] And there is some truth to this. When Horkheimer delivers his inaugural lecture as director of the Institute, "The Present Situation of Social Philosophy and the Tasks of an Institute for Social Research" in 1931, he sets out to reinvigorate philosophy by radically reimagining it. Against the dominant intellectual trends of his time, especially phenomenology and positivism, which he saw as antitheoretical movements, Horkheimer envisions a Marxist critical theory that would blend social philosophy and empirical research. But nowhere does he identify the state or political life as a distinct area of concern. Indeed, he rejects arguments for the primacy or autonomy of politics, seeing politics instead in its interaction with social, economic, cultural, and psychological forces. Horkheimer does not presume politics to be the main engine of historical change, nor does he see political life—the life of the ordinary citizen or the life of the revolutionary—as the necessary foundation of human flourishing. And in the early 1930s, the forecast for a workers' revolution in Germany was already darkened by fascist mobilization. Almost from its beginnings, the Frankfurt School has fallen under suspicion of what Terry Eagleton (2003: 31) describes as a "gentrified version" of revolutionary Marxism, "disillusioned and politically toothless."

Still, the first project Horkheimer launched as director was a multidisciplinary study of authority and the family, a project animated by the political crisis in Germany (and beyond) and aimed at the social, economic, cultural, and psychological conditions for fascism. In other words, politics is the prime occasion for Institute research and its driving concern. Though multidisciplinary, this early study addressed a core concept in political theory and political science—the concept of authority. When considered in connection with other canonical writings on authority, from Max Weber and Hannah Arendt, for example, the Frankfurt School adds an important perspective. What is especially significant is how a political concept of authority gets seated in the institution that the liberal political tradition typically places outside of politics: the family. The problem of authority draws Horkheimer into the family, which is also the place that contemporary readers might look for this tradition's contribution to political theory. Horkheimer's inaugural research shines a spotlight on the family as a political institution—arguably *the* political institution—and as a legitimate object of social scientific interest. He leads the Institute to elaborate on the dialectic already established in Hegel's political thought and developed by Engels, the dialectic that binds the family to the State. But where Horkheimer and his associates go beyond Hegel and Engels is in conceiving of the psychological dimensions of authority and historical change. Getting into the family ultimately requires getting into psychoanalysis and the psychological structure of a class society.

This early research was published as *Studien über Autorität und Familie: Forschungsberichte aus dem Institut für Sozialforshung* (*Studies on Authority and the Family: Research Reports from the Institute for Social Research*), a sprawling 850-page presentation of the Institute's empirical observations, methodology, and intent, with introductory essays by Horkheimer, Erich Fromm, and Marcuse (1987).[8] It was printed in Paris in 1936, and soon after Adorno would join Horkheimer in America and begin preliminary research that would lead to *The Authoritarian Personality*. Any assessment of the political theory of the Frankfurt School might well begin with the *Studies* and with Horkheimer's (1975) lengthy introduction. There he explains why the family takes a leading role in the study of authority. First, because it offers an instance of authority in a discrete form and setting. This allows for the development and refinement of diverse research methods—historical, comparative, and conceptual. Second, and more importantly, because the family is the human being's first acquaintance with authority, the first experience of authoritarianism, and the most powerful agent of assimilation to that experience in all of its other forms. In other words, the family matters not only for reproducing the social order, as Marxist feminists have long argued, but for orienting human beings to authority and adapting them to authoritarianism. In these early studies, Horkheimer is beginning to think of the fascist state in terms of the fascist family, and vice versa—an argument I am suggesting is also at the core of *The Authoritarian Personality*.[9] He conceives of the fascist family not as an ideological project (though it was certainly that) but as a social structure and a set of social relations. It is in this structure and through these relations that primary politicization occurs. Primary politicization means something more specific and more general than what is typically meant by the term *socialization,* or the internalization of the norms, practices, and ideologies of the larger society. Primary politicization refers to a basic orientation to authority, whatever its content. It is not about the adoption of certain beliefs or values, but about a disposition toward domination. The family is the institution that prepares its members to assume their place in a social hierarchy, adhere to the principle of inequality, and accept the rule of authority, rational or not. The family is where we first become political subjects.

Horkheimer says a few things about authority that compare with arguments made by Weber and Arendt, but with a distinctive spin. Like Weber, he recognizes a basic conflict between traditional and rational authority—and the terrifying possibility that this conflict might be mediated or overcome in a "charismatic" leader. But he rejects tradition, formal law, and charisma as sources of a genuinely legitimate or rational authority, without entirely giving up the idea that a source might be found elsewhere. Like Arendt, Horkheimer sees authority in crisis, this mostly as a result of the collapse of tradition on the one hand and the rise of reaction on the other. Arendt (1977: 91) even suggests that authority has "vanished from the modern world"—though much of her analysis shows that it only ever really existed as a *political* practice with the ancient Roman Senate. Arendt also notes the basic link between authority and the family. She considers how Plato and Aristotle turned to the household for models of authority, but also how they ultimately believed that political authority must be grounded in the polis, in the distinctive experience of freedom that only the citizen knows. The household could only offer models of authority indistinguishable from domination and tyranny.

Arendt follows the Greek valorization of the polis as the space of freedom—and the household as the domain of necessity—but her own discussion of authority is constantly stumbling on these efforts. "Aristotle's example is . . . of great relevance," Arendt (1977: 119) says, "because it is true that the necessity for 'authority' is more plausible and evident in child-rearing and education than anywhere else. That is why it is so characteristic of our time to want to eradicate even this extremely limited and politically irrelevant form of authority." What is so curious about this passage is that the best (and only?) evidence of the concept of authority—the authority of parents and teachers—is also alleged to be irrelevant to the case. Arendt must exclude child-rearing and education from political relevance in order to preserve her concept of politics. But she also takes these forms of authority for granted, because she assumes the household and the classroom to be spaces of natural domination and inequality. She is incredulous at the idea that parenting or education might be premised on a radical equality or a meaningful freedom. Arendtian equality is an achievement, reserved for some adults, not a starting point assumed by all. Arendtian equality assumes and requires inequality to give shape and boundary to the space of appearances. The result, beyond the rarified realm of the political, is a troubling incapacity to see authoritarianism in the household or the school—or, what's worse, proffer its justification.

Horkheimer's approach opens up to a more radical antiauthoritarianism (even if he never entirely pursues it), in part because he sees authoritarianism in a general psychoanalytic frame: as indicating a deficit of real authority. Authoritarianism is itself a symptom of the crisis in authority. It indicates the *absence* of authority, not its abundance. Authoritarianism is compensatory, not expressive. Horkheimer saw the need for an alternative to the authoritarian family, where Arendt could see only the inevitable "tyranny of the household" and the neat assumption that political actors brought no family drama into theater of politics. Horkheimer saw that alternative in the pursuit of a properly "rational authority"—an authority that he still presumed to be vested in fathers.

Arendt idealizes the polis, but Horkheimer tends to idealize the patriarchal family as the disappearing space of intersubjectivity. He valorizes strong fathers (and weak mothers) for the forms of character they cultivate, against an array of social pressures. He presumes the benefits of patriarchal authority without much consideration of its costs. He also presumes women to be a largely conservative force in political life, less for their particular beliefs than for their structural position and their investments in a traditional moral economy. But it is his own conservatism that explains his deference to a patriarchal concept of authority and his ultimate disinterest in the idea of the revolutionary or democratic family, even against insights pointing in that very direction. Pursuing the idea of the revolutionary or democratic family would have put the Frankfurt School into conversation with utopian socialist and radical feminist movements, connections that Marcuse did pursue. But even Marcuse adheres to the Law of the Father, as the essential object against which sons rebel and assert their autonomy. He too lamented the decline of patriarchal authority, for the corresponding collapse of a dialectic that he presumed played out largely between fathers and sons

(Marcuse 1970). Early critical theory reads as an opening, but also a missed opportunity for the development of a more radical critique of the family, one that connects fascism to patriarchy and a durable democracy to a real equality in the household.

Also like Arendt, Horkheimer insists that authority be distinguished from both force and persuasion. Authority, for Horkheimer, is a power that does not need to persuade, because it is already accepted and internalized. Authority does not use force to gain this acceptance as much as it will use violence to demonstrate and display it. An authority appealing to persuasion or force is an authority already in danger, already at risk of becoming authoritarian. Authority is not the power to impose punishment, but the near certainty that punishment will be called justice. The whole system of laws, beliefs, practices, customs, and institutions that Horkheimer terms *culture* depends upon authority, which it is endlessly consolidating and reproducing throughout that system. As T. H. Marshall (1937: 4) puts it in his excellent commentary on *Studies*, authority "becomes part of the pattern that it is its function to preserve, and takes root in the minds of those whom it enables to live according to that pattern." For the early Frankfurt School, psychoanalytic concepts were essential to discover how authority "takes root" in the individual subject and how a certain family pattern gets reproduced as a general social relation. This is a view of the family, not only as a site of social reproduction, where the requirements of "culture" get reproduced in everyday life, but as *itself* the relationship that gets reproduced throughout society. The family matters because we tend to replicate its dynamics and its irrationalities across a range of social relations. The principle of authority in the family produces a whole social order in its dysfunctional image. Here is Marshall, again: "The translation of the logic of utility into the illogic of authority gives meaning and color, *one might almost say personality*, to a culture" (5; my emphasis). But, of course, they *did* say personality.

Though Horkheimer develops a psychoanalytic framework for critical theory, it is decisively *not* in the direction suggested by Freud's *Group Psychology and the Analysis of the Ego* (1959). *Group Psychology* does not even mention the family as a significant social group—an omission that is especially surprising given that the psychoanalytic project is rooted in a family drama. Freud discusses the church and the army as two dominant examples of groups that endure in time (as opposed to spontaneous or temporary groupings), but neglects the family as an arena of "group psychology" or as an institution that shapes the development of mass movements. Horkheimer steers the psychoanalytic critique of fascism decisively away from the analytic assumptions of mass psychology and the psychology of the crowd. Even when Adorno takes up the analysis of *Group Psychology*, in his 1951 essay "Freudian Theory and the Pattern of Fascist Propaganda," it is less for the development of a mass psychology and more for a portrait of an archaic family drama, with father figures and father substitutes and their stunted, narcissistic children (Adorno 1987).[10] Fascism is not about the return of the repressed or the eruption of buried id impulses, but the reproduction of rigid archaisms in and through civilization.

Wilhelm Reich is another touchstone for the development of a psychoanalytic critique of fascism, still within the paradigm of mass psychology but closer to the Frankfurt School in his Marxism and political application of Freudian concepts. *The Mass Psychology of Fascism*, published in 1933, advances "political psychology" well beyond the rudimentary formulations of *Group Psychology*. Here is how Reich describes it:

> Political psychology has a sharply delineated task. It cannot, for instance, explain the genesis of class society or the capitalist mode of production (whenever it attempts this, the result is always reactionary nonsense—for instance, that capitalism is a symptom of man's greed). Nonetheless it is political psychology—and not social economy—that is in a position to investigate the structure of man's character in a given epoch, to investigate how he thinks and acts, how the contradictions of his existence work themselves out, how he tries to cope with this existence, etc. (Reich 1970: 16)

Reich also termed his approach a "character-analytic psychology," building on his earlier character analysis and adapting it to Marxist social theory. Reich's idea of an investigation into the structure of man's character under specific historical conditions is an important predecessor to the early Frankfurt School—and here we might recall that the original title for *The Authoritarian Personality*, the title Adorno preferred, was *The Fascist Character and the Measurement of Fascist Trends* (Wiggershaus 1995: 411).[11] The problem with Reich's "character-analytic psychology" is that it still tended to treat character as an individual matter and treat masses as the aggregates of individual egos. It still tended to assume that the problem of fascism was the problem of the crowd, of depersonalized masses, as opposed to deeply personal relationships and dynamics in the family. Reich's analysis is too limited by the assumptions of mass psychology, whereas the Frankfurt School pursues a different kind of "political psychology"—focused on the family and the formation or deformation of character that occurs there. And though it purports to deal with the family, *The Mass Psychology of Fascism* leaves largely unexamined the relationship between the family structure in a given epoch and the political character produced in that structure and according to its image.

Personality is arguably closer to what Horkheimer and Adorno were trying to get at anyway, for its link to terms like *person, persona,* and *personhood* and the importance of these terms in the theory and practice of juridical authority. Though *personality* risks an overly individuated and arbitrary application of political psychology, and *character* seems to preserve a link with history and society, the theory of the authoritarian personality is a theory of history and society. It is not an account of how individual madness becomes general, but how a general disorder takes root and expresses itself in individual cases. *The Authoritarian Personality* is a fitting sequel to the *Studies on Authority and the Family,* another attempt to answer the question of how fascism gains a foothold in a liberal society. It shows that anti-Semitism, white supremacy, xenophobia, racist nationalism, and fascist commitments are not minor or fringe phenomena, but deeply embedded in the foundation of American life. *The Authoritarian Personality* is social philosophy and critical theory at its most ambitious and audacious. It names a general historical disorder, tries to account for the proliferation of "syndromes" that indicate it, and locates a primary cause of disorder in the bourgeois family. The political implications of this "personality theory" are radical and reach into the most intimate of human relations, though the book has been criticized as conservative and timid. And while it is typically passed over as marginal to the theoretical project of the early Frankfurt School, *The Authoritarian Personality* is arguably the closest that critical theory has come to the integration of social philosophy and empirical methods at the core of Horkheimer's inaugural vision.

Collaborations

The Dialectic of Enlightenment is the collaborative text that formed an intellectual tradition. It might also be taken as an experiment in antiauthoritarian writing, where the individual author gives up authority without giving up authorship, where difference and disagreement surface in the work as a feature and not a flaw, where contradictions remain unresolved and the principle of nonidentity saturates both content and form. *The Authoritarian Personality* is also the product of a collaboration between the Institute and a team of psychologists, led by Else Frenkel-Brunswik and R. Nevitt Sanford, at the University of California, Berkeley. It is probably the fate of all of Adorno's coauthors to be overshadowed by his tremendous legacy and impact, but

Frenkel-Brunswik's contributions to *The Authoritarian Personality* are essential to making sense of its theoretical contributions. She was responsible for the interview material, as well as research design and methodology, and her efforts are critical to the conceptual part of the argument as well.[12]

Her biography is fascinating and deserves more attention than it can be given here. She was born Else Frenkel in 1908, to an observant Jewish family in Lemberg, a small Polish town in what was then the Austro-Hungarian Empire. She received her PhD in psychology at the University of Vienna, where she was deeply involved in the intellectual circles that had formed around psychoanalysis and logical positivism, associationism and Gestalt psychology. From 1931 to 1938 she was lecturer and research associate at the Psychological Institute at the University of Vienna, working with the celebrated psychologist Charlotte Bühler. There she met Egon Brunswik, who would become her husband—a relationship that met with strong disapproval from all members of her family, with the exception of her father, with whom she maintained a close connection. After the German invasion in 1938, the couple fled to the United States, where Brunswik was offered an appointment in the psychology department at the University of California, Berkeley. Though she was as brilliant and qualified as her husband, university rules against nepotism barred Frenkel-Brunswik from receiving a faculty appointment at Berkeley. She took a position as a research psychologist at the university's Institute of Child Welfare, where she conducted personality research and studied racial discrimination in children. As she began her collaborative work with Adorno, Daniel Levinson (who was her student at Berkeley), and Sanford on the adult authoritarian personality, she launched an independent investigation into the causes of ethnocentrism in young children and adolescents. Some of her responses to criticisms of *The Authoritarian Personality* and refinements to its basic arguments are based on findings from this secondary research. Frenkel-Brunswik's collaborations with the Institute extended beyond work on *The Authoritarian Personality*. She was consultant to the staff at the University of Oslo and spent a year there as a Fulbright Scholar in the mid-1950s. This was just after Brunswik took his own life, ending his prolonged struggle with illness, and the loss had a devastating impact on her. After her husband's death, the psychology department at the University of California finally extended her an offer to join the faculty, but it was too late. She killed herself in 1958, just before her fiftieth birthday.

As a psychology student in Vienna in the 1930s, Frenkel-Brunswik argued for the integration of psychoanalysis, clinical research, and academic psychology. If the early Frankfurt School had been working at the intersection of social philosophy, political sociology, and psychoanalytic theory, Frenkel-Brunswik was merging the insights of psychoanalysis and general psychology. "Whereas psychoanalysis has been asking, 'Which drive?' and general psychology has been asking, 'Which effect?,'" she writes, "a unified theory should ask 'Which effect out of which drive?'" (Frenkel-Brunswik 1940: 176). A unified theory combined the best insights and applications of distinct scientific methods. She insisted on the *science* of psychoanalysis—that it was a science and its principal discoveries were demonstrable and defensible. Against positivist attacks on psychoanalysis as pseudoscience, Frenkel-Brunswik (1954) compared it to Einstein's atomic theory: *it does not need verification, just confirmation*. And it was, paradoxically, the democratic structure of American society that allowed for the scientific confirmation of a pervasive authoritarian personality. "Since the prevalent political organization in America is not a totalitarian one," she writes, "such an attitude must be explained psychologically as well as sociologically, for only when the existing institution leaves room for genuine preference do psychological and social factors become important" (Frenkel-Brunswik 1952: 50). It is not when masses are coerced, but when they are shown to *prefer* fascism, to want hierarchy and domination and the division of human beings into unequal races, to desire these things seemingly against their rational interests and their natural impulses—this is the moment that the social sciences cannot do without Freud. Psychoanalysis offers a scientific approach to the study of the irrational in culture and identifies the family as the primary incubator of this irrationalism.

As a researcher at Berkeley, Frenkel-Brunswik argued for a multidisciplinary approach to the human sciences: "In our psychological description we found ourselves concerned with parental figures, with authority, with child-training, mating behavior and so forth. All of these are concepts frequently referred to by sociologists" (Adorno et al. 1950: 255–56). Psychological developments pushed her toward social research, whereas the early Frankfurt School moved in the other direction. But they met in the family, where they saw a fascist character first being formed and which helped to explain the prevalence of deeply antidemocratic attitudes in a nominally democratic society. Frenkel-Brunswik's treatment of the family is mostly limited to ideological transmission by the parents and child-rearing, especially disciplinary practices. She believed severe discipline and harsh punishment, particularly when unpredictable and explosive, were linked to authoritarian personalities and ideologies (Adorno et al. 1950: 256–57; Frenkel-Brunswik 1951). She thought that those who were raised in rigidly hierarchical families were likely to be defensive of hierarchy and deferential to authority. She believed racist parents were likely to raise racist children, but also that parenting practices more generally had a profound impact on ideological formation.

Again, Frenkel-Brunswik did not take up the sexual division of labor in the family or the larger context of relations between the sexes, between adults and children, or between social classes and groups. She did not deal with larger patterns of social domination or their impact on the family. She never specifies the difference between an "authoritarian" family and an abusive family—or whether the distinction itself is overdrawn. And she never deals with the disturbing fact that mothers are more often the perpetrators of child abuse in the family, or how this forces us to rethink the circuits of control in the authoritarian household. She was not necessarily a feminist. Still, psychoanalysis—what Shulamith Firestone (1970: 38) would later describe as a "misguided feminism"—offered her a view of the authoritarian family, the authoritarianism *of* the bourgeois family, where her insights anticipate some of the pioneering voices in radical feminism. And speaking of Firestone, *The Dialectic of Sex* posits that the liberation of women and the liberation of children are part of the same revolutionary project. Firestone believed psychoanalysis was essential for feminism, even if Freud tended to naturalize the historical dynamics he described. Frenkel-Brunswik was a scientist, not a militant, and believed psychoanalysis essential not only for descriptions, but also for explanations. "Freud's signal contributions to sociology and political science," she writes, "are his interpretation of human behavior from the standpoint of its latent, unconscious, irrational, and archaic aspect and his emphasis on the formative experience of early childhood, dreams, and fantasies" (Frenkel-Brunswik 1952: 48). Even minor discoveries, like the "closeness of opposites, first observed by Freud in discussing the vicissitudes of instincts," helped to make sense of general behavior patterns (63). And she was a liberal, not a revolutionary. She did not propose the abolition of the bourgeois family. But she did suggest that it was breeding fascists.

One of the key claims of *The Authoritarian Personality* is that fascism is not just a political ideology, that it runs deeper than specific beliefs. Fascism is a psychological structure. Correspondingly, the fascist family is not an ideological designation for right-wing parents or families that adhere to racist beliefs. The fascist family is a social structure. Not every fascist is a product of this family. And not all of its products are fascist. But *The Authoritarian Personality*, as well as corresponding secondary research, posits a correlation between authoritarian personalities and an "authoritarian home regime"—a regime marked by distant authority, strict hierarchy, sex segregation, harsh discipline, and arbitrary violence (Adorno et al. 1950: 258).

In a section on the interview material and family research, Frenkel-Brunswik writes,

> Prejudiced subjects tend to report a relatively harsh and more threatening type of home discipline which was experienced as arbitrary by the child. Related to this is a tendency apparent in families of prejudiced subjects to base interrelationships on rather clearly defined roles of dominance and submission in contradistinction to equalitarian policies. (Adorno et al. 1950: 256–57)

She sees racial hatred in a general psychoanalytic vein: as self-hatred turned outward, the projection of despised parts of oneself onto another, compensation for feelings of weakness. These dynamics are set in motion by specific family patterns, distinguished by "fearful subservience" and "prescribed roles," "surface conformity without integration," and "a relative lack of mutuality in the area of emotion" (257–58). The overall picture she draws is very sketchy, of the authoritarian and "democratic" family alike.[13] She admits that mapping family patterns can be a matter of emphasis or expectation, that the team was unable to conduct a separate study of siblings or ideological differences between family members, and that observations about gender difference remain impressionistic. Still, some tendencies are striking:

> In line with the fact that the families of the prejudiced, especially those of our male subjects, tend to be father-dominated, there is a tendency in such families toward a dichotomous conception of sex roles and a relative separation of sexes within the family. . . . By and large, the prejudiced man has more possibilities available to him to compensate for underlying weakness. He may do so by demonstrating his independence, or by implicit or explicit assertion of his superiority over women. Prejudiced women, with fewer outlets at their disposal for the expression of underlying feelings, show . . . stronger underlying hostilities and more rigid defenses than their male counterparts (259).

The authoritarian family is organized according to a rigid hierarchy of sex. This may be unsurprising, but more the point is how this sexual hierarchy produces a whole range of dysfunction in all of its members. The repression of women in the family (and in society) might mean they are especially prone to racist reaction.

This is also the section of *The Authoritarian Personality* where some basic differences between the authoritarian family and the antiauthoritarian family come into view: "One of the most important differences as compared with the family of the typical high scorer is that less obedience is expected of the children. Parents are less status-ridden and thus show less anxiety with respect to conformity and are less intolerant toward manifestations of socially unaccepted behavior" (Adorno et al. 1950: 259). Since the unprejudiced child as a rule does not seem to have to submit to stern authority—a fact supported by interviews with the parents—he can afford in his later life to do without strong authority, and he does not need to assert his strength against those who are weaker (277).

Frenkel-Brunswik is careful to note, as all of the authors do throughout the study, that the typical low-scorer is by no means "an unmitigated ideal" and the typical high-scorer ought not be "blamed as an individual for his or her bias" but rather "be considered the outcome of our civilization" (Adorno et al. 1950: 261). It is likely that more blame is due to racists who persist in their racism and pass it on to their children, not less. Still, a generous reading also sees how Frenkel-Brunswik is refusing to individualize the problem or idealize any family or personality type. The point seems to be that the authoritarian family is status-anxious in a status-obsessed society. (The authoritarian family today, shaped by the success of neoliberalism in remaking all domains of human life into arenas of capitalist investment, probably endures its status anxiety differently.) It is a highly disciplinary regime, where the main purpose is social conformity and the main value is obedience. Parental authority comes down to the rule of the stronger over the weaker. And those who learn to live under these conditions may find they can't live by any other rule.

There is another way, suggested but never elaborated in the book. They are families organized according to more egalitarian principles and practices, including the relaxation of sex roles and liberation of children from arbitrary discipline and violence. They are families formed through "mutuality" and "more affection, or more unconditional affection," "less surrender to conventional rules," and a "greater richness and liberation of emotional life" (Adorno et al. 1950: 258–60). Not without conflicts, anxieties, and guilt, these families also produce egos equipped to handle them. Children in "democratic" families do not entirely escape the dysfunctions of life in a postwar capitalist society, nor is the family figured here as a "refuge" from society, as it occasionally figures elsewhere in the canons of critical theory. Frenkel-Brunswik admits that these families produce all sorts of dissatisfactions and frustrations, as all families do. But, crucially, they tend *not* to produce fascists.

Of the personality variables that comprise the F-scale, which include "mechanization, standardization, stereotypy, dehumanization of social contacts, piecemeal functioning, rigidity, intolerance of ambiguity and a need for absolutes, lack of individuation and spontaneity, a self-deceptive profession of exalted ideals, and a combination of overrealism with bizarre and magical thinking as well as irrationality with manipulative opportunism," Frenkel-Brunswik (1974: 264) argues that the intolerance of ambiguity is ultimately decisive. This reinforced her earlier research on the intolerance of ambiguity as a perceptible personality variable (Frenkel-Brunswik 1949). It was, for her, an indication of the lasting impact of the authoritarian family and the pathologies it engenders, above all the division of the world into good and evil, strong and weak, self and other, us and them. The authoritarian personality is a type bent on maintaining these divisions and the forms of social domination they rationalize. He (or she) was raised on the authority of authoritarians and is lost without it. Ambiguity throws this authority into question. It brings disorder to the ordered violence of domination.

The principle of ambiguity in Frenkel-Brunswik might ultimately contradict the ideal of a "rational authority" in early critical theory, one that could be distinguished from a domination that gets rationalized and reproduced. It might push her psychological research closer to the philosophy of Simone de Beauvoir, whose *Ethics of Ambiguity* (1947) is also an antifascist effort. Ambiguity surely complicates any nostalgia for the "authority" of the patriarchal family, found all over the early Frankfurt School. It is no surprise that this nostalgia is more muted in *The Authoritarian Personality* and the innovations to a basic Freudian apparatus more extensive and imaginative. Adorno's collaborations were well chosen.

The Authoritarian Personality is an exercise in antifascism. One of its understated aspirations is the refutation of Nazi psychology. E. R. Jaensch was among the most prominent Nazi psychologists. He published *Der Gegentypus (The Anti-type)* in 1938, the first major study to argue that the psychology of perception could be used to index personality "types." He also posited the emergence of a new human type—or "anti-type"—characterized by ambiguity and irresolution. Jaensch called it the S-type—weak and effeminate, eccentric and individualistic, prevalent among Jews, communists, "Orientals" and foreigners, homosexuals, radicals, poets, and other deviants. Its opposite was the J-type—determined and definitive, manly and resolute, a predominant psychological type among true Germans and an ideal Nazi. *The Authoritarian Personality* has been mistakenly seen as a simple inversion of Jaensch's typology, where one's hero is the other's villain (Brown 1965). What Jaensch calls stability, the authors of *The Authoritarian Personality* call rigidity. And ambiguity, in both, is an antifascist principle. But one of the many surprises of the theory of the authoritarian personality is the prominence of the family in shaping and directing perceptions, an argument that goes well beyond anything in Nazi psychology. Jaensch believed personality types to be the result of race and race mixture. The theory of the authoritarian personality posited the primary importance of our basic social institutions, especially the family. Nazi psychology remained under the spell of an individualism disguised as blood and soil.

Besides, the refutation of Nazi psychology and the recovery of Freud for antifascist social science is no minor achievement or accomplished by mere inversion. Beyond Jaensch "an important feature of the Nazi program, it will be recalled, was the defamation of anything that tended to make the individual aware of himself and his problems, not only was 'Jewish psychoanalysis' quickly eliminated but every kind of psychology except aptitude testing came under attack" (Adorno et al. 1950: 164). Antifascist social science is the rediscovery of the individual and his problems, which necessarily leads beyond what is individual—beyond psychology and psychoanalysis—to what is social and historical. Making the individual aware of himself, for a tradition of thought schooled in psychoanalysis, means making him aware of early and formative social relations, those that get reproduced throughout his life in so many different arenas. In this context, consider that Adorno's (2005) indirectly political piece of wartime writing, *Minima Moralia*—his "melancholy science"—draws so many of its images of "damaged life" from the bourgeois household. And so many of his images of freedom are found in escaping it.

That's because a fascism lives there.

Notes

I am grateful to all of the participants at the conference on *The Authoritarian Personality* at Hunter College, CUNY, in November 2016. Thanks are also due to Andy Polsky and the Dean's Office at Hunter College for their support for that event. I presented earlier versions of this paper for the Critical Social Theory Group at McGill University and the Political Theory Colloquia at Yale University and the University of Minnesota. Thanks to all in attendance.

1   The collection edited by Christie and Jahoda (1954) features critical commentaries from a variety of perspectives. This volume also includes an article by Else Frenkel-Brunswik responding to some of the criticisms of *The Authoritarian Personality*.

2   The exceptions are typically—and predictably—feminists who engage the Frankfurt School. Axel Honneth does discuss the family in *Freedom's Right*, as a moral domain more than a political institution, where human beings first begin to recognize others. And he invokes the arguments of *The Authoritarian Personality* directly: "The time has past [sic] when the bourgeois family was a hotbed of authoritarian behavioral characteristics that could not nourish ego-strength because of its empty, disciplinarian character. In today's families, under favorable economic conditions, children can experience early on what it means to participate as individuals in shared cooperation" (Honneth 2014: 175). Honneth retains from the first generation the view of the family as the set-

ting for a political education, but because he does not see hierarchy and domination there, the lesson is one about recognition. Honneth believes the problem of the authoritarian family is obsolete because he believes the issue lies primarily with a particular parenting style, as opposed to a general structure that enables it. Given that the family does not exist apart from larger social relations and determinations, it is no surprise that "today's families" have traded a strict disciplinary power for different instruments. Whether the structure of the bourgeois family permits *anyone* to experience what it means to participate as individuals in shared cooperation is precisely what this intellectual tradition, in its more radical iterations, calls into question.

3   *The Authoritarian Personality* expands on early Institute studies of prejudice and anti-Semitism, but Frenkel-Brunswik had also been working with Sanford on anti-Semitism and authoritarian ideology among college women and, before that, developing instruments of personality research and studying the mechanisms of self-deception.

4   Frenkel-Brunswik began her formal training and research under the direction of Charlotte Bühler, working on the psychology of biography. She agreed that biographical details matter and adopted a developmental approach to personality, but she would ultimately reject Bühler's view that psychological development had an empirical basis in the human life span.

5   Hortense Spillers (1987) takes up this issue in her blistering critique of the Moynihan report.

6   For what it's worth, her own anecdotal experience was quite different: Frenkel was very close with her father. And, of course, the vast research on child abuse and violence in the home, far from anecdotal, suggests a very different story: that mothers, not fathers, are more often the perpetrators of violence against children (US Department of Health and Human Services 2012). This is on one level unsurprising, given how much more time on average mothers spend with their children than fathers. On another level, it complicates the conventional image of domestic violence.

7   For a sophisticated version of this argument, see Wolin 1993.

8   Leo Lowenthal also contributed to these studies and to the larger project of developing a critical theory of fascism, though his essay was not included in the original publication.

9   Here my account differs a bit from that of Jan Baars and Peer Scheepers (1993), who emphasize the influence of Fromm's notion of psychological syndromes on *The Authoritarian Personality*.

10   As Jessica Benjamin (1988) has already shown, mothers are notably absent from or peripheral to this drama.

11   The different applications of the concept of *character* in critical theory deserve more attention than I can give them here. I have touched on the psychoanalytic idea of character in Reich and others, but Adorno's use of the term would have also been informed by Walter Benjamin's work, especially his 1921 essay "Fate and Character." In Benjamin, character is a historical form and mythological residue.

12   M. Brewster Smith (1997: 163) insists on "the relatively minor role of Frankfurt Institute émigré Theodor Adorno, who won the citation count for alphabetical reasons." He further speculates that Frenkel-Brunswik and Sanford were the principal authors of the work, that she was not the senior author but "that from early on, it was a fortunate and mutually complementary partnership." Though I disagree with Smith's assessment of

the complex authorship of *The Authoritarian Personality*, he is among the few commentators to address it.

13   She does elaborate on the elements of the democratic family in some of her supplementary publications. Features include equality, ambiguity of roles, mutual respect, and a nonthreatening home environment (see Frenkel-Brunswik 1952, 1974).

References

Adorno, Theodor W. 1987. "Freudian Theory and the Pattern of Fascist Propaganda." In *The Essential Frankfurt School Reader*, edited by Andrew Arato and Eike Gebhardt, 118–37. New York: Continuum Books.

Adorno, Theodor W. 2005. *Minima Moralia: Reflections on a Damaged Life*. Translated by E. F. N. Jephcott. London: Verso.

Adorno, Theodor W., Else Frenkel-Brunswik, Daniel J. Levinson, and R. Nevitt Sanford. 1950. *The Authoritarian Personality*. New York: Harper and Row.

Arendt, Hannah. 1977. *Between Past and Future: Eight Exercises in Political Thought*. New York: Penguin.

Baars, Jan, and Peer Scheepers. 1993. "Theoretical and Methodological Foundations of the Authoritarian Personality," *Journal of the History of the Behavioral Sciences* 29, no. 4: 345–53.

Bataille, Georges. 1985. "The Psychological Structure of Fascism." In *Visions of Excess: Selected Writings, 1927–1939*, edited by Allan Stoekl, 137–60. Minneapolis: University of Minnesota Press.

Beauvoir, Simone de. 1976. *The Ethics of Ambiguity*. Translated by Bernard Frechtman. New York: Citadel Press.

Benjamin, Jessica. 1988. *The Bonds of Love: Psychoanalysis, Feminism, and the Problem of Domination*. New York: Pantheon Books.

Brown, Roger, ed. 1965. "The Authoritarian Personality and the Organization of Attitudes." In *Social Psychology*, 477–546. New York: Free Press.

Christie, Richard, and Marie Jahoda, eds. 1954. *Studies in the Scope and Method of "The Authoritarian Personality."* Glencoe, IL: Free Press.

Eagleton, Terry. 2003. *After Theory*. New York: Basic Books.

Firestone, Shulamith. 1970. *The Dialectic of Sex: The Case for Feminist Revolution*. New York: Farrar, Straus and Giroux.

Frenkel-Brunswik, Else. 1940. "Psychoanalysis and Personality Research." *Journal of Abnormal and Social Psychology* 35, no. 2: 176–97.

Frenkel-Brunswik, Else. 1949. "Intolerance of Ambiguity as an Emotional and Perceptual Personality Variable." *Journal of Personality* 18, no. 1: 108–43.

Frenkel-Brunswik, Else. 1951. "Prejudice in Children." *Idea and Experiment* no. 1: 7–9.

Frenkel-Brunswik, Else. 1952. "Interaction of Psychological and Sociological Factors in Political Behavior." *American Political Science Review* 46, no. 1: 44–65.

Frenkel-Brunswik, Else. 1954. "Meaning of Psychoanalytic Concepts and Confirmation of Psychoanalytic Theories." *Scientific Monthly* 79, no. 5: 293–300.

Frenkel-Brunswik, Else. 1974. "Environmental Controls and the Impoverishment of Thought." In *Selected Papers*, edited by Nanette Heiman and Joan Grant, 261–91. New York: International Universities Press.

Freud, Sigmund. 1959. *Group Psychology and the Analysis of the Ego*. Translated and edited by James Strachey. New York: Norton.

Gordon, Peter E. 2017. "The Authoritarian Personality Revisited: Reading Adorno in the Age of Trump." *boundary 2* 44, no. 2: 31–56.

Honneth, Axel. 2014. *Freedom's Right: The Social Foundations of Democratic Life*. New York: Columbia University Press.

Horkheimer, Max, ed. 1987. *Studien über Autorität und Familie: Forschungsberichte aus dem Institut für Sozialforshung* (*Studies on Authority and the Family: Research Reports from the Institute for Social Research*). Lüneburg, DE: Dietrich zu Klampen.

Horkheimer, Max. 1975. "Authority and the Family." In *Critical Theory: Selected Essays*, 47–128. New York: Continuum.

Hyman, Herbert H., and Paul B. Sheatsley. 1954. "'The Authoritarian Personality': A Methodological Critique." In Christie and Jahoda, *Studies in the Scope and Method*, 50–122.

Jaensch, E. R. 1938. *Der Gegentypus*. (*The Anti-type*). Leipzig, DE: Barth.

Jay, Martin. 1973. *The Dialectical Imagination: A History of the Frankfurt School and the Institute of Social Research, 1923–1950*. Berkeley: University of California Press.

Marcuse, Herbert. 1964. *One-Dimensional Man: Studies in the Ideology of Advanced Industrial Society*. Boston: Beacon Press.

Marcuse, Herbert. 1970. "The Obsolescence of the Freudian Concept of Man." In *Five Lectures: Psychoanalysis, Politics, and Utopia*, 44–61. Boston: Beacon Press.

Marshall, T. H. 1937. "Authority and the Family." *Sociological Review* 29, no. 1: 1–19.

Martin, John Levi. 2001. "'The Authoritarian Personality,' 50 Years Later: What Lessons Are There for Political Psychology?" *Political Psychology* 22, no. 1: 1–26.

Moynihan, Daniel P. 1965. *The Negro Family: The Case for National Action*. Washington, DC: Office of Policy Planning and Research, US Department of Labor.

Reich, Wilhelm. 1970. *The Mass Psychology of Fascism*. Edited by Mary Higgins and Chester M. Raphael. New York: Farrar, Straus and Giroux.

Samelson, Franz. 1993. "The Authoritarian Character from Berlin to Berkeley and Beyond: The Odyssey of a Problem." In *Strength and Weakness: The Authoritarian Personality Today*, edited by William F. Stone, Gerda Lederer, and Richard Christie, 22–43. New York: Springer.

Shils, Edward. 1954. "Authoritarianism: 'Right' and 'Left.'" In Christie and Jahoda, *Studies in the Scope and Method*, 24–49.

Smith, M. Brewster. 1997. "The Authoritarian Personality: A Re-Review 46 Years Later." *Political Psychology* 18, no. 1: 159–63.

Spillers, Hortense J. 1987. "Mama's Baby, Papa's Maybe: An American Grammar Book." *diacritics* 17, no. 2: 64–81.

US Department of Health and Human Services, Administration for Children and Families, Children's Bureau. 2012. *Child Maltreatment Report*. www.acf.hhs.gov/sites/default/files/cb/cm2012.pdf.

Wiggershaus, Rolf. 1995. *The Frankfurt School: Its History, Theories, and Political Significance*. Cambridge, MA: MIT Press.

Wolin, Sheldon. 1993. "Reason in Exile: Critical Theory and Technological Society." In *Technology in the Western Political Tradition*, edited by Arthur M. Melzer, Jerry Weinberger, and M. Richard Zinman, 162–89. Ithaca, NY: Cornell University Press.

Andrew Poe

Expressions of a Fascist Imaginary:
Adorno's Unsettling of Cathexis

> Fascism sees its salvation in giving the masses not
> their right, but instead a chance to express themselves.
> —Walter Benjamin, "The Work of Art in the Age of
> Mechanical Reproduction"

To Work a Miracle

In the 1951 essay, "Freudian Theory and the Pattern of Fascist Propaganda," Adorno (2001: 141) reflects on the psychological basis of fascism, claiming, "Even the fascist leader's startling symptoms of inferiority, his resemblance to ham actors and asocial psychopaths, is . . . anticipated in Freud's theory. For the sake of those parts of the follower's narcissistic libido that have not been thrown into the leader image but remain attached to the follower's own ego, the superman must still resemble the follower and appear as his 'enlargement.'"[1] This connection, between leader and follower, depends on the macro-reflection that the leader offers, appearing to increase the potency and agency of those on whom the enlargement depends for its content. Adorno continues, "Accordingly, one of the basic devices of personalized fascist propaganda is the concept of the 'great little man,' a person who suggests both omnipotence and the idea that he is

The South Atlantic Quarterly 117:4, October 2018
DOI 10.1215/00382876-7165883 © 2018 Duke University Press

just one of the folks, a plain, red-blooded American, untainted by material or spiritual wealth. Psychological ambivalence helps to work a social miracle. The leader image gratifies the follower's two-fold wish to submit to authority and to be the authority himself" (Adorno 2001: 142).

The follower's twofold wish, to both submit and ascend as authority, facilitates a complex social-psychic phenomenon—wherein fascist subjects become both divided and doubled, folded over on themselves in such a way that their psyche is both their own and not their own. This appears as a social miracle, it seems, because the division/doubling is without cause. As Peter Gordon (2017) argues,

> in this analysis fascism becomes simultaneously truth *and* untruth: On the one hand, it holds out to the masses the promise of a collective release from the constraints of bourgeois civilization with its demand that all instinct (and perhaps especially violence) submit to a pathological repression. Condemning this repression as pathological, it presents itself as the "honest" or "forthright" acknowledgement of everything one is not supposed to say or do. On the other hand, it offers merely the *performance* of this release through the fantasy of an identification with a leader who offers *both* the experience of masochistic submission *and* the illusion that he is just like his followers. This is fascism's "social miracle," which, like all miracles, serves as a dream of redemption without providing any actual transformation from the social conditions of unhappiness.
>
> The ambivalence of the follower allows for a loosening, such that the double quality of the fascist leader—revealed in propaganda as the great little man—produces a counterdouble in the follower.

The collective efforts of the sociological project known as the *Authoritarian Personality* aim to explain at least part of this process of the social miracle of fascism. Following Horkheimer's (Adorno et al. 1964: 1) thinking in his introduction, we might ask how anyone could be "susceptible to antidemocratic" or fascist propaganda today. This question takes on special significance now, more than seventy-five years after Horkheimer first asked it. In the essay that follows, I am especially interested in a refined form of this question—namely, whether or how the social miracle Adorno names is itself antidemocratic. At issue here is whether fascism's "social miracle" might always be a threat to democratic politics, and the latent political energies that linger in such a democratic fantasy.[2]

For a resource to encounter this question, I turn to a perhaps surprising site—chapter 16 of *The Authoritarian Personality*, titled "Prejudice in the

Interview Material." This is one of several chapters that Adorno self-authored in *The Authoritarian Personality* project. At first gloss, this chapter may seem especially benign, attempting, as Adorno explains, "to examine the relation of anti-minority prejudice to broader ideological and characterological patterns" (Adorno et al. 1964: 605). The evidence presented within this chapter highlights how, at least in the mid-twentieth century, "anti-Semitism gradually all but disappeared as a topic," becoming one among many manifestations of intolerance. Indeed, Adorno wonders whether, with the dispersal of the subterranean energies once evident in this deep-seated prejudice, there was a proliferation of possible new sites for social, political, and economic division.[3] While anti-Semitism may, for the contemporary moment of 1950, appear to be subverted, Adorno and other authors associated with *The Authoritarian Personality* worried rightly that such forces could cluster again, seeking new objects of hatred and pathways for antiminority violence.

Following through on this speculation, Adorno set out a task to discover differential patterns within the general structure of prejudice, with a specific focus on the function of prejudice. He theorized that "subjects who are prejudiced *per se*, but with whom it is relatively accidental against what group their prejudice is directed" might be a possible resource for the rejuvenation of fascism, and within the United States.

In the essay that follows, I focus on one very specific window that opens up in this account of prejudice in general—Adorno's use of the idea of cathexis in his analysis of the interview of subject #5051—referred to as the "Boy Scout Leader." As I hope to show, Adorno's subtle engagement with cathexis—the psychoanalytic referent for a charged investment of psychic and emotion energy in a person or thing—can serve as a resource for making sense of the double division on which fascism's propaganda depends.[4] As Shannon Mariotti (2014: 421) reminds us, "for Adorno, democracy itself is premised on a citizenry free and able to exercise its critical capacities in everyday life, to resist the given based on what they have learned from listening to the non-identical." Fascist propaganda ruptures that premise, collapsing any frame for resistance.

I begin my analysis with an explication of cathexis, including Adorno's use of psychoanalytic theory to encounter social and political phenomena. Significant here may be Adorno's use of cathexis, as opposed to the German referent of *Besetzung*. I suggest, by following Freud's English translator's vocabulary rather than Freud's own German vocabulary, that Adorno opens up an avenue for interpreting prejudice along a distinct pathway that breaks from Freudian structures. The second section of the paper offers a close reading of the Boy Scout Leader's interview, keeping this alternative theory of cathexis in mind. Here I show how Adorno's use of cathexis clarifies the logics of prejudice that would otherwise be obscured by a reading of the Boy Scout Leader as reasoning through Besetzung. Significant here is what happens to the stranger as the subject of prejudice, given this alternative translation. The third section utilizes Adorno's minute reference to Edgar Allan Poe's short story "Murders in the Rue Morgue" as a window into the consequences of thinking on prejudice released from an object, and the political and social results of a liberated cathexis.[5] I then conclude with remarks on the idea of the scapegoat that seems to motivate Adorno's anxiety and how democrats might begin to share that social worry.

My central aim is to explicate how, in Adorno's analysis of the notion of cathexis,[6] we see a ground for both fascist political psychologies, as well as—I hope—the possibility of their interruption.

Objects of a Fascist Character

The perceived danger that prejudice might pose to democratic citizenry frames the authoritarian personality, almost as its tantamount and unquestioned authority. If the prejudgment of another forms the basis of the horrific fantasy of authoritarianism that the democrat might imagine, the fear of prejudice itself poses a fundamental risk to democracy's own culpability with regard to its own founding prejudice. In his foreword to these "Studies in Prejudice," Horkheimer reminds us that "at this moment in world history anti-Semitism is not manifesting itself with the full and violent destructiveness of which we know it to be capable" (Adorno et al. 1964: v). And yet the possibility of the resurgence, or "outbreak," of anti-Semitism and similarly antiminority hatreds is something that democratic society must always already concern itself with. There is a view here, in Horkheimer's own words, of a prejudice lurking, a constant danger, and one that might—as a threat, even before it is manifest—malform the democratic. As Horkheimer asks, "what tissues in the life of our modern society remain cancerous, and despite our assumed enlightenment show the incongruous atavism of ancient peoples?" (Adorno et al. 1964: v). If democrats fantasize about prejudice as cancer, how cancerous is the fantasy itself?

Perhaps here we see something of the pathology that begins with the authoritarian personality. What is the project that would attempt to name one's enemy? Again, as Horkheimer explains, "our aim is not merely to describe prejudice but to explain it in order to help in its eradication" (Adorno et al. 1964: vii). (Though maybe, as I think we will see through analysis later on, we also begin to see here a difference in Horkheimer's thinking, along with the psychologists from UC Berkeley who helped formulate the study, and Adorno's own project on fascist character.) Horkheimer seems to stand as the voice of social scientific rationality in his condemnation of prejudice and its underlying logics. Later, Horkheimer explicitly elaborates on this point, explaining that "the superstitious belief in witchcraft was overcome in the seventeenth and eighteenth centuries, after men had become more and more under the influence of the results of modern science. The impact of Cartesian rationalism was decisive . . . [demonstrating] that the previously accepted belief in the immediate effect of spiritual factors on the realm of the corporal is an illusion" (Adorno et al. 1964: ix–x). From Horkheimer's perspective, the study should operate on a similar premise of trial—the eradication of new witches.

The present moment, at least for Horkheimer and others in the *Authoritarian Personality* study, was a moment of pause in prejudice—a moment when democracy was not so hampered by prejudice. (Hard to believe they could fantasize this was the case in 1950, though we might think this was simply a comparison—after the fascist rise to power in Europe in the early twentieth century, the American manifestation of fascism seemed nascent.) Prejudice here, for Horkheimer, was not simply "pre-judgement" of the other, but specifically the logic of irrational social prejudgment that leads to an "authoritarian type"—one that threatens "to replace the individualistic and democratic type" (Adorno et al. 1964: x). The *Authoritarian Personality* project begins in a complicated anxiety, in defense of the democratic against the authoritarian, but under a threat that risks its own foundation.

Yet Adorno himself calls our attention to a more subtle study, not on this or that prejudice, but on the very form of prejudice per se. Despite the concerns we might have regarding the frame of the *Authoritarian Personality*, if the study begins in an anxiety on anti-Semitism, interests shift to "antiminority prejudice as a socio-psychological prejudice per se" (Adorno et al. 1964: 605). What precisely is prejudice per se? As Adorno examines it, it is prejudice that has developed in such a way that "it is relatively accidental against what group the prejudice is directed" (609). While once we might have focused on the case of prejudice against Jews that manifests itself as anti-Semitism, Adorno moves our attention (at least in the chapters he was responsible for) to the general form of prejudice, and of prejudice in general. In what reads as a jab to the other authors of the study, he quips, "Naturally, these processes come to the fore in the dialectics of the interview rather than in the scales, which hardly allow the subject freely to 'express' himself" (611).

It seems, for Adorno anyway, that to find prejudice per se, we need to look somewhere else than in systems and scales.

The logic of prejudice per se that Adorno identifies as latent within those prejudices manifest in the interview materials used to support the study is one of cathexis. As he explains it, "as soon as (the subject) has achieved a specific and concrete counter-cathexis, which is indispensable to his fabrication of a social pseudo-reality, he may 'canalize' his otherwise free-floating aggressiveness, and then leave alone other potential objects of persecution" (Adorno et al. 1964: 611). Prejudice per se appears, a posteriori, through the countercathexis of a concrete prejudice. Tracing the pathway of cathexis should point us to how prejudice operates before such attachments become energized.[7]

A word on cathexis, so as to orient us to this phenomenon. *Cathexis* (κάθεξις) often gets read as Freud's psychoanalytic theory of emotional investment. As one theorist observes, "Freud comes to endorse a principle of conservation of the original libidinal cathexes of the ego, such that the original reservoir of libido is maintained, and there is a net balance between how much of it is cathected to the ego (ego-libido) and how much of it is cathected to objects (object-libido), so that an increase in one entails a decrease in the other."[8] The ego navigates the world through the investment of psychic/emotional energies placed onto objects/persons/things. Cathexis, then, is a charge of emotional energy, felt as an intense commitment to a gratifying object.

The etymological origins of cathexis show us something of the logic here. From the Greek *káthexis*, we might best imagine this as a process of "keeping" or a "keeping a hold on," as felt through our attachment to an object. Not that we are keeping a hold on it, or it is keeping a hold on us, but that both are keeping a hold on each other. To invest an object with psychic charge, in cathexis, links one to the object and vice versa. In psychoanalysis, then, cathexis is the emotional charge itself, but also the act of committing oneself to an object or body or thing.

It had been thought that Freud first articulated the concept in his famous 1895 text *Studies on Hysteria*. Except he didn't.

The word Freud uses for cathexis is actually *Besetzung*. A translation of the German *Besetzung* would be something like a "taking possession of" / a "seizing"/ an "occupation," and this is how Freud himself later translated the word in letters and other texts.[9] Similarly to *káthexis*, it can be read as a "keeping"/ a "holding"/ a "setting up." But in Besetzung there is a deeper meaning, a kind of analog to electricity (excitation / surge). While Freud would have translated *Besetzung* as "charge" or "occupation" or "investment," the much more ancient term *cathexis* was invented in 1922 by Freud's translator James Strachey (Ornston 1985: 394). Freud himself found Strachey's translation very far removed from his original intent.

Why would Strachey take what appeared to be a rather benign word and elevate it, through his translation, to the level of abstract concept? Strachey, it seemed, worried that American psychoanalysts "seemed to think that if they could be told the 'right' translation the meaning of *Besetzung* would automatically be conveyed to them. I believe that if the 'right' translation can be fixed upon a word with no ostensible meaning at all, people may be induced to try and discover what the meaning really is" (Ornston 1985: 394). While Strachey didn't always take such liberties with Freud's concepts, Besetzung seems to have struck him as one such opportunity, one to create a false front by which theorists could enter into the complex logic of Besetzung, and there begin to uncover the puzzles of what such an occupying charge of emotional energy might entail for the ego-subject.

Here, in Strachey's mistranslation, we find an opportunity. For already, because of Strachey, cathexis has a kind of double logic—the etymologies of the Greek and the German, working with and against each other, creating an energy in the concept itself.

And yet, perhaps even more surprising than Strachey's use of cathexis for the German Besetzung may be Adorno's adoption of the concept. Throughout much of his writings in exile, Adorno uses the term *cathexis* specifically, rather than relying on the original German concept of *Besetzung*. Following his use of this concept, I argue, may allow us to uncover the radical quality of "prejudice per se" made manifest in cathexis.

Expressing Prejudice

Of the many chapters of the study of prejudice in *The Authoritarian Personality*, chapter 16 on the interview materials is perhaps the most deceptive. While many of the chapters have overt theoretical claims, this chapter seems to present itself in the words of those being interviewed, along with Adorno's own editorial reflections. And yet here, I argue, in the voices of those subjects who are meant to evince prejudice, do we find a manifestation of more—of prejudice per se.

The first interview subject we encounter in the chapter is #5051—the Boy Scout Leader—who is described as having strong but unconscious fascist leanings. In response to an interview question on anti-Semitism, #5051 explains,

Sometimes we hear that the average Jew is smarter in business than the average white man. I do not believe this. I would hate to believe it. What the Jew should learn is to educate their bad individuals to be more cooperative and agreeable. Actually there is more underhandedness amongst Armenians than there is amongst Jews, but the Armenians aren't nearly as conspicuous and noisy. Mind you, I have known some Jews whom I consider my equal in every way and I like very much. (Adorno et al. 1964: 605)

#5051 seems to experience a dispersal of prejudice, releasing anti-Semitism even while directing those same hate-filled energies to another object. The voice of the "we" seems to isolate him from his hatred, while also later working to accelerate it. (The "I" that manifests itself does so first as a negation, "I do not," and then through strong affect of aversion, "I would hate.") As Adorno observes, "While the paranoid is beset by an over-all hatred, he nevertheless tends to pick his enemy—to molest certain individuals who draw his attention upon themselves: he falls, as it were, negatively in love. And yet, that negative love can be redirected to new enemies / new sites, so long as the energy itself remains preserved" (611). That negative love appears when #5051 settles on the Armenians as the object of aversion. While the interview question draws the subject's attention to Jewish identity, his negative love only manifests itself through the negation of the more hated love object.

Why would Adorno refer to this as negative love? What sort of love is negated (or is negative love its own unique form of love)? If love presents itself as an object of attraction (*eros*), or of equal relation (*philia*), or of universal and divine association (*agape*), how would it be negative? We might read the object as the source of repulsion, as generating unequal relation. If the Christian love that has come to characterize the West is love of the neighbor as one's self, the act wherein one becomes another, then negative love—in its most radical instantiation—might manifest itself as the denial of that equation. Maybe?

Adorno's negative love as the concrete experience of cathexis seems here to depend on the othering and exclusion of another. Here, I would suggest that Adorno is struggling with a sociological category once prominent in German academic discourse, and it may be helpful to contrast his thinking on the othering of #5051 with Georg Simmel's sociological account of the stranger.

Endeavoring to articulate the limits of social groups, Simmel hoped to rethink the stranger as a means of outlining those limits.[10] In his essay *Der Fremde*, Simmel (2010: 143) asserts, "The stranger (is not) the wanderer who comes today and goes tomorrow, but rather (is one) who comes today and stays tomorrow—the potential wanderer, so to speak, who, although he has gone no further, has not quite got over the freedom of coming and going."[11] The stranger, Simmel argued, poses—as a potential wanderer—challenges to the limits of group: The stranger is *here*—in the group, committed to the group, working and living with the group—and yet he can always leave. The stranger is thus defined by his freedom to exit, and *that he does not*. This sociological redefinition of the stranger as potential wanderer offers a means to imagine the conceptual limits of communities through a rearticulation of what it means to be *in* but not *of* a group.[12] The distinction between stranger and, say, foreigner is made clearer in the German—where stranger is *Fremde* (*coming* from other customs, languages, places; with an implied sense of now *being* here), and foreigner is *Ausländer* (literally "from outside the land").

While Adorno was critical of Simmel's sociology, it may not be wrong to hear echoes of German sociological categories in Adorno's thinking. Crucial here is Adorno's attention to #5051's language of exclusion. That #5051 is willing to name groups, and express resentment and hate toward groups, even as persons in those groups can be of equal legal status, may offer a manifestation of the logic of stranger that Simmel observed in prewar Germany. Adorno (Horkheimer and Adorno 2002: 166–67) reflects, "In the world of mass production, stereotypes replace intellectual categories. Judgment is no longer based on a real act of synthesis but on blind subsumption. . . . a regression to judgment without judging. . . . The perceiver is no longer present in the process of perception. He or she is incapable of the active passivity of cognition, in which categorical elements are appropriately reshaped by preformed conventional schemata and vice versa, so that justice is done to the perceived object." #5051, through the form of prejudice per se, begins to experience judgment without judging. According to Simmel (2010: 143), "(The stranger) is fixed within a certain spatial circle—or within a group whose boundaries are analogous to spatial boundaries—but his position within it is fundamentally affected by the fact that he does not belong in it initially and that he brings qualities into it that are not, and cannot be, indigenous to it."

Adorno illustrates that #5051 judges the stranger as being here, *in* the community. But his strangeness comes from the qualities he has that are not from here. The effect of this recognition is the possibility of openness. Knowing that the stranger is estranged from the group presents the opportunity to think through the limits of the group, particularly the boundaries that define the group as such. The qualities that make the stranger "strange" appear as moments of difference with regard to the community (either as "strange" qualities the group lacks, or the absence of qualities essential to the group).

Of course, the possibility of openness entails the chance of closure. The group can reify its boundaries and reject the stranger, thus preserving itself and the stranger as distinct from each other. But whether the group performs this option is not itself the consequence of the stranger, but of the affect of the group. Here we see the manifold forms of misrecognition, and in all its violence.

Xenophobic charge, like the sort #5051 feels for the Armenians, is made all the more potent because it is a manifestation of prejudice per se. #5051's redirection of the affective pathways of aversion highlight for us who is strange for him. Xenophobia, and the related elements of nationalism or exclusion that fetishize "foreigners," may require an architecture of prejudice that depends on the concept of strangeness and the negative love of that stranger as the site of that directed affect. The stranger—being present, and still strange—is the theoretical location whereupon communities can begin to examine the nature and structure of their own limits. As the stranger remains as such, the group is forced by this very fact to continue to maintain openness, at least with regard to the stranger. Thus, Simmel (2010: 147) explains, "the stranger is close to us insofar as we feel between him and ourselves similarities of nationality or social position, of occupation or of general human nature. He is far from us insofar as these similarities extend beyond him and us, and connect us only because they connect a great many people."

Locating the stranger could open communities to an experience of universality while reminding them of its impossibility. This would be the manifestation of agape made apparent in Christian love. But Adorno pivots here, using #5051 to illustrate how exactly the moment of the stranger, as fantasized through cathexis, might result in a negative love instead.

The consequences of this concept of *stranger* are far-reaching for democratic politics. Isolating strangers as either internally excluded or as foreigner has the anathematic consequence of malforming the openness on which democratic politics depends (Honig 2003). Seeing the nearness and farness of the stranger, combined together and evoked by our experiences of their strangeness, creates an opportunity to delineate those boundaries, which too often become stabilized around democratic communities. It is the awareness of the position and presence of strangers that opens democracies to this questioning of boundaries and disables (if momentarily) the psychological structures set by conforming to the community.

What is it to be in negative love with a stranger? Here, the lurking notion of cathexis becomes increasingly useful. As Axel Honneth (2012: 62) puts it, "the act of imitating a concrete second person, which draws upon libidinal energies, becomes transmitted, so to speak, onto the object by endowing it with additional components of meaning that the loved figure of attachment perceives in the object. The more second-person attitudes a subject can attach to this same object in the course of his libidinal cathexis, the richer in aspects the object will ultimately appear in objective reality." That richness can result in a full and positive love of another. But Adorno introduces us to the possibility that exactly that same mechanism might manifest itself in the uncritical negation. Here it is still love, still attachment and attraction and charge, but toward a person or group whom one defines as already alien and other.

Doubles

In his reflections on the Boy Scout Leader's interview testimony, Adorno offers us a unique analogue by which to parse the meaning of his unique prejudice. According to Adorno, the cathexis apparent in #5051's experience of prejudice is reminiscent of Edgar Allan Poe's short story "Murders in the Rue Morgue." In what at first might appear an odd comparison, Adorno (1950: 609) explains, #5051's prejudice per se parallels the auditory frameworks of Poe's detective fiction, "where the savage cries of an orangutan are mistaken by bystanders as words of all kinds of different foreign languages, to wit, languages particularly strange to each of the listeners who happen to be foreigners themselves." Just as the bystanders believe they are bearing witness, through sound, to the traces of many foreigners who could be guilty of murder, so too does #5051 have the capacity to direct unstable detection to many different objects he perceives as strange. Adorno claims, "The primary hostile reaction is directed against foreigners per se, who are perceived as 'uncanny.' This infantile fear of the strange is only subsequently filled up with the imagery of a specific group, stereotyped and handy for this purpose."

This should, I think, strike us as strange.[13] At first, this reference to the orangutan in the Rue Morgue might seem odd or out of place, but I argue that narrative stands as an opening into Adorno's conception of such prejudicial energies.

To make sense of the parallels, the story Adorno refers to has several key elements worth recounting. Poe's story begins in a summation of events reported in the evening news clips of the *Gazette des Tribunaux*. The story begins, "Extraordinary Murders.—This morning, about three o'clock, the inhabitants of the *Quartier St. Roch.* were roused from sleep by a succession of terrific shrieks, issuing, apparently, from the fourth story of a house in the

Rue Morgue, known to be in the sole occupancy of one Madame L'Espanaye, and her daughter, Mademoiselle Camille L'Espanye" (Poe 1992: 147). Poe presents an unfolding narrative of a spectacle, first in sound and then in sight. The newspaper report describes horrific events of unknown violence taking place in strange and indistinguishable screams: "As the party rushed up the first flight of stairs, two or more rough voices, in angry contention, were distinguished, and seemed to proceed from the upper part of the house" (147). As the spectacle transforms from sound to sight, the report moves from an uncertain orientation of action to a grounding of place. The police and witnesses (neighbors, friends, and strangers, all mixed together) invade the domicile, only to discover that it has already been invaded by another. The report explains, "The apartment was in the wildest disorder— the furniture broken and thrown about in all directions. There was only one bedstead; and from this the bed had been removed, and thrown into the middle of the floor" (147). In this condition of disorder, everything is uncertain. At first, there is only evidence of violence, but not yet a body. Then, just as sound led to sight, disorder leads to the certainty of death. The reporter describes "an unusual quantity of soot being observed in the fire-place, a search was made in the chimney, and (horrible to relate!) the corpse of the daughter, head downward, was dragged therefrom; it having been thus forced up the narrow aperture for a considerable distance" (148). In the freshness of the violence, the still-warm body becomes a vivid object of the nearness of danger, and the spectacle that is also event.

And yet the mystery continues, for the violence discovered is itself still disordered by the conditions that framed it. All witnesses will testify to having heard multiple voices, and yet there is only one body. As the search continues, the investigation uncovers the body of Madame L'Espanaye, "her throat so entirely cut that, upon an attempt to raise her, the head fell off. The body, as well as the head, was fearfully mutilated—the former so much so as scarcely to retain any semblance of humanity" (Poe 1992: 147–48). The report of events creates a scene where bourgeois life has been invaded—the home is itself the site of horrific violence, and from an unknown source. The double murder of two women, literally torn apart, provokes a scene of insecurity. The article begins a logic of rationality to uncover what person would have committed such an act. Until the person can be identified, the energy of the story will remain sublimely potent, and all will cast about for someone to cast their judgment upon.

Poe's narrative unfolds from this newspaper article, following the protagonist Dupin and an unnamed narrator as they explore various bits of evidence. Especially important for the structure of the story are the strange voices—languages that sound both familiar and unfamiliar—heard by witnesses coming from the scene of violence. Here there are obvious intonations of foreign invasion and provocations of xenophobia. Poe summarizes a variety of responses to these voices, which becomes the central clue to the mystery of the murder. Isidore Musèt, the gendarme, explained that he arrived at the house in question at three o'clock in the morning, having "found some twenty or thirty persons at the gateway, endeavoring to gain admittance" (Poe 1992: 149). The gendarme forcibly entered the building, leading the way to the scene of violence. On the way, Musèt explained, "the shrieks were continued. . . . They seemed to be screams of some person (or persons) in great agony—were loud and drawn out, not short and quick" (150). Made clear in the gendarme's depositions were the presence of two voices in heated dispute, one which he described as that of a "gruff" French woman and the other as "shriller" and "foreign." That second voice was specifically characterized as "a very strange voice," by which Musèt meant that he was entirely uncertain as to whose voice it was. He explained that he "could not be sure whether it was the voice of a man or of a woman. Could not make out what was said, but believed the language to be Spanish" (150).

Poe presents us with a pattern of uncovering, but always in the negative. Another witness, Henri Duval, whom Poe describes as "a neighbor, and by trade a silver-smith," was one of the first witnesses to follow the gendarme onto the premises. He too explained that he heard a "shrill voice," though he suspected it was an "Italian." Like Musèt, Duval was not certain of what he did hear, but merely clear on what he did not, claiming he "was certain it was not French. Could not be sure that it was a man's voice. It might have been a woman's. Was not acquainted with the Italian language" (Poe 1992: 150). This pattern of witnessing continues through the report. Another witness, William Bird, a local tailor by trade, testified that he too heard the voices in question. But, like the others, he identified the "gruff" voice as that of a Frenchman. As for the other, Bird could only be certain that this voice was not the voice of an Englishman. Perhaps it was the voice of a German, and maybe a woman? Bird was clear in his testimony that he "does not understand German" (150). Witness after witness, when deposed, testifies to what is present and what is absent. And, in what is absent, they seem to maintain the clearest certainty.

In this fictional city, the voice one hears is always the voice of another—always the voice of another person. The sounds of the city are foreign voices—seemingly recognizable as human, but also only as foreign. As Poe

(1992: 155) describes, "the witnesses . . . agreed about the gruff voice; they were here unanimous. But in regard to the shrill voice, the peculiarity is— not that they disagreed—but that, while an Italian, an Englishman, a Spaniard, a Hollander, and a Frenchman attempted to describe it, each one spoke of it as that of a foreigner." Not one of the witnesses could understand what the voice said; each one gave it a different name. Here Poe presents us with a portrait of the most minimal voice—the voice that does not speak.

,

—''—...

'————'———

'— . . . ————'''''' . . . . . . '' . . . . —'————'' . . . ——''—

The two options Poe offers as the source of this voice (one more true than the other, each grounded in unique prejudices) are a madman or an orangutan. In these options, we see the outside limits of the human—the unreasoned and the animal—both distinct in their expression of self, and each capable of receiving the dispersal of energy that would explain the unexplainable—the murders which could not be committed by mere human because too horrible. This characterization of the boundary of the human, and the narrative exploration of the deconstruction of that boundary, fit well with Adorno's imaginary. As Horkheimer and Adorno (2002: 202) explain in *Dialectic of Enlightenment,*

> in popular fairy tales the metamorphosis of humans into animals is a recurring punishment. To be imprisoned in an animal body is regarded as damnation. To children and peoples, the idea of such transformations is immediately comprehensible and familiar. Believers in the transmigration of souls in the earliest cultures saw the animal form as punishment and torment. The mute wildness in the animal's gaze bears witness to the horror which is feared by humans in such metamorphoses. Every animal recalls to them an immense misfortune which took place in primeval times. Fairy tales express this dim human intuition. But whereas the prince in the fairy tale retained his reason so that, when the time came, he could tell of his woe and the fairy could release him, the animal's lack of reason holds it eternally captive in its form.

Turning back to the Boy Scout Leader, Adorno's window into his prejudice reveals a troubling logic of the anxiety of the human, and the limits of the human, in the dispersal of prejudice. Adorno compares the Boy Scout Leader with "the potentially fascist character," claiming that "as soon as he has achieved a specific and concrete counter cathexis, which is indispensable to his fabrication of a social pseudo reality, he may canalize his otherwise free-floating aggressiveness and then leave alone other potential objects of persecution" (Adorno et al. 1964: 611). Returning to that passage now, we perhaps see more of what was informing Adorno's reflections on the function of prejudice per se in #5051's thinking. Adorno explains, "The manipulative individual avoids the danger of psychosis by reducing outer reality to a mere object of action: thus, he is incapable of any positive cathexis. He is even more compulsive than the authoritarian, and his compulsiveness seems to be completely ego-alien: he did not achieve the transformation of an externally coercive power into a superego." #5051 has an internal reality that parallels the city with unrecognizable voices. Just as the violence that unfolds in the apartment is unthinkable as nonhuman, and thus puts the reader in the position of finding the criminal to whom to secure our own negative love, #5051 experiences his own prejudices as insecure unfoldings of pervasive violence.

Of course, prejudice is not simply an individual framework, and Adorno highlights for us how this pathway of prejudice per se could become the basis for that charge that mobilizes masses in favor of the pathological democratic leader. As one theorist notes, "the leader's ordinary and even absurd characteristics (those characteristics that individuals think they have in common with the leader and make him or her an 'ordinary person,' 'one of us') allow the ego to transfer to the leader the cathexes that remained attached to the individual, while the leader's display of supernatural strength attracts the attachment of the self to its megalomaniac ego-ideal" (Baeza 2016). Significant in how #5051 exemplifies prejudice per se and the cathexis of negative love is the possibility that such energy could become the foundation for a radical antidemocratic politics. It is hard to recognize the orangutan—indeed, many would seem to try their very hardest to misrecognize him.

Twin for the Scapegoat

As a resource to encounter prejudice per se, I have turned to Adorno's "Prejudice in the Interview Material" (chapter 16 of *The Authoritarian Personality*). This was one of only a few solo-authored chapters of Adorno's in the *Authoritarian Personality* project. As I have tried to illustrate, Adorno attempts to examine the relations of "anti-minority" prejudices and to link them to "broader ideological and characterological patterns." On the surface, this chapter is quite literally a reporting of prejudice in the voices of interview subjects. But we may miss hearing those voices at first. I argue that Adorno's review of these interview materials offers a critical engagement with a dispersal of prejudicial energies (once directed into feelings of anti-Semitism, and now into new resources of social, political, and economic division). Clear pathways for this dispersal form through what Adorno names, borrowing from Freud's translator, as cathexis.

#5051's negative love is, admittedly, a microscopic moment in the overarching argument of *The Authoritarian Personality*. But Adorno's subtle engagement with the Boy Scout Leader's investment of psychic and emotional energy can, I think, serve as a resource for making sense of the pathways of prejudice per se and the link between this form of prejudice and the fascism imaginary.

There is a concrete danger in how we experience prejudice, in that the form of our prejudice works a logic of destructiveness upon us. If we turn back to the start of chapter 16, Adorno explains that "the 'object' of unconscious destructiveness, far from being a superficial 'scapegoat,' must have certain characteristics in order to fulfill its role. It must be tangible enough; and yet not too tangible, lest it be exploded by its own realism" (Adorno et al. 1964: 608). The origins of scapegoating lie in the Mosaic tradition of sacrificing one goat, and leaving its twin to wander in the wilderness. Indeed, the proper definition of scapegoating may be, "In the Mosaic ritual of the Day of Atonement (Lev. xvi), that one of two goats that was chosen by lot to be sent alive into the wilderness, the sins of the people having been symbolically laid upon it, while the other was appointed to be sacrificed."[14] How to not be a superficial scapegoat, but a true scapegoat? Since members of those already included cannot admit their latent aggressions, they project their cathexis upon the out-group—which produces a true scapegoat through its charge.

The twin that wanders cannot be a "superficial scapegoat," but instead must serve its proper function.

Notes

1   Adorno's continued references to the fascist imaginary, even after the publication of *The Authoritarian Personality*, afford us an opportunity to consider his thinking in a fuller context. This essay on Freud is an important example of that sustained thinking.

2   There is some worry that Adorno offers a flat contrast between the authoritarian and the democratic. Counter to this position, I see Adorno as offering the opportunity to read techniques of fascism that may engage the democratic imaginary. For a review of these criticisms, see Hammer 2006, especially 62–64.

3   For related studies on prejudice and social boundaries, see, for example, Nancy 1991, Kristeva and Roudiez 1991, Honig 2003, Young and Allen 2011, Allen 2006, and Hayward 2007.

4   I am especially indebted to Shannon Mariotti (2014) and her arguments in "Adorno on the Radio: Democratic Leadership as Democratic Pedagogy."

5   I take inspiration from James Martel's reading that takes Poe's politics seriously. See, for example, "Rendering the World into Signs: Alexis de Toqueville and Edgar Allan Poe," chapter 4 in Martel 2013.

6   As Peter Gordon (2016: x) argues, "critical theory, after all, is not a homeland, but a method. It is a strategy of reflection that aims to trouble all forms of untroubled cathexis—even the cathexis with critical theory itself."

7   As Steven Helmling (2009: 9) observes, "the moment called cathexis in psychology, thought's affective investment in the object, is not extrinsic to thought, not merely psychological, but rather the condition of its truth. Where cathexis atrophies, intelligence becomes stultified." For further reflections on Adorno's thinking on psychoanalysis, see Dahmer 2012.

8   Especially useful here are Baeza's (2016) reflections on psychoanalytic concepts in Adorno's thought.

9   The original argument regarding Freud and Strachey was made in Ornston 1985.

10   Simmel's essay "The Stranger" appears in *On Individuality and Social Forms: Selected Writings*. The most significant discussions of Simmel's efforts are Schuetz 1944, where Schuetz compares the stranger's psychology with that of the in-group; and Gurevitch 1988.

11   Relatedly, Simmel's model for this reconceptualization of the concept of stranger is the Jew in late nineteenth-century Europe. For a discussion of the identity politics of European Jews during this period, see Markell 2003, especially chapter 5, "Double Binds: Jewish Emancipation and the Sovereign State."

12   For a recent critique of the concept of groups, and the dangers of misperceiving their distance from actual sociological phenomena, see Brubaker 2006. While I agree with Brubaker's critique of the concept of groups and the danger of reification of group identities, the concept of the stranger can still be sociologically identified as differentiated from perspectives that are part of the group-building projects Brubaker identifies.

13   This move should surprise us, given Adorno's critique of Benjamin on similar grounds. See Feldman 2011: 336–40.

14   See "scapegoat, n." Oxford English Dictionary Online. www.oed.com/view/Entry/1719 46?rskey=6O6iR6&result=1 (accessed November 18, 2017).

References

Adorno, Theodor W. 2001. "Freudian Theory and the Pattern of Fascist Propaganda." In *The Culture Industry: Selected Essays on Mass Culture*, edited by J. M. Bernstein, 132–57. London: Routledge.

Adorno, Theodor W., et al. 1964. *The Authoritarian Personality . . . [by] T.W. Adorno, Else Frenkel-Brunswik, Daniel J. Levinson, R. Nevitt Sanford, Etc. [In Collaboration with Other Writers. A Reduced Photographic Reprint of the Edition of 1950]*. New York: Wiley and Sons.

Adorno, Theodor W., and Max Horkheimer. 1987. *Dialektik der Aufklärung (Dialectic of Enlightenment)*. In Vol. 5 of *Max Horkheimer: Gesammelte Schriften*. Frankfurt am Main: Fischer Verlag.

Allen, Danielle S. 2006. *Talking to Strangers: Anxieties of Citizenship since Brown v. Board of Education*. Chicago: University of Chicago Press.

Baeza, Natalia. 2016. "Adorno's 'Wicked Queen of Snow White': Paranoia, Fascism, and the Fate of Modernity in *Dialectic of Enlightenment.*" *European Journal of Psychoanalysis*, October.

Benhabib, Seyla, Ian Shapiro, and Danilo Petranović, eds. 2007. *Identities, Affiliations, and Allegiances.* Cambridge: Cambridge University Press.

Brubaker, Rogers. 2006. *Ethnicity without Groups.* Cambridge, MA: Harvard University Press.

Dahmer, Helmut. 2012. "Adorno's View on Psychoanalysis." *Thesis Eleven* 111, no. 1: 97–109.

Feldman, Karen S. 2011. "Not Dialectical Enough: On Benjamin, Adorno, and Autonomous Critique." *Philosophy and Rhetoric* 44, no. 4: 336–62.

Gordon, Peter E. 2016. *Adorno and Existence.* Cambridge, MA: Harvard University Press.

Gordon, Peter E. 2017. "The Authoritarian Personality Revisited: Reading Adorno in the Age of Trump." *boundary 2* 44, no. 2:31–56.

Gurevitch, Z. D. 1988. "The Other Side of the Dialogue: On Making the Other Stranger and the Experience of Otherness." *American Journal of Sociology* 93, no. 5: 1179–99.

Hammer, Espen. 2006. *Adorno and the Political.* London: Routledge.

Hayward, Clarissa. 2007. "Binding Problems, Boundary Problems: The Trouble with Democratic Citizenship." In *Identities, Affiliations, and Allegiances*, edited by Seyla Benhabib, Ian Shapiro, and Danilo Petranović, 181–205. Cambridge: Cambridge University Press.

Helmling, Steven. 2009. *Adorno's Poetics of Critique.* London: Continuum.

Honig, Bonnie. 2003. *Democracy and the Foreigner.* Princeton, NJ: Princeton University Press.

Honneth, Axel. 2012. *Reification: A New Look at an Old Idea.* Oxford: Oxford University Press.

Horkheimer, Max, and Theodor W. Adorno. 2002. *Dialectic of Enlightenment: Philosophical Fragments.* Stanford, CA: Stanford University Press.

Kristeva, Julia, and Leon S. Roudiez. 1991. *Strangers to Ourselves.* New York: Columbia University Press.

Mariotti, Shannon L. 2014. "Adorno on the Radio: Democratic Leadership as Democratic Pedagogy." *Political Theory* 42, no. 4: 415–42.

Markell, Patchen. 2003. *Bound by Recognition.* Princeton, NJ: Princeton University Press.

Martel, James R. 2013. *Textual Conspiracies: Walter Benjamin, Idolatry, and Political Theory.* Ann Arbor: University of Michigan Press.

Nancy, Jean-Luc. 1991. *The Inoperative Community.* Minneapolis: University of Minnesota Press.

Ornston, Darius. 1985. "The Invention of Cathexis and Strachey's Strategy." *International Review of Psychoanalysis* no. 12: 391–99.

Poe, Edgar Allan. 1992. *The Collected Tales and Poems of Edgar Allan Poe.* New York: Modern Library.

Schuetz, A. 1944. "The Stranger: An Essay in Social Psychology." *American Journal of Sociology* 49, no 6: 499–507.

Simmel, Georg, and Donald N. Levine. 2010. *On Individuality and Social Forms: Selected Writings.* Chicago: University of Chicago Press.

Young, Iris Marion, and Danielle S. Allen. 2011. *Justice and the Politics of Difference.* Princeton, NJ: Princeton University Press.

Samantha Rose Hill

Elements of Authoritarianism

> It is the nature of the calamitous situation existing
> today that even the most honorable reformer who
> recommends renewal in threadbare language
> reinforces the existing order he seeks to break by
> taking over its worn-out categorical apparatus and
> the pernicious power-philosophy lying behind it.
> False clarity is only another name for myth.
> —Theodor Adorno, *The Dialectic of Enlightenment*

What are the sociopsychological conditions that make fascism possible? Why are some individuals more susceptible than others to fascist propaganda? These are two of the questions that underpin Theodor Adorno's work on the authoritarian personality in the 1950s.

The Authoritarian Personality is a formidable text that occupies some nine hundred pages. Widely praised, and criticized for its methodology, the work offers a variegated portrait of authoritarianism in the twentieth century. While there are many threads in the work worth picking up on, this essay considers the theme of thought patterns in Adorno's chapter "Politics and Economics in the Interview Material." Looking at the relationship between the culture industry and the successful dissemination of fascist propaganda,

The South Atlantic Quarterly 117:4, October 2018
DOI 10.1215/00382876-7165895 © 2018 Duke University Press

I distill the various elements of authoritarianism that Adorno identifies throughout his writing.

Formal Constituents of Fascist Propaganda

In "Politics and Economics in the Interview Material," Adorno considers what he calls the formal constituents of political ideology—that is, the overall patterns and thought patterns that shape political opinion. How have certain characteristics like reproducibility, mass production, and reification shaped the distribution and reception of fascist propaganda?

The constituent elements of political ideology are applicable to both low and high scorers on the F-scale, and pose a broader threat to democracy, generally understood. This particular chapter, Adorno tells us, was born out of the shortcomings of methodology to predict accurately certain attitudinal outcomes like anti-Semitism in the general population. Overall patterns evidence the limitation of individual traits and characterizations, which were utilized in measuring fascist tendencies. The intimate connection between psychology and ideology cannot be subject to what Adorno calls a simple reduction to terms of personality. The determinant that blurs the distinction between high and low scorers is the general cultural climate, "and particularly the ideological influence upon the people of most media for molding public opinion" (Adorno et al. 1950: 655). There are thought patterns that pervade distinctions between people who are more or less inclined toward fascism, and these thought patterns are what we should be attuned to and wary of.

Thought patterns are generally understood to be those linguistic and logical ways in which we default to thinking. They indicate how we operate on a daily basis moving through life, and give form to the way we understand the world and experience. We learn these thought patterns from an early age, when our parents teach us how to name objects, draw distinctions between things we encounter, and shape the way we come to encounter our own desires and wishes.

In an essay titled "Freudian Theory and the Pattern of Fascist Propaganda," Adorno discusses how fascist propaganda does not create fascism, but rather appeals to certain latent personality traits that already exist within people. And one need not be a master of Freudian theory to understand how to appeal to the general masses. For example, the psychology of the masses, which can quickly turn violent, can be mobilized rhetorically through the use of ad hominem attacks and irrational emotional aggressiveness. This move shifts the gaze of the many onto the few, and is what Adorno refers to as a "clear-cut device." Speech devices like the use of ad hominem attacks and irrational emotional aggressiveness have the power to shape thought patterns, and they are deployed with precision toward a specific political end (Adorno 1982: 119). The mechanical rigidity of speech patterns used by fascist figureheads expresses certain psychological aspects about their mentality. Adorno writes, "The speeches themselves are so monotonous that one meets with endless repetitions as soon as one is acquainted with the very limited number of stock devices. As a matter of fact, constant reiterations and scarcity of ideas are indispensable ingredients of the entire technique" (119). The scarcity of ideas necessary for successful propaganda is a form of condensation that eliminates the need for thinking, or reasoning, altogether. The propaganda material sells a fascist brand that represents the political and psychological characteristics of the leaders. The production of mass rhetoric is designed and systematized to appeal to mass thinking and deploys a number of rhetorical strategies in order to appeal to the masses, which are typified as deindividualized, irrational, and easily influenced, prone to violent action and regressive tendencies.

In order to win the favor of the masses and turn them against their own interests, the fascist demagogue must create an artificial bond with them. It is this bond that turns individuals into masses, where each becomes devoted and loyal to the leader. Working with Freud's text, Adorno argues that this is done by appealing to certain qualities of our libidinal nature. The mobilization of our libidinal drives in a group setting is a pleasurable experience. We are literally whipped into the frenzy of the crowd, and taken over. As individuals, we experience pleasure actually or vicariously, according to Freud, and this kind of mass libidinal investment is a form of feminine self-surrender, which is associated with a masochistic and submissive personality. Adorno (1982: 122) says, "For us it would be enough to say that in a group the individual is brought under conditions which allow him to throw off the repressions of his unconscious instincts." Fascism does not create anything new in people; it draws out what is already there, unconsciously repressed.

The first element of fascist propaganda is the universality of its appeal. Fascists appeal to the libidinal drive, which is common to all people. It is the libidinal drive that enables us to form psychic attachments beyond our own immediate selves. Psychological mechanisms transform our primary sexual energy into a feeling that holds the masses together, and this is accomplished through what Freud terms *suggestibility*. This suggestibility is a kind of screen that conceals the love relationship created through ego-object investment.

The libidinal pattern of fascism is authoritarian, and uninhibited love is molded into obedience to the leader and group. Adorno (1982: 123) notes, "It is one of the basic tenets of fascist leadership to keep primary libidinal energy on an unconscious level so as to divert its manifestations in a way suitable to political ends." That is, we are not conscious of our libidinal investments in the loved-object who is the fascist leader. And because we are not conscious agents, the energy we invest into this loved-object can be directed toward certain political ends. Repression is necessary then for the formation of mass society—the active repression of consciousness. The irrational, authoritarian aim of fascist propaganda can be successfully disseminated only if individuals remain repressed. The image of the leader animates the image of the primal father, and this draws out a passive, masochistic attitude that requires individuals to surrender their will. Identification, the next element, forms a bond between the leader and followers, and is a form of erotic bind.

On the one hand, Adorno's writing on the authoritarian personality can be read as a study of individuals who submit to authoritarian figures and operate within a kind of mass psychology; on the other it can be read as a character study of fascist figureheads who mobilize individuals through authoritarianism. Who is this leader, the prototypical fascist that people identify with? The great little man, or fascist demagogue, is a person who suggests both omnipotence and the idea that he is just one of the folks. He appears absolutely narcissistic, and borrows his power from collective strength. In public, his speeches are identified by an absence of a positive program, the presence of threat and denial, a quality of averageness, and an inability to love. The individual in the crowd gives up his own ego ideal (his self) and substitutes it for the group ideal as it is embodied in the leaders, submitting to authority, and so becoming an authority himself by extension.

Adorno (1982: 127–41) identifies several elements that allow the authoritarian leader to command psychological devices or instruments. These include:

- Identification: The leader can guess the psychological wants and needs of those susceptible to his propaganda because he resembles them psychologically.
- Distinction: The leader is distinguished from the mass by a capacity to express himself without inhibition, speaking to what is latent in them.
- Oral character: Leaders are generally oral characters with a compulsion to speak incessantly. His speech is freely associative, and he posits a temporary lack of ego control.

- Irrationality: The spell leaders cast over their followers relies on language devoid of rational significance. Leaders make rational use of irrationality, exploiting their own psychology, turning their unconscious outward.

The aims of fascist propaganda propagated by these great little men are mostly irrational insofar as they contradict the material self-interests of those who embrace them. In his speech, the authoritarian leader creates a continuous threat of danger, war, and the sense that calamity could strike at any moment. Rationalism itself is turned into a rhetorical device that mobilizes irrational ideas rationally toward a political end. Adorno tells us that it would be impossible for fascism to win the masses through rational arguments, and its propaganda therefore must be deflected from discursive thinking. It must be oriented psychologically, emotionally, and affectively to mobilize irrational, unconscious, and regressive tendencies characterized by repression.

The psychology of fascism is engendered by manipulation. Psychological dispositions do not cause fascism; fascism is defined as a psychological area that can be successfully exploited by the forces that promote it for non-psychological reasons of self-interest. When the masses are aroused by fascist propaganda they are not spontaneously given to something new, but reverted to a regression of their psychology. The psychology of the masses, then, is a means to domination, and the means to liberation from fascism— and the possibility of resistance—is rational thinking.

Understanding the Ununderstandable

Adorno's sociopsychological approach to the distribution and success of fascist propaganda leaves us with a question of consumption. How is it that we receive political information, propaganda, news? How do we take in these mediums? Throughout "Politics and Economics in the Interview Material," which summarizes many key claims in *The Authoritarian Personality*, Adorno consistently returns us to questions of thinking, reason, and judgment. In the deluge of political news, where is there a possibility for self-reflective critical thinking? That is, how might we move away from the easily repeatable, threadbare, irrational language of fascist and authoritarian propaganda toward a more individual, particular approach to language and thinking?

Themes of authorship and listening recur throughout *The Authoritarian Personality*. Among the many qualities of authoritarianism outlined in this text is the desire to be told how the world is in neat little information packets. There is a constant deferral of self-narration among authoritarian types who find themselves drawn toward the fascist leader. There is a willing adoption of another's voice, which allows one to feel connected to something or someone greater than one's self.

In the section "Ticket Thinking and Personalization in Politics," Adorno discusses how the subject does not reach politics and economics in a direct way, but rather has to "contend with it in an indirect, alienated way" (663). Despite the alienation that most people experience in relation to political and economic institutions, they are aware that those institutions have an impact on their fate. Foreign forces give form to the lives of individuals who have no control over them and can exercise little individual agency within them. This apparent reality combined with the anxiety and confusion that defines complex political issues leads individuals to embrace "certain techniques of orientation"—mechanisms that allow us to navigate through things that we do not know. Adorno writes,

> These means fulfill a dual function: on the one hand, they provide the individual with a kind of knowledge, or with substitutes of knowledge, which makes it possible for him to take a stance where it is expected of him, whilst he is actually not equipped to do so. On the other hand, by themselves they alleviate psychologically the feeling of anxiety and uncertainty and provide the individual with the illusion of some kind of intellectual security, of something he can stick to even if he feels, underneath, the inadequacy of his opinions." (Adorno et al. 1950: 664)

In this passage, we see a number of authoritarian elements merge. The simplicity of a narrative that is easily repeatable allows one to possess a comfort in expressing their opinions. They need not formulate these political or economic opinions themselves, but can happily defer to one in whom they both see themselves and believe to be stronger and smarter than they are. As much as the authoritarian leader bolsters his ego and persona by acting as the voice of a movement, the association with his fame, wealth, and/or success bolsters the individuals who make up his movement. The masses repeating the slogans and rhetoric of the great little man is a way of extending one's self.

Adorno describes how an attempt to understand the "ununderstandable," a concept paradoxical in itself, leads to a paradoxical solution. Authoritarian subjects tend to employ two devices that contradict each other—stereotypy and personalization. Simplistic divisions enable us to cope with the chaotic nature of the world and create a form of organization. "Good and bad," "we and the others," "I and the world," and so forth (Adorno et al. 1950:

664). These divisions become stubborn beliefs and repetitive thought patterns that allow one to organize what is unfamiliar and challenging. These affirmative thought patterns and narratives—what is called stereotypy—mean that one inhabits a kind of boiled-down reality, neatly delineated by choices: "The stereotype, while being a means of translating reality in a kind of multiple-choice questionnaire where every issue is subsumed and can be decided by a plus or minus mark keeps the world as aloof, abstract, 'nonexperienced' as it was before. The opposition of alienation and anxiety caused by the coldness of politics is met with personalization. And both psychic reflexes are remainders of childhood, and inadequate to reality" (664).

A good example of this is how we are primed to consume news media as adults. There is a discrepancy between the amount of training we receive as individuals by and large to discern the veracity of political news and the constant flood of political news we receive. Adorno emphasizes two aspects of political ignorance: The first is that "being intelligent today means largely to look after one's self, to take care of one's advantages whereas idle curiosity is discouraged" (Adorno et al. 1950: 662). The second is the effect industrial culture has had on participation in politics. Not on voter turnout, but rather on the ways in which we consume political news and form political opinions. We generally consume political news during leisure time, within the same setting and framework as any other form of entertainment: "Political news and commentary like all other information poured out by the radio, the press, and the newsreels, is generally absorbed during leisure time and falls, in certain ways, within the framework of entertainment" (663). The effect both aspects have on political life is similar. Individuals are dissuaded from participation because they do not see the point in bothering with things that have little to no bearing on their lives, and because they view politics through the lens of entertainment as a kind of drama which is always disappointing, and which has no quick payoff.

How do we understand what cannot be understood? How can we understand all of the political news that floods the media and our devices? Political information cannot directly help us further our individual aims in reality, and at the same time, it cannot fully fulfill the function of entertainment by allowing us to escape reality entirely. Adorno describes this frame of mind, which is characterized by ignorance and confusion as a "lack of political experience in the sense that the whole sphere of politics and economics is aloof from the subject. The subject does not reach the political sphere with concrete innervations, insights, and reactions but has to contend with it in an indirect and alienated way" (Adorno et al. 1950: 663). And despite the foreign character of politics, those topics that seem perceptibly out of reach have a great impact on an individual's fate.

How do we cope with these problems and anxieties that we have not been trained to understand? In other words, how do we listen to and consume the news? And then how do we articulate smart individual political opinions? Adorno answers this by returning to the development of devices. We develop mechanisms, devices, or techniques that allow us to process the amount of information we receive. We rely on logical thinking apparatuses that allow us to assume positions on political questions, which means our political opinions are not so much judgments, but rather reflections of internal thought patterns that allow us to make sense of the world. The means developed to alleviate anxiety generated by the news "provides the individual with a kind of knowledge, or with substitutes for knowledge, which make it possible for him to take a stand where it is expected of him, whilst he is actually not quipped to do so" (663).

We need not buy into the sociopsychology behind Adorno's theory of stereotypy and personalization in order to see how political machinery uses media to create anxiety and fear. Or to see how contemporary media disperses information, which is "ununderstandable," but offers the illusions of knowing, being in the know, of allowing the individual to appear up to date on what is going on. The development of devices, of thought patterns that rely on certain ways of listening to information and thinking about the world, makes individuals susceptible to Nazi propaganda. And we might even say that these thought patterns or devices for thinking are authoritarian in their nature—dividing the world in objects and experiences that can be easily understood. And it is this systematization of the world through thought patterns that enables the perversion of reason into an instrument that rationalizes the irrational, bleeding reality into fiction, fiction into reality.

Odysseus and Instrumental Reason

In *The Dialectic of Enlightenment* Adorno and Max Horkheimer recount the story of Odysseus, the prototype of modern bourgeois man.[1] Elements of authoritarianism emerge in the play between desire and recognition when Odysseus encounters the sirens. In order safely to pass the sirens, he must keep a safe distance. As Adorno and Horkheimer (2007) put it, Odysseus "throws himself away in order to live." And through language emptied of all meaning, he saves himself. Odysseus's mastery is constituted within and against the natural world. "Odysseus lives according to the ancient principle which originally constituted bourgeois society. One had to choose between cheating and going under" (Adorno and Horkheimer 2007: 48–49). The modern bourgeois man is like Odysseus, guided by cunning and reason. He hears what he wants to hear, enjoying the pleasures of the sensual realm without the risk of succumbing to his senses. He exercises control over his bodily self, and there is a certain indulgence in his bounded consumption. Assuaging desire in this way allows him to take what he wants without recognizing the other, the other who makes what he wants possible at all. This instrumental reason allows him to objectify those who are perceived as dangerous, unwieldy, and unknown, yet somehow alluring and desirable. He makes use of the other in a way that is pleasing and beneficial to himself.

This Odysseus man, the man of enlightened, instrumental reason who can harness nature, understands the use value of simplification. Reason does not imply logic or sense making, and it permits sense experience only to a certain extent. Pleasure must be repressed and experience must be ordered, regulated, and organized. A safe distance is maintained through self-narration from those elements that might undermine one's ability to steer clearly. In this way, the bourgeois subject is freed from all guidance. Reason need not be well formed according to certain moral standards for it to succeed in mastery. It is not the thought as it is expressed through language in reality, but rather the "agency of calculating thought, which arranges the world for the purposes of self-preservation and recognizes no function other than that of working on the objects as mere sense material in order to make it the material of subjugation" (Adorno and Horkheimer 2007: 65). What we see in this formulation, in Adorno and Horkheimer's critique of the limits of Kantian reason, is how thinking and the product(s) of thought are formulated and reified within the cultural apparatus. So that individual human beings are thought of as objects that can be manipulated and administered too, an invariable mass that can be repeated and replaced.

Simplification and systematization are essential to both mechanized capitalist production and fascist propaganda. Seen from the perspective of the consumer, of ordinary citizens, these commodity goods—ends produced mostly through invisible processes—appear before us as desirable objects that contain not only an ideology but also a metaphysical certainty. That is, concepts and metaphysical goods like happiness are embodied in commodities. In this simplified system that packages and represses experiences of living into consumer goods, individual experience is lost. Adorno and Horkheimer (2007: 65–66) continue:

The senses are determined by the conceptual apparatus in advance of perception; the citizen sees the world as made *a priori* of the stuff from which he himself constructs it. Kant intuitively anticipated what Hollywood had consciously put into practice: images are precensored during production by the same standard of understanding which will later determine their reception by viewers. The perception by which public judgment feels itself confirmed has been shaped by that judgment even before the perception takes place.

Reason exercised as a systematic science levels out individual experience, predetermining perception before it has the possibility of occurring. This Enlightenment thinking expels difference and otherness by necessity of simplification. Each individual is nothing more than that for which he or she has been produced. The multitude of human actions and desires are perceived as flattened planes, and the only pleasure that matters is that of those who are shaping public opinion.

Odysseus's denial of nature in man—his denial of the rower's pleasure—allows him to exercise domination. He is an authoritarian hero who uses what harsh measures he must in order to survive, to continue in his domination, and he does this through restraint, repression, self-affirmation, and self-renunciation. The use of language is instrumental; without meaning, it only reinforces the orders of domination. In this way, Enlightenment thinking exploits the difference between word and thing through language.

Critical Thinking as a Means to Resistance

The demand for organization, the rejection of chaos, a fear of the unknown enables a simplified view of the world where self-reflective thinking is no longer necessary. It is enough to consume a sense of self through mediated objects; one need not turn inward to think about one's self as an individual. The ego is cathected into a world where order is given value and social hierarchy offers a sense of certainty. To challenge these principles is to then challenge the individual who has adopted them. As Adorno reminds us in *The Authoritarian Personality*, this challenging can provoke underlying violent tendencies. So while not thinking seems to be a quality valued by those who seek comfort and knowledge in the material world, thinking in certain ways is perceived to be a threat to one's way of life. There is an ascription to this understanding by those who embrace a passing life, and there are those who treat this understanding as a device that can be used to manipulate and control those who desire an ordered version of the world. An Odysseus who commands, and workers who put wax in their ears, who sacrifice their own sense perception of the world, so that they may move another forward.

And this is why Adorno writes that

> all modern fascist movements, including the practices of contemporary American demagogues, have aimed at the ignorant; they have consciously manipulated the facts in a way that could lead to success only with those who were not acquainted with the facts. Ignorance with respect to the complexities of contemporary society makes for a state of general uncertainty and anxiety, which is the ideal breeding ground for the modern type of reactionary mass movement. Such movements are always "populist" in and maliciously anti-intellectual." (Adorno et al. 1950: 658–59)

Just as the authoritarian distances himself from nature in order to arrange it in a way that can be mastered, individuals are distanced from politics and economics in a way that requires simplified narratives that do not necessarily have to be reflective of reality or individual experiences in the world. The rowers, or workers, experience the siren's song differently from Odysseus. They do not get to partake in any of the pleasure; they know only of its danger.

Note

1   *The Authoritarian Personality* and *The Dialectic of Enlightenment* undertake very similar projects in trying to offer accounts of authoritarian and fascist elements within society. A question that underscores both texts is: How was totalitarianism possible?

References

Adorno, Theodor W. 1982. "Freudian Theory and the Pattern of Fascist Propaganda." In *The Essential Frankfurt School Reader*, edited by Andrew Arato and Eike Gephardt, 118–37. London: Bloomsbury.

Adorno, Theodor W., and Max Horkheimer. 2007. *The Dialectic of Enlightenment*. Stanford, CA: Stanford University Press.

Adorno, Theodor W., Else Frenkel-Brunswik, Daniel J. Levinson, and R. Nevitt Sanford. 1950. *The Authoritarian Personality*. New York: Harper and Row.

Michael Stein

The Authoritarian Personality and the Limits of American Social Science

In the age of "Trumpism," where white suprema-
cists, the alt-right, and the president's contempt
for the judiciary have renewed liberal fear of
authoritarianism and fascism, revisiting Adorno
et al.'s landmark study, *The Authoritarian Personality*, is a worthwhile enterprise. Despite seeming
parallels and contemporary evocations, I do not
believe the study illuminates the politics of our
contemporary moment. It does, however, demonstrate the promise and limits of American social
science and, in doing so, problematize the relationship between politics and the study of politics.
The encounter between Max Horkheimer,
Adorno, Samuel Flowerman, and other stateside
colleagues who collaborated on the American
Jewish Council's (AJC) Studies in Prejudice series
produced tensions, especially in the *Authoritarian
Personality* study, between behavioral social science and critical theory that were ultimately unre-
solvable. Exploring the nature of these tensions is
important for our present moment where the legacy of the study lives on in the disciplines of political science and political psychology as well as the
popular press.

In order to draw out this tension, I focus on
two interrelated dimensions of the study. First,

The South Atlantic Quarterly 117:4, October 2018
DOI 10.1215/00382876-7165911   © 2018 Duke University Press

I consider the authors' understanding of the enterprise they were engaged in, the assumptions of the work, and, briefly, the legacy of *The Authoritarian Personality* on contemporary political psychology in particular and social science in general. Second, I suggest some ways that the assumptions and knowledge produced in *The Authoritarian Personality* and subsequent quantitative social science[1] prefigure the political, sanctify the politics of the moment, and circumscribe an impoverished political imaginary unsuitable for grappling with the profound challenges faced by American democracy today.

In addition to my own reading of the text, in order to make this argument I engage substantially with the work of two interlocutors. Peter Gordon (2017), in "The Authoritarian Personality Revisited: Reading Adorno in the Age of Trump," traverses similar ground and importantly emphasizes Adorno's unpublished remarks on the study that largely called the logic of the enterprise into question and exemplified the tension between method and theory. On a broader but similar terrain, Sheldon Wolin's landmark essay "Political Theory as a Vocation," published nearly twenty years after *The Authoritarian Personality*, squarely challenged the ascendance of behavioralism and its expression in American political science. While Wolin is taking on his own discipline, the insights are generalizable to method in the social sciences. The blistering criticism he offers, alongside his view of epic theory, is as potent today as when it was written, perhaps even more so as the techniques and hegemony of quantitative social science are now dominant. Engaging Wolin in my reading of *The Authoritarian Personality* offers a harsher evaluation of the tension between American social science and critical theory than Gordon's gracious reading allows, and one that is necessary in order to understand the nature and limits of our contemporary intellectual and political inheritances whose consequences extend far beyond the page.

Authoritarians: Discovered or Produced?

Adorno and Horkheimer's involvement in the Studies in Prejudice research program, an initiative of the AJC's Department of Scientific Research, is both a strange departure for the authors of *The Dialectic of Enlightenment* and a thematically consistent project focused on the nature of anti-Semitism. The disconnect is embodied in the competing approaches of the two efforts. In the case of *The Dialectic of Enlightenment*, Adorno and Horkheimer approached the increasing standardization of society through a dialectical lens engaging with philosophy, literature, and consumer culture. In their work for AJC, especially in Adorno et al.'s collaboration, the dialectical orientation is subsumed and limited by the influence and methods of American social science. This difference in approach was the central issue in Horkheimer and Flowerman's relationship, and their competing visions for the direction of the Department of Scientific Research were irreconcilable. Horkheimer preferred "large-scale, long-term and theory-oriented research," while Flowerman was interested in "quick results and methodologically well-grounded research" (Wiggershaus 1994: 397). What resulted was a mixed bag that slanted toward method but was imbued with theoretical underpinnings. The primary ongoing intellectual legacy of *The Authoritarian Personality* is similarly slanted toward method in that it produced a measure of authoritarianism that remains operative today.

The foreword to the Studies in Prejudice series, authored by Horkheimer and Flowerman, and the preface to *The Authoritarian Personality* by Adorno et al., provide insight into the way the projects were conceived, or at least presented, by those carrying them out. They are worth considering in the context of the tension between theory, and more specifically critical theory, and American social science. What they reflect is a faith in actionable knowledge and the power and role of education, as well as an unfounded expectation of paradigm-shifting science.

The foreword approaches the problem of anti-Semitism in a medicalized fashion, suggesting that it is a "social disease" that the social scientist, much like the "biologist or the physician, can study . . . in the search for more effective ways to prevent or reduce the virulence of the next outbreak" (v). Furthermore, the authors ask, "what within the individual organism responds to certain stimuli in our culture with attitudes and acts of destructive aggression?" Framing the approach in this manner pathologizes prejudice, rendering it an essential characteristic of the species that can be identified, studied, and perhaps even treated. Understanding prejudice as a biological and/or psychological feature, the social scientist has the potential to discover the root causes (in this case anti-Semitism) endemic in humanity (organisms). While the emergence of these latent elements is stimulated by "our culture," the condition of their activation seems consequential rather than dialectical given the essential nature of humanity's susceptibility to "social disease." In other words, if the root of prejudice lies within us, it is merely awakened or invigorated by culture (society) and not dynamically produced by it.

For the authors, the task was to identify this cancer and in doing so have real cultural and political effect. Adorno et al. expressed this optimism with sincerity and painted a peculiar portrait of the role of the intellectual as well as the nature of scientific discovery. Highlighting this portrait is important because it allows us to consider the role we imagine for the intellectual. Consider how the authors of *The Authoritarian Personality* imagined their task, responsibility, and effect:

> The implications and values of the study are practical as well as theoretical. The authors do not believe that there is a short cut to education which will eliminate the long and often circuitous road of painstaking research and theoretical analysis. Nor do they think that such a problem as the position of minorities in modern society, and more specifically the problem of religious and racial hatreds, can be tackled successfully either by the propaganda of tolerance or by apologetic refutation of errors and lies. On the other hand, theoretical activity and practical application are not separated by an unbridgeable gulf. Quite the contrary: the authors are imbued with the conviction that the sincere and systematic scientific elucidation of a phenomenon of such great historical meaning can contribute directly to an amelioration of the cultural atmosphere in which hatred breeds. (Adorno et al. 1950: 7)

This attempt to bridge the gulf between theory and method arguably failed, but even so, the belief in the ameliorating effects of science deserves more attention. In support of the claim that scientific elucidation of a phenomenon can directly contribute to the amelioration of the negative effects of that phenomenon, the authors offer two historical examples. The first is the impact of Cartesian rationalism on the superstitious belief in witchcraft, and the second is the revolution between parents and children brought about by Freud's demonstration of the prime importance of the events of childhood.

I have a difficult time making sense of these examples. In general, I understand that the work of scientists broadly conceived to include the category of the intellectual can have an impact on culture, politics, and society. On the other hand, I am dubious of what I sense as a teleology of enlightenment: faith in science, the knowledge it produces, and the presumed consequences of that knowledge. Perhaps this concern is unwarranted and merely reflects my suspicion of empiricism due to the ascendance of behavioralism, positivism, and normal science in the social sciences. At the same time, if we take the claim seriously and evaluate the effect of *The Authoritarian Personality* on political psychology, we are hard-pressed to identify parallels with the effects of Cartesian rationalism or Freudian theory.

For example, in January 2016 research conducted by Matthew MacWilliams purported to show authoritarianism as the key variable distinguishing Trump supporters. The press seized upon this finding because the implication seemed to prove the sentiment of those on the Left who viewed the rhetoric of Trump as echoing an era of fascism. Finally, there was some proof of the fascist appeal Trump had flirted with since descending the escalator of Trump tower and calling Mexicans rapists. MacWilliams's (2016b: 4) account, based on a December 2015 poll, utilized four questions concerning child-rearing that political psychology scholars have deployed since 1992 to measure authoritarian attitudes among Americans. Is it more important for a child to have independence or respect for elders? Obedience or self-reliance? Curiosity or good manners? Be considerate or well behaved? In asking the questions, MacWilliams found that among Republican primary voters, Trump supporters were more likely than any other group within the Republican electorate to score as authoritarian.

For over thirty years, these four questions have served as a fascism scale (F-scale) for political psychology whose genealogy leads to *The Authoritarian Personality*. Reading the son and the father together illuminates the peculiarity of each and the limitations of both. Adorno's F-scale sought to overcome the self-censorship possible in the previous scales devised to identify prejudice by asking indirectly about the individual's prejudices. This ambiguity was thought to have the effect of identifying deep-seated personality traits that predisposed people consciously and unconsciously toward fascist ideals, while the previous scales measured anti-Semitism and ethnocentrism. The questions that the research team developed attempted to tease out "unconscious forces" or "deep-lying psychological needs." The following examples, taken from the long list of the full survey (F-scale), give a sense of the less-than-subtle endeavor:

> 3. America is getting so far from the true American way of life that force may be necessary to restore it.
>
> 23. He is, indeed, contemptible who does not feel an undying love, gratitude, and respect for his parents.
>
> 35. There are some activities so flagrantly un-American that, when responsible officials won't take the proper steps, the wide-awake citizen should take the law into his own hands.
>
> 50. Obedience and respect for authority are the most important virtues children should learn.
>
> 70. To a greater extent than most people realize, our lives are governed by plots hatched in secret by politicians. (Adorno et al. 1950: 226–27)

From the responses to these questions, Adorno et al. (1950: 228) developed a number of variables that "were thought of as going together to form a single syndrome, a more or less enduring structure in the person that renders him receptive to antidemocratic propaganda." These included conventionalism, authoritarian submission, authoritarian aggression, anti-intraception, superstition and stereotypy, and power and toughness.

Political psychology has refined (or simplified) this approach further to separate behavior from opinions. Feldman and Stenner, whom MacWilliams cites, put both the concern and the solution this way:

> One of the major problems with F-scale-type measures is that they include items that are often uncomfortably close to the consequences of authoritarianism that we are interested in explaining. The measure of authoritarian predispositions we use in our analysis taps the respondent's subscription to alternative child-rearing values. The measure arrays respondents on a dimension that runs from a belief at one end that children should be well-behaved, obedient, and respectful of elders, to a view at the other end that children should be independent, responsible, and curious. (Feldman and Stenner 1997: 747)

According to Feldman and Stenner, question 50 regarding obedience is the enduring contribution of the original F-scale. In their view, it gets to the heart of authoritarian conviction without explicitly mentioning consequences or views that such a conviction is receptive to embracing. As a result, it is a more reliable or objective measure of an authoritarian personality. By refining the variable, social scientists and pollsters can easily incorporate authoritarianism into their research and measure it alongside other variables in search of statistically significant relationships.

This process of refinement is a strange one because it does not offer or center on a persuasive account about why we should see opinions on "child-rearing values" as definitive of an authoritarian personality. For Feldman and Stenner as well as MacWilliams, this "fact" about the world seems settled, but we should be wary of where such confidence comes from. Perusing MacWilliams's references one notices Adorno et al.'s *Authoritarian Personality* study and Erich Fromm's *Escape from Freedom* as the foundational references—those that temporally and politically inform future inquiries into authoritarianism. In large part, the subsequent works listed seek to operationalize, simplify, or reorient the knowledge of these touchstones—especially *The Authoritarian Personality*. In a sense, we can view this as a conceptual and instrumental genealogy of authoritarianism—a process of reification by American social science whereby the origins and nature of the "fact" of authoritarianism become obscured by the deployment of the concept in measures of public opinion. The bold conclusions and short explanations published by MacWilliams testify to the success of this reification. The conventions of his publication are commonplace, well within the accepted form of the literature, but what is notably missing, and not of concern to such literature, is an actual account of the nature of the phenomenon measured. Before returning to this question, a brief consideration of the theoretical claims and implications in *The Authoritarian Personality* is necessary.

Broadly speaking, in the account of Adorno et al. (1950), the nature of the authoritarian personality is framed under the specter of Freud. The weight of this specter is demonstrated in the equivocation of the Cartesian rationalism with Freud's insights on the primacy of the child-parent relationship mentioned earlier. Held up as examples of transformational knowledge, *The Authoritarian Personality* sought to marshal Freud's insights into a research program whose results had the potential to stand up to the horror and threat of fascism. The resulting study, though arguably more theoretically engaged than the subsequent research, also commits a level of mystification through quantification and lays the foundation for the work of American social science concerned with authoritarianism that followed.

While informed by Freud, Adorno et al. describe the nature of the authoritarian personality in their own way. In the preface, mentioned earlier, the nature of the problem is described as primordial, ancient in origin, and endemic to the organism (human species). In other places in the study, it is variously described as an assemblage of elements forming a syndrome, unconscious needs, and deep personality traits. While not all of these renderings are necessarily essential, by which I mean fundamental or absolute in nature, they do function that way in terms of the logic of the study, its techniques, and its rationale.

For instance, devising a scale and carrying out interviews with a cross section of the population presupposes that what you are looking for can be identified in the general population and found in some proportion within the group, and that what is found is an essential character trait of the individual. In other words, with the right tool (scale) it becomes possible to unearth a truth about *us*, measure its prevalence, and ultimately mitigate its effects. It is from this perspective that I read chapter 20, "Genetic Aspects of the Authoritarian Personality," which considers the hereditary impact in two of the case studies. Going beyond merely identifying authoritarian character, the two case studies consider what it would take for each subject to achieve "personality integration." In the case of "Mack," therapy may be effective; it "seems unlikely that his *personality* will change, [but] there is good reason to believe that his *behavior* can be controlled" (Adorno et al. 1950: 816). The behavior may be controlled, but the *personality* remains constant—essential.

Freudian theory notwithstanding, what evidence or arguments are necessary to support the claim that ethnocentrism, anti-Semitism, and authoritarianism can be understood as resulting from the activation of personality traits within individuals and, furthermore, that these traits can be identified and measured? If we are to take political psychology and the work of MacWilliams and others seriously, surely they need an answer. Instead, what we find is not only a lack of an answer but also a lack of recognition that the question is meaningful. In a section titled "theory and hypotheses," Mac-Williams (2016a: 717) offers the following:

> First, whether authoritarianism is conceptualized as an individual personality trait forged in the crucible of childhood (Adorno et al. 1950), a socially-learned attitude (Altemeyer 1981a, 1988, 1996, and 2006), or as a predisposition (Stenner 2005), authoritarians are described as rigid thinkers who perceived the world in black-and-white terms (Adorno et al. 1950; Altemeyer 1981a, 1988, 1996; Duckitt 1989; Feldman 2003; Feldman and Stenner 1997; Hetherington and Weiler 2009; Jost et al. 2003; Lavine et al. 2005; Stenner 2005). Uniformity and order are authoritarian watch words. Authoritarians obey. They seek order. They follow authoritarian leaders. They eschew diversity, fear "the other," act aggressively toward others, and, once they have identified friend from foe, hold tight to their decision.

While it is beyond the scope of this paper to speak to the accuracy of MacWilliams's characterization of all of the references cited, his identification of three separate conceptualizations of the nature of authoritarianism is problematic. These competing and overlapping theories suggest quite different things about the nature of the "authoritarian" and in doing so unmoor, or at least require additional theorization in order for us to be persuaded by, the certainty that the four child-rearing questions are definitive of the pathology. Moreover, without a conceptualization that speaks to child-rearing opinions as demonstrative of psychological structures that predispose individuals to fascism, any statistical relationships that are identified by the pollster require mediation and are not authoritative.

Aside from the conceptualization of authoritarianism MacWilliams attributes to Adorno et al. above, neither of the other two concepts—predisposition or rigid thinking—speak to the nature of the relationship between children and parents or suggest a psychological structure or personality trait that can be identified and quantified by this series of four questions. Due to the weight of the literature he cites and the conventions of Americanist political science, he is not required to offer such an account. What makes his account authoritative in this context is his deployment of a measure that is generally agreed upon in this field despite its conceptual weakness and ambiguity. Its authority relies on a process of reification where techniques of statistical data gathering and analysis eclipses the credibility or persuasiveness of the underlying categories upon which the edifice of objective knowledge is erected. In other words, the conceptual poverty of the measure is transubstantiated into verifiable and provable knowledge.

Another angle from which we can examine the limits of this conceptual poverty is by contrasting the purported goals and motivations of Adorno et al. and MacWilliams. In the wake of the horrors of fascism, authoritarianism, and the Holocaust, the American Jewish Committee commissioned the Studies in Prejudice series, of which *The Authoritarian Personality* was one part, in order to understand how such horrors could occur in seemingly advanced societies. Adorno et al. sought to identify root causes, which led them to develop the various scales. Perhaps recognizing the danger of their approach, they emphasized the need for both theory and practice and the hope that together they might produce knowledge capable of ameliorating the dangers of fascism. As they put it, "theoretical activity and practical application are not separated by an unbridgeable gulf" (ix). The hegemony of American social science, however, makes it difficult for the practitioners to recognize that any gulf exists.

It is possible, even likely, that Adorno et al. overestimated the ability to bridge this gulf and committed the original sin that MacWilliams reenacts. Gordon (2017: 36–37) cogently lays out this concern:

> As later critics would observe, the AP study seemed to commit an unwarranted reification of consciousness when they announced in the book's opening pages that they had identified nothing less than a "new anthropological type." In identifying this new type, Adorno et al. had troubled the possibility for a dialectical understanding, one that may have made bridging the gulf possible. "Instead of enforcing a dialectical image of the relation between the psychological and the social, it tended to reify the psychological as the antecedent condition, thereby diminishing what was for critical theory a sine qua non for all interdisciplinary labor joining sociology to psychoanalysis. The recent work by MacWilliams (which reflects formidable research effort and should not be lightly dismissed) would appear to reflect this understanding of psychology as the prior explanatory variable because of the way it tries to isolate "authoritarianism," as if it were a stable category for sociological analysis prior to other affiliations or identifying social factors.

For MacWilliams, the context and motivation are quite different. Working within the Americanist tradition of political science, he aimed to answer the following question: "who decides when party elites don't?" (MacWilliams 2016a: 716). Prior to the last presidential election, it was orthodoxy that the party would decide, through "invisible primaries," who the presidential nominee would be. When Trump emerged from a large field of challengers, this orthodoxy was upended. MacWilliams argues that "authoritarian voters" responded to Trump's "us vs. them" rhetoric and that the failure of the Republican establishment to get behind a single candidate allowed Trump the opportunity to surge. Ultimately, what is at stake in this inquiry is the ability of Americanist political science to explain Trumpism, a phenomenon that their models and theories failed to predict or imagine. In light of that failure, they return to statistical analyses to conduct a postmortem of an election that has already been decided and whose consequences must now be endured in order to develop the next set of theories and relationships that will be challenged by future events that do not fit the model.

If an important task of Americanist political science is to explain events that have already occurred through statistically significant relationships drawn from and among public opinion surveys, the knowledge their work offers is going to be limited both conceptually and practically. Despite these limits, its legitimacy and hegemony reigns supreme in the academy, and a generalized hubris is widespread in the quantitative social sciences. The legitimacy of this "normal science" lies in its methodologies and the conceptual choices such methodologies obscure. This fidelity to a knowable world that can be translated in and understood through categorization, quantification, and analysis typifies the base assumptions at work. Society can be studied by social scientists in much the same way atomic particles are studied in physical sciences. The incongruity between studying human beings and particles can be overcome with methodological and statistical adjustments, as the difficulty is one of technique rather than kind.

The tension or gulf between critical theory (as well as theory more broadly conceived) and American social science is complex and long-standing. In the foregoing, I have attempted to demonstrate some aspects of this tension by putting into conversation the conceptual underpinnings of *The Authoritarian Personality* and the work of MacWilliams of which *The Authoritarian Personality* is a genealogical touchstone. By highlighting the process of reification at work in both and ascendant in the latter, I hope to have shown the conceptual and theoretical limits of American social science—at least in this context. This modest contribution draws inspiration from previous attempts to reckon with the behavioral revolution, and I now turn to Sheldon Wolin's landmark essay, "Political Theory as a Vocation," whose insights remain as penetrating today as when they were published nearly fifty years ago.

Published in 1969, Wolin's essay confronted the impact of the behavioral revolution on the study of politics and called the growing affinity for methods into question. By drawing out the underlying idea of method and contrasting it with the corresponding idea of theory, Wolin was able to tease out the core assumptions endemic to each, assess the consequences, and illuminate the choices made when one embraces method or theory as a vocation. In order to excavate the underlying idea of method he employs a "Kantian type of question, What must the world be like for the methodist's knowledge to be possible?" (Wolin 1969: 1064). Rendered this way the question is not how you conceive the world, but what world is conjured by your assumptions. Wolin (1969: 1064–65) identifies the following features of the idea of method by drawing upon assumptions of the "'movement' of political behavior":

> The first item was: "Regularities. These are discoverable uniformities in political behavior. These can be expressed in generalizations or theories with explanatory and predictive value." It follows that the methodist is in trouble when the world exhibits "deformities" or emergent irregularities. As the unhappy state of theories of "development" or "modernization" suggests, similar trouble appears when the world manifests "multiformities."

Assuming regularity in political behavior is a consequential choice, one that justifies the search for such regularities and the methods necessary to find and establish them. Paradoxically, when irregular events occur, it is not the assumption and enterprise that is challenged but merely an isolated regularity that is shown to be irregular or the emergence of a different pattern. This is precisely the challenge and limit MacWilliams faced when the "invisible primary" theory failed to predict or explain Trump's nomination. Rather than rethink the assumptions that framed the "invisible primary," the impulse is to return to the same methods (and assumptions) to explain the irregularity and ground it in other theories of political behavior.

A more troubling problem for political scientists and others who see themselves as "normal scientists" in the sense meant by Thomas Kuhn in *The Structure of Scientific Revolutions* is that their work does not rest on a paradigmatic theory (see Wolin 1969: 1064). Rather, as Wolin points out, it stands on a collection of assumptions, including and related to those listed previously. For him, this "framework of assumptions . . . is the ideological

paradigm reflective of the same political community which the normal scientists are investigating" (1064). In other words, if political scientists start
with the assumptions of the political community that they are studying, they
mistake their particular horizon for a universal one. As a result, encounter-
ing irregularities over time would be the norm, and by claiming to produce
scientific knowledge, political science in its search for regularity contributes
to the normalization of the very structures of society that it seeks to study—
structures of domination, exclusion, and exploitation.

The assumptions of methodism, and the techniques they enable,
eschew background political knowledge gained through engagement with
the messy web of social, historical, and political factors. This type of political
education cannot be easily rendered into forms that are suitable for the methodological tools of political scientists. At the same time, this knowledge is
indispensable for understanding the world around us. The gulf between theory and method in the contemporary study of politics is irreconcilable. In an
exaggerated sense, the choice is between certainty or its promise and conceptual poverty on one hand and nuance, context, and conceptual depth on the
other. Wolin (1969: 1073) frames the choice in an even more colorful way:

> An impoverished mind, no matter how resolutely empirical in spirit, sees an
> impoverished world. Such a mind is not disabled from theorizing, but it is
> tempted into remote abstractions which, when applied to the factual world,
> end by torturing it. Think of what must be ignored in, or done to, the factual
> world before an assertion like the following can be made: "Theoretical models
> should be tested primarily by the accuracy of their prediction rather than the
> reality of their assumptions." No doubt one might object by pointing out that
> all theorizing does some violence to the empirical world. To which one might
> reply, that while amputations are necessary, it is still better to have surgeons
> rather than butchers.

The concept of vision, for Wolin, refers to a broader political education and
knowledge he sees as necessary for the theorist to possess. Precisely because
this knowledge evades the toolbox of methods due to its nature, it serves as a
source of creativity to be drawn upon by theorists as they see the world
around them.

The normal scientist may rightly object that the framing of the choice
described above is condescending and privileges a romantic view of the theorist consumed with difficult texts and ideas. They may also be likely to reject
the claims of conceptual poverty I have levied. Even so, this is simply to
make the choice to be the butcher, to accept the assumptions and commit to

a view that the world should be examined by techniques of analysis that can produce statistically provable knowledge. The failure to see the nature of this choice reflects the hegemonic position of method in social sciences and reaffirms the reifying character of the techniques deployed.

In contradistinction to the normal scientist, Wolin offers the figure of the epic theorist to convey his view of the nature and perspective of theory. The epic theorist "aims to grasp present structures and interrelationships, and to re-present them in a new way. Like the extraordinary scientific theory, such efforts involve a new way of looking at the familiar world, a new way with its own cognitive and normative standards" (Wolin 1969: 1078). Instead of reflecting the world as it imagines itself to be from the perspective of the existing order, epic theory seeks to make the common strange and in doing so open spaces for new ideas and practices which may ameliorate and overcome the limitations and suffering of the status quo. This is the second hallmark of epic theory, intentions of "public concern." In my mind, such a view shares deep affinities with critical theory and dialectical mediation.

Conclusion

By way of conclusion, I will briefly summarize what I take to be the contributions of this essay before offering an assessment of the political consequences of these contributions in the present moment. The preceding analysis has attempted to demonstrate the limits of American social science by examining the tension between method and theory. In order to do this I have drawn attention to how this tension plays out in *The Authoritarian Personality* as well as contemporary works of political psychology informed by Adorno et al.'s study. What I have found is a persistent and unbridgeable gulf between method and theory where the former offers seemingly knowable, objective, repeatable, and actionable knowledge about the world and the latter offers unverifiable particularity, nuance, and contingency. Method seeks to analyze the world as it is screening out complicating questions about base assumptions at work in the existing power structure and the enterprise of "normal science." Theory seeks to apprehend not only the dynamics of the present moment but also the forces that have shaped the present and to develop new horizons of our political imagination.

At this point, it will come as no surprise to the reader that where amputation is concerned I prefer the surgeon to the butcher. I find it hard to believe that Horkheimer and Adorno truly saw the *Authoritarian Personality* study as a way to enrich and advance the understanding of anti-Semitism due to its focus on the individual in vacuo. There is reasonable evidence that Adorno had his doubts about this focus on the individual, describing in his unpublished remarks on *The Authoritarian Personality* that "we remain, so to say, in the realm of 'reactions,' not of stimuli" (Gordon 2017: 43). This concern is echoed in Adorno's 1951 essay "Freudian Theory and the Pattern of Fascist Propaganda," which provides a much richer engagement between Freudian theory and the dynamics of fascism than *The Authoritarian Personality*, taking inspiration from Leo Lowenthal and Norbert Guterman's *Prophets of Deceit*, another text in the AJC series on prejudice. Adorno (1951: 135–36) writes,

> Psychological dispositions do not actually cause fascism; rather, fascism defines a psychological area which can be successfully exploited by the forces which promote it for entirely nonpsychological reasons of self-interest. . . . The content of Freud's theory, the replacement of individual narcissism by identification with leader images, points in the direction of what might be called the appropriation of mass psychology by the oppressors. To be sure, this process has a psychological dimension, but it also indicates a growing tendency towards abolition of psychological motivation in the old, liberalistic sense. Such motivation is systematically controlled and absorbed by social mechanisms which are directed from above. When the leaders become conscious of mass psychology and take it into their own hands, it ceases to exist in a certain sense.

This understanding of fascism is quite different from the one put forward in *The Authoritarian Personality*. Instead of an individual conceived largely in vacuo, possessing essentialized character traits that can be identified and quantified, here we have an account of fascism that includes not only individual and mass psychology but also leaders with interests who seek to exploit such tendencies. This alternative conceptualization requires us to apprehend the whole and deessentializes and deindividualizes the enterprise. Importantly, in the passage quoted above, Adorno recognizes the impact (a type of observer effect) of those in power becoming conscious of mass psychology and exploiting it for their own advantage.

These concerns found little voice in *The Authoritarian Personality* despite the significant consequences to the logic of the study they represent. As I have described above, these concerns have little traction within American social science because they run contrary to the logic and assumptions of quantitative social science. The resulting conceptual blindness and lack of *vision* mistakes "reactions" for "stimuli" resulting in important political choices, which are uncritically or even unknowingly made. To choose method is to embrace a knowable world capable of being apprehended in the abstract by data and fed by empirical technique. By "discovering" truths about the world, method regularizes the status quo by presenting current configurations of power as normal.

More importantly, the statistical methods and techniques deployed by the social scientist are largely indistinguishable from those deployed by the industry of political consultants, campaign professionals, and communication specialists. This professional apparatus fuels much of the punditry and beltway common sense, and is the dominant frame through which cable news apprehends political events and communicates what matters to viewers. These "wonks" pull back the covers of the American electorate in order to predict the outcome based on the data as well as shape interventions to effect outcomes based on that data. Imagine how MacWilliams's survey data might be apprehended and operationalized by consultants, pundits, and politicians. He has demonstrated through statistical models that authoritarians are a key part of Trump's base and that their influence in electing Trump upended conventional wisdom about presidential nominations. This data can be operationalized in a number of ways: for the pundit it is a fact to be embraced or reviled; for the consultant it provides a measure to utilize in a campaign; for the communications specialist it suggests new possibilities for messaging; and for the politician it may incentivize attention to this segment of the electorate. While these data are useful (if not necessarily effective), they are based on an impoverished conceptual edifice and as a result will be of marginal value in helping us understand our contemporary political moment, the past it emerged from, and the horizon of possibility that is our future.

Notes

This essay was first presented at "*The Authoritarian Personality*, Revisited" conference at Hunter College in November 2016. I am grateful for the feedback I received and the conversations among the participants, and to Robyn Marasco for organizing the event and this special issue.

1   In this essay, I equivocate behavioralism, positivism, empiricism, normal science, quantitative social science, methodism, and statistical analyses for the purposes of my argument. One can certainly trace differences among these terms (and concepts), and while this may be quite important for social science practitioners, I believe my equivocation is justified for the purposes of this paper and most importantly my argument. Furthermore, the temporal frame and source material of this paper introduce such terminology, which I read as consistent, and feel based upon that reading it is appropriate to put them into conversation in this way.

References

Adorno, Theodor W., and Max Horkheimer. 2002. *Dialectic of Enlightenment: Philosophical Fragments*. Edited by Gunzelin Schmid Noerr. Translated by Edmund Jephcott. Stanford, CA: Stanford University Press.

Adorno, Theodor W., Else Frenkel-Brunswik, Daniel J. Levison, and R. Nevitt Sanford. 1950. *The Authoritarian Personality*. New York: Harper and Row.

Adorno, Theodor W. 1982. "Freudian Theory and the Pattern of Fascist Propaganda." In *The Essential Frankfurt School Reader*, edited by Andrew Arato and Eike Gephardt, 118–137. New York: Continuum.

Feldman, Stanley, and Karen Stenner. 1997. "Perceived Threat and Authoritarianism." *Political Psychology* 18, no. 4: 741–70.

Gordon, Peter. 2017. "The Authoritarian Personality Revisited: Reading Adorno in the Age of Trump." *boundary 2*, no. 2: 31–56.

Lowenthal, Leo, and Norbert Guterman. 1949. *Prophets of Deceit: A Study of the Techniques of the American Agitator*. New York: Harper and Row.

MacWilliams, Matthew. 2016a. "Who Decides When the Party Doesn't? Authoritarian Voters and the Rise of Donald Trump." *Political Science and Politics* 49, no. 4: 716–21.

MacWilliams, Matthew. 2016b. "The One Weird Trait That Predicts Whether You're a Trump Supporter." *Politico*, January 17. www.politico.com/magazine/story/2016/01/donald -trump-2016-authoritarian-213533.

Wiggershaus, Rolf. 1994. *The Frankfurt School, Its History, Theories, and Political Significance*. Translated by Michael Robertson. Cambridge, MA: MIT Press.

Wolin, Sheldon S. 1969. "Political Theory as a Vocation." *American Political Science Review* 63, no. 4: 1062–82.

Barbara Umrath

A Feminist Reading of the Frankfurt School's Studies on Authoritarianism and Its Relevance for Understanding Authoritarian Tendencies in Germany Today

Dating back to the 1930s and 1940s, the Frankfurt School's studies on authoritarianism have
gained renewed attention among a broader public
in recent years. In an attempt to understand
authoritarian tendencies in the present, political commentators and analysts, journalists, and
scholars alike return to the analyses of the so-
called first generation of critical theory. In particular, the rise of right-wing movements and their
electoral success in countries that hitherto were
considered well-established democracies—represented in the United States by the alt-right and
Donald Trump, in France by Marine Le Pen and
the *Front National*, in Germany by a wave of anti-
refugee/anti-"Islamization" mobilizations and the
Alternative für Deutschland (Alternative for Germany [AfD])—makes the Frankfurt School seem
relevant again.

On January 17, 2016, the online news outlet
Politico published a piece by political scientist
Matthew MacWilliams that argued authoritarianism was the variable that most reliably predicted
an individual's support for Trump. In his poll that
included 1,800 registered voters across the country, self-identified Democrats as well as Republi-
cans and Independents, authoritarianism was

The South Atlantic Quarterly 117:4, October 2018
DOI 10.1215/00382876-7165927   © 2018 Duke University Press

operationalized simplistically, using nothing more but four questions as predictors. From a feminist perspective, however, it is interesting that all of them pertained "to child-rearing: whether it is more important for the voter to have a child who is respectful or independent; obedient or self-reliant; well-behaved or considerate; and well-mannered or curious" (MacWilliams 2016). According to MacWilliams, neither political affiliation, income, education, race, gender, nor age was as reliable an indicator of a person's support for Trump than what is often considered a "not really political," "merely individual and private" attitude: people's approach toward rearing children.

Although MacWilliams did not directly refer to the Frankfurt School, five months later, with Trump all but guaranteed the nomination as presidential candidate of the Republican Party, intellectual historian Peter Gordon followed up in *boundary 2* with a detailed discussion of the 1950 study *The Authoritarian Personality*, which paid specific attention to Theodor W. Adorno's contribution (Gordon 2017). Trump's election as president of the United States in November 2016 spurred further references to the Frankfurt School: on November 17, 2016, in the German weekly *Die Zeit*, Gero von Randow finds in the Frankfurt School's analyses a nightmarish relevance for understanding the rise of Trump, Le Pen, and the AfD. Alex Ross's December 5, 2016, article in *The New Yorker* was titled "The Frankfurt School Knew Trump Was Coming." On December 27, 2016, the online news magazine *Vox* published an interview with Stuart Jeffries, longtime contributor to the *Guardian* and author of *Grand Hotel Abyss: The Lives of the Frankfurt School* (2016), under the title "If You Want to Understand the Age of Trump, Read the Frankfurt School."

From a feminist perspective, it is striking that none of these contributions directly drawing on the Frankfurt School addresses questions of gender, family, or sexuality—despite the fact that these issues figure prominently within contemporary right-wing movements. Starting from this observation, the purpose of this essay is twofold. First I am to show that critical analyses of gender, family, and sexuality have been an integral part of the Frankfurt School's studies on authoritarianism. Abstaining from considering these questions not only risks missing crucial dimensions of contemporary right-wing movements, but also falls short of the Frankfurt School's original approach. This essay's second purpose is to discuss the relevance of the approach developed by the Frankfurt School in the 1930s and 1940s for a feminist analysis of authoritarian tendencies at the beginning of the twenty-first century.

In the first part of this essay, I will show that the aforementioned authors' failure to consider questions of gender, family, and sexuality is no coincidence. Rather, it mirrors a dominant reading of the Frankfurt School that hastily overlooks those theorists' analyses of these areas, treating them as negligible, not part of what makes the Frankfurt School's approach distinctive. In a second step, I will challenge this reading. Returning to the *Studien über Autorität und Familie* (*Studies on Authority and the Family*, [1936] 1987) and *The Authoritarian Personality* (1950) as well as drawing on further primary sources, I will point out how critical analyses of gender, family, and sexuality have been integral to the Frankfurt School's studies on authoritarianism.[1] In the third and final section of this essay, I will address authoritarian tendencies in the present. Focusing on the German right-wing party AfD and a phenomenon called *Anti-Genderismus* (antigenderism), I will argue that from a feminist perspective, it is not so much the *concept* of the authoritarian *character*, but rather the Frankfurt School's *overall approach* to authoritarianism that is productive for understanding contemporary developments.

Gender, Family, and Sexuality in the Frankfurt School: Absent or Sidelined?

According to most secondary literature, the Frankfurt School theorists never really concerned themselves with questions of gender, family, or sexuality.[2] No matter if one turns to the detailed studies on the history and development of the Frankfurt School by Martin Jay ([1973] 1976) and Rolf Wiggershaus ([1986] 1988), the rich intellectual biographies of individual members, like Detlev Claussen's (2003) portrait of Adorno or John Abromeit's (2011) otherwise excellent study of Max Horkheimer, or to shorter paperback introductions like those of Christoph Türcke and Gerhard Bolte (1994), Helmut Dubiel (1988), or Michael Schwandt (2009), a consistent pattern emerges: emphasis is placed on the Frankfurt School's efforts to move beyond the narrow, economistic understanding of Marx that, at the beginning of the twentieth century, dominated the labor movement and its parties. We learn that at the outset of critical theory stands the rejection of what can be called traditional Marxism, a certain reading of Marx that takes societal developments, at least in the last instance, to be reducible to economic tendencies and class struggle. Being well aware of the shortcomings of such an approach, the secondary literature continues, the Frankfurt School expanded and updated Marxian thought by combining philosophical reflections with interdisciplinary empirical research and integrating insights of Freudian psychoanalysis. Whereas traditional Marxism is marked by a predominant concern with relations of production, it is stressed that the Frankfurt School's critical social theory (*Gesellschaftstheorie*) put the *relation* between economy, culture, and psyche at its center, paying particular attention to how societal relations of domination and power are internalized by and reproduced within the individual. While all of the above is indeed characteristic of the Frankfurt School's approach, from a feminist perspective, though, equally noteworthy is what most secondary literature fails to discuss explicitly and in more detail: that critical analyses of gender, family, and sexuality were an integral part of the Frankfurt School's attempt to develop a critical theory of twentieth-century bourgeois society.

With respect to the 1936 *Studies on Authority and the Family*, this becomes particularly visible. In the secondary literature, the first major research project of the Institute for Social Research under its new director, Horkheimer, is presented as the beginning of the Institute's concern with authority. Attention is focused primarily on Erich Fromm's famous concept of the authoritarian or sadomasochistic character. A good case in point here is Helmut Dubiel's introduction to critical theory, in which the family vanishes from the title of the chapter. It simply reads: "The Authoritarian Social Character" (Dubiel 1988, 40).[3] While the relation between this concept and patriarchal structures within the family is briefly hinted at, the detailed historical and sociological analyses of the family that constitute the major part of the anthology are barely mentioned. Described as a mere "collection of data and material" (Türcke and Bolte 1994: 25), they do not seem worthy of further consideration. Discussion is for the most part limited to Horkheimer's and Fromm's contributions, that is, the first 130 pages of an anthology of more than 850 pages, with some authors, in addition, referring to rather brief discussions of the family in later works by Frankfurt School theorists. Without considering the Frankfurt School's analyses of the family in detail, it is then argued that the authoritarian character was understood as the result of a demise of patriarchal authority *within the family*.[4] Moreover, the secondary literature suggests the Frankfurt School theorists took this to be equivalent to a decline of patriarchal (gender) relations *within society at large*. According to this reading, the Frankfurt School theorists unambiguously identified the authoritarian character as the product of what psychoanalyst Alexander Mitscherlich (1963) later described as a "fatherless society" (Dubiel 1988: 61–62; Jay [1973] 1976: 127, 324; Wiggershaus [1986] 1988: 176–77).

In the following section, I will show that the Frankfurt School's position on this question is more nuanced. More importantly, I will point out how analyses of gender, family, and sexuality have been integral to the Frankfurt School's studies on authoritarianism from the very beginning.

Patriarchal Structures and Rigid Identities: The Studies on Authoritarianism

In his 1931 introductory speech as director of the Institute for Social Research, Horkheimer ([1931] 2009: 32) announced that the question of the relation between the economic life of society, the psychical development of individuals, and the changes in the realm of culture in the narrower sense would stand at the center of forthcoming activities. While in his presentation Horkheimer suggested that in order to inquire into these relations the Institute would focus on "a particularly significant and salient social group, namely . . . the skilled craftspeople and white collar workers in Germany" (32), archival sources indicate that the concern with a particular social group was soon to be replaced by a focus on a particular social institution: the family. It was by means of extensive analyses of the family that the Institute sought to develop a comprehensive critical social theory of modern society (Institut für Sozialforschung n.d.). Thus, what was published in 1936 as *Studies on Authority and the Family* actually started out as a research project not on authoritarianism, but on the family. It was only in the course of the research process and with the unfolding of political developments that the concept of authority became more central (Horkheimer 1934).

While most secondary literature focuses on the latter, paying only scant attention to the family, in fact, it is the *relation* between authoritarian structures within the family and society at large that stands at the center of the anthology. By focusing on the family, the Frankfurt School theorists describe how, with the emergence of modern capitalism, structures of authority do not simply disappear, but rather assume new forms. As Horkheimer argues in his introductory essay to the 1936 anthology, the old feudal authorities had been dethroned, the individual—from a feminist perspective one would have to add: as long as it was male and white—had been declared free. Yet, and this is decisive from the Frankfurt School's perspective, only to find itself confronted with societal relations that, once again, appear as beyond the individual's own control because they are not recognized for what they are: the result of social practices, but taken as givens to be accepted. Drawing on the Marxian critique of commodity fetishism and reification to make this point, Horkheimer pays particular attention to the congealed and hierarchized relation between entrepreneur and worker. At the same time, however, he extends Marx's argument to the relation between husband, wife, and children, arguing that the separation of public and private realm and a gendered division of labor result in a reification of patriarchal authority within the family (Horkheimer [1936] 2002: 73–89, 105). The father-husband appears as "master of the house" because of his "seemingly natural characteristic" of earning or at least possessing the money (105). Horkheimer thus highlights that what at first glance appears as personal authority in fact rests on social structures: the authoritarian role of the patriarchal father-husband is analyzed as the product of a gendered division of labor and the separation of public and private spheres characteristic of bourgeois society. This, however, does not imply it automatically disappears if the father-husband loses his position as a breadwinner. According to Horkheimer, the "psychic and physical power" of the patriarchal father-husband has to be understood as originating with his "economic power," while at the same time exhibiting a "capacity for resistance" (123).

That the *Studies on Authority and the Family*, rather than describing a mere decline of patriarchy, trace how, with the emergence of capitalism, patriarchal structures both within the family and beyond persist exactly by undergoing certain transformations, however, only becomes fully visible if the often neglected historical, economic, and legal analyses of the family are taken into consideration. In his 337-page manuscript "Beiträge zu einer Geschichte der autoritären Familie" ("Contributions to a History of the Authoritarian Family"), Ernst Manheim ([1936] 1987) gives a detailed account of the historical transformations of family structures. Further critical discussion of the gendered division of labor that renders wife and children economically dependent on the father-husband and as such represents an important source of patriarchal power can be found in the contributions by Andries Sternheim ([1936] 1987), Hilde Weiss ([1936] 1987), and Karl August Wittfogel ([1936] 1987). Ernst Schachtel ([1936] 1987), in a study that in many ways anticipates later feminist legal theory, analyzes how, at the beginning of the twentieth century, patriarchal rule within the family and hierarchical gender relations within society are further sustained by the regulations of modern law.[5]

Against the backdrop of detailed historical, economic, and legal analyses of the transformation of patriarchal structures with the advent of capitalism Fromm develops his famous concept of the sadomasochistic or authoritarian character. These analyses do not represent a separate project barely related to the study of authoritarianism—quite the contrary. Fromm's concept is not simply psychological, it is *socio*-psychological. According to him, the patriarchal structure of the family in bourgeois society plays a decisive role in the formation of the sadomasochistic character: the patriarchal father represents a child's first contact with societal authority. By submitting to the arbitrary demands of the patriarchal father, the child learns not to question the way things are. Rather, he or she develops a disposition to bow readily to those perceived as strong and tread on the supposedly weak (Fromm [1936] 1987: 82–92). This disposition, then, at later points in life, is continuously reproduced in relation to authorities beyond the family. Domination and subordination are simply taken as givens. The critical question whether a life beyond the bourgeois status quo might better suit the needs of humankind is never asked (Fromm [1936] 1987: 95–110, 114–22, 132).

As the 1936 *Studies on Authority and the Family* makes very clear, the Frankfurt School theorists understand the sadomasochistic or authoritarian character as the product of bourgeois society. Far from being the exception, it represents the average social character of a thoroughly problematic society. In other words, the 1936 studies comprehend authoritarianism as born out of bourgeois society. Bourgeois society, in turn, is not understood as marked by one principal contradiction, as traditional Marxism would have it. Rather, it is the coming together and mutual entwinement of capitalist and patriarchal structures that gives rise to authoritarianism.

No longer the exclusive product of the Frankfurt School, but the result of joint efforts with the American Jewish Committee, in the later study on *The Authoritarian Personality* (1950) the sociotheoretical dimensions of the 1936 anthology recede into the background—without altogether disappearing.[6] In contrast to the earlier project, the intention of this later study was to identify the fascist potential in a democratic country like the United States, or, as the authors put it, to identify "implicit pre-fascist tendencies" (Adorno et al. 1950a: 224). Thus, *The Authoritarian Personality* in an important way differentiates Fromm's early concept: distinguishing between authoritarian and nonauthoritarian character structures, it accounts for the fact that, even in a society as problematic as the bourgeois one, not everyone by necessity becomes a potential fascist. Moreover, paying particular attention to ideologies, *The Authoritarian Personality* further deepens the Frankfurt School's approach to authoritarianism.

One of the major lessons still to be learned from *The Authoritarian Personality* is the necessity to analyze what its authors dubbed "broad ideological trends" (Adorno et al. 1950b: 14). Their original focus, not surprisingly in the context of the Holocaust, had been on anti-Semitism. However, early in their research these scholars had come to the conclusion that, unlike public opinion surveys, critical social research cannot take anti-Semitic views as isolated opinions on particular issues. Instead, they argued, opinions regarding particular issues need to be understood in relation to other opinions and attitudes. Thus, in addition to a first scale measuring anti-Semitic attitudes and opinions (A-S scale), two more scales were constructed for the measurement of ethnocentrism (E scale) and politico-economic conservatism (PEC scale), and finally a fourth, the most famous one: the so-called F scale, with the F standing for fascism (14). The first three scales intended to measure what the authors called ideological "surface opinions" (Adorno et al. 1950a: 223)—in their case: a person's views and beliefs regarding Jewish people, issues of race, and political and economic questions. The purpose of the F scale, however, was different. This last scale was meant to show that apparently disparate ideological "surface opinions" were in fact closely related and thoroughly intertwined insofar as they could be traced back to what the researchers described as "deeper, often unconscious forces," as "enduring psychological dispositions in the person" and "underlying antidemocratic trends in the personality" (223). As the wording already indicates, these studies, too, were informed by the psychoanalytic distinction between conscious and unconscious dimensions of the human personality. In other words, the F scale aimed beyond mere views and opinions. It was interested in how certain ideological beliefs are rooted in a person's psychic makeup or character structure. In order to gain a deeper understanding of these unconscious dimensions and the personality as a whole, in addition to the F scale, select participants were interviewed and asked to participate in a thematic apperception test, a psychoanalytically inspired testing procedure (Adorno et al. 1950b: 16–19).

From a feminist perspective, one might ask why no scale for measuring sexism or homophobia was constructed. Does this mean that, unlike the research project of the 1930s, the later study on *The Authoritarian Personality* was simply not interested in or ignorant of questions of gender, family, and sexuality? As a closer look reveals, the case was quite the contrary. Eight out of thirty-eight items on the original F scale referred to gender relations, family structures, and expectations toward parents and children as well as attitudes toward homosexuality, sex crimes, and sexual morality in a more general sense (Adorno et al. 1950a: 226–27). After subjecting the preliminary scale to statistical analyses, several items were excluded for insufficient reliability (242–47). The final scale, consisting of thirty items, still featured five items that related to (homo-)sexuality and expectations regarding children and parents (255–57). This already indicates that the researchers considered attitudes pertaining to gender, family, and sexuality not as something merely personal, but as indicative of an embrace or rejection of authoritarian tendencies. Moreover, particular attention was paid to gender, family, and sexuality in the analyses of the interview material. In this respect, an important finding was that subjects who revealed pronounced ethnocentric, anti-Semitic, and/or conservative attitudes regarding political and economic concerns (individuals that the researchers dubbed "high-scorers") at the same time exhibited strong conformity with prevailing norms of masculinity and femininity—both when asked to describe themselves and their ideals (Frenkel-Brunswik 1950: 404, 428–29). As Else Frenkel-Brunswik elaborates, high-scoring men emphasized traits commonly associated with masculinity like "determination, energy, industry, independence, decisiveness, and will power," while frowning upon weakness, dependence, and passivity in men (428). Similarly, high-scoring women "tend(ed) to think of themselves as feminine and soft; no masculine trends (were) being admitted" (428). They listed "as the ideal the same traits which they mentioned in their self-description" (431). At an unconscious level, however, in both high-scoring men and high-scoring women, the researchers found considerate ambivalence about and difficulties in complying with the role ascribed to one's gender. While similar ambivalence and difficulties were found in low-scoring subjects, what distinguished the high-scorers was their inability to admit and integrate strivings commonly associated with the opposite gender. Instead, such tendencies were met with "rigid and counterphobic defense" (441). Those parts of the self that did not conform to prevailing ideals of masculinity or femininity were repressed—a repression that Frenkel-Brunswik considers to be nothing less than "one important source of hidden aggression toward the opposite sex—and toward other people generally" (405).

Contemporary Authoritarianism from a Feminist Perspective Informed by the Frankfurt School

So far, I have shown that, while frequently sidelined in the secondary literature, critical reflections on gender, family, and sexuality were in fact an integral part of both the *Studies on Authority and the Family* and the more famous later study on *The Authoritarian Personality*. Given that these studies date back to the 1930s and 1940s, some aspects, of course, are now dated. In the decades following the youth, student, and women's movements of the 1960s and 1970s, gender relations as well as relations between parents and children have changed in considerable ways. As Andrea Maihofer (2014) points out based on a broad overview of recent research, overall family arrangements have become more diverse, norms regarding masculinity and femininity more flexible. In this context, Fromm's insight into the relation between patriarchal family structures and authoritarian character formation loses much of its explanatory power. Similarly, one can doubt that rigid identification with traditional norms of masculinity and femininity is still as reliable an indicator of authoritarian personalities as Frenkel-Brunswik found in the 1940s.

Moreover, the concept of an authoritarian *character* seems problematic today. While widespread in the mid-twentieth century, since then it has been criticized for its functionalism, suggesting an all-too-neat integration of the individual into society (Knapp 1993: 97–99; Schmidt 2009: 295–96; Wiggershaus [1986] 1988: 176). In addition, feminists have argued that the Frankfurt School's concept not only overemphasizes the role of the father while neglecting that of the primary caregiver, the mother, it also privileges the son's experience without further considering that of the daughter (Benjamin [1977] 1994a: 149; a. [1978] 1994b: 311; Jagentowicz Mills 1987: 97, 112–13, 148; Rumpf 1989: 19–20, 26, 34–44). Thus, they pointed to androcentrism underlying the concept of the authoritarian character.

These difficulties, however, do not mean we have to discard the Frankfurt School's studies on authoritarianism altogether. To be sure, their concrete historical insights into how gender, family, and sexuality relate to authoritarianism capture a different moment within the development of bourgeois society; rather than referring to an authoritarian character or personality, today it seems preferable to speak of authoritarian tendencies or dispositions, or simply authoritarianism. At the same time, from a feminist perspective, the Frankfurt School's more general insight that understanding authoritarianism requires taking a closer look at questions of gender, family, and sexuality still remains crucial. Moreover, if read alongside each other, the Frankfurt School's *Studies on Authority and the Family* and *The Authoritarian Personality* offer nothing less than a comprehensive approach to authoritarianism—one that is based on a critical social theory of modern bourgeois society, while at the same time considering ideological and sociopsychological dimensions. In the remainder of this essay, I will argue that such a perspective is productive not only for understanding the new German right-wing party AfD, but also for identifying authoritarian tendencies in the so-called political center.

A feminist perspective informed by the Frankfurt School understands authoritarianism not as the mere opposite of, but rather as a negative potential inherent to bourgeois society. Expanding on the Frankfurt School's insight that it is insufficient to describe bourgeois society as merely capitalist, I would like to suggest it is best comprehended as structured by manifold, mutually entangled relations of dominance and power. In such a society, as Fromm puts it, everyone finds him- or herself in a "system of dependencies" (Fromm [1936] 1987: 117), superordinated in one sense, subordinated in others. This, in turn, means that authoritarian inclinations cannot be limited to certain groups of people. It is not just the less affluent or unemployed parts of the "native" population that tend to be attracted to right-wing movements. Nor does the reference to decades of neoliberal destruction of the welfare state suffice as an explanation for the rise of the Right. A similar point, I think, could be made with reference to another major authoritarian current in the present: Islamic fundamentalism. Its attraction, unfortunately, is by no means limited to the less educated and affluent, nor can it simply be explained by pointing to experiences of exclusion and racism. Based on a critical social theory that accounts for the manifold relations of dominance and power that constitute bourgeois society, a feminist perspective informed by the Frankfurt School thus pays attention to the similarly multifaceted forms of authoritarianism. Moreover, it rejects attempts to explain the rise of these tendencies by identifying "objective," structural causes as overly simplifying. For as much as authoritarianism in its different guises cannot be understood without problematizing the capitalist, patriarchal, racist, and anti-Semitic structures built into bourgeois society, as *The Authoritarian Personality* has shown, even in such a society not everyone by necessity develops an authoritarian "character."

When it comes to the AfD, a feminist perspective informed by the Frankfurt School renders a fairly different picture than that dominating in a broader public. There, the AfD is often portrayed as a single-issue party—in its origins as Euroskeptic, these days as predominantly concerned with closing the borders and rejecting a presumed "Islamization." Following the Frankfurt School with its insight that ideological trends need to be studied in relation and that any discussion of authoritarianism must consider questions of gender, family, and sexuality, we can see that the AfD's image of the family, which has been aptly described as "reminiscent of the 1950s" (Kemper 2016: 9), is just as much a part of its ideology as is nationalism, ethnocentrism, and the upholding of a capitalist ideology of performance and individual achievement. More precisely: the AfD's positions on gender, family, and sexuality are a genuine part of its increasing radicalization. This can be seen by taking a closer look at its most recent statements and programs. In its general policy statement (2016) as well as its program for the 2017 federal elections, the AfD presents itself as committed to the equality of men and women as guaranteed by the constitution. However, it is as an essential part of "German culture" and in contrast to the disrespect of women and girls presumed typical of "Islamic cultures" that equality between men and women is embraced (AfD 2016: 54–55; 2017: 12, 35).[7] At the same time, more substantial gender equality policies are vigorously opposed. Quotas, for example, are rejected as "detrimental to performance, . . . unjust," said to "often create renewed and new discrimination" (AfD 2016: 54–55) or even discredited as unconstitutional (AfD 2017: 12, 40). The AfD's overall position regarding sexual and gender diversity is, to put it mildly, not characterized by tolerance, let alone acceptance: recent curricular reforms designed to no longer present nonheterosexual orientation or nonbinary gender identities as deviations are rejected as "ideologically motivated experiments of premature sexualization" meant to "unsettle" and "confuse" children and teenagers about their sexual orientation (AfD 2017: 41). They are charged with emphasizing "homosexuality and trans-sexuality in classrooms" and making "our children . . . the plaything to the sexual orientation of a noisy minority" (AfD 2016: 53). Against these "state-sponsored programs of reeducation" (2017: 41), the AfD declares its commitment "to the traditional family as a guiding principle" (AfD 2016: 40) and explicitly rejects attempts to broaden the definition of family beyond that of a heterosexual couple with children (AfD 2017: 40). While not directly championing a gendered division of labor, its programs lament a presumed "discrimination of [*sic*] full-time mothers," a "misconceived view of feminism, which favours women with a career above mothers and housewives" and promise that the AfD will support families so that they can "freely choose" to take care of small children and elderly relatives at home instead of "being forced" to rely on professional providers (AfD 2016: 36–37, 40; AfD 2017: 39). What the AfD seems most worried about in the first place, however, is not so much the erosion of a gendered division of labor, but the relatively low birth rates among native Germans and the comparatively higher rates of the immigrant population—interpreted as a negative trend toward the "self-abolishment of Germany" ("Selbstabschaffung Deutschlands"). In order to stop this trend, it proposes a paradigm shift toward a national population policy that promises financial incentives for larger families, stigmatizes abortion, and encourages starting families at a young age, especially among academics (AfD 2016: 40–42; AfD 2017: 37–39). Refugees, in contrast, should have no right to family unification (AfD 2017: 31). Again, we can see that questions of gender, family, and sexuality play a major role within the AfD's ideology. They are intricately linked to its process of radicalization, the increasing dominance of the "völkisch" extreme right current within the party.[8]

While a feminist perspective informed by the Frankfurt School can thus contribute to a broader understanding of the AfD's ideology, it does not stop at analyzing right-wing tendencies that are easily identified as such. Rather, following *The Authoritarian Personality*, it further inquires into the more hidden authoritarian potential within broader strata of society. With respect to this, in the German-speaking context a phenomenon called *Anti-Genderismus* (antigenderism) deserves particular attention.[9] In a nutshell,

Anti-Genderismus can be characterized as a discourse that rejects the concept of gender, public policy based on this concept, and the academic field of gender studies as its origin. In order to understand Anti-Genderismus, it is important to know that over the last twenty-something years the English *gender* has found entrance into German political and academic discourse. The reason is that in German there is only one word, *Geschlecht*, for what in English is distinguished as *sex* and *gender*, where the first refers to the physical, biological, and "natural" dimensions of *Geschlecht*, and the second to grammatical, cultural, and social ones. In fields like public policy, education, and social work, today the originally English *gender* instead of the German *Geschlecht* is often preferred in order not only to make clear that one's emphasis is on sociocultural dimensions, but also to account for the fact that, from the epistemological perspective advanced by gender studies and most commonly associated with Judith Butler, there is no *concept* of sex beyond gender.

The perspective advanced by contemporary gender studies certainly irritates everyday assumptions about sex as the "ground" or "basis" on which gender difference develops. We have grown up with the idea that binary sexual difference is rooted "in nature." Understanding the ways in which we assign sex to bodies as sociohistorical processes runs contrary to our everyday intuition. In my teaching, students often have difficulty grasping this idea and regularly fall back on "commonsense" arguments at one point or another. Anti-Genderismus, however, has a different quality—a quality that, as I would like to suggest, can only be fully grasped from a sociopsychological perspective. Distorting what is basically an epistemological point, proponents of Anti-Genderismus suggest that talking about gender is tantamount to denying the existence of Geschlecht per se, and thus what they consider a natural or biological fact. While Anti-Genderismus is an integral part of the AfD's ideology (AfD 2016: 51, 54; AfD 2017: 40–41), it is by no means limited to the right-wing spectrum of society. Over the last couple of years, antigenderist stances have been granted ample space in renowned newspapers like *Die Welt* (Strausberg 2015), *Süddeutsche Zeitung* (Weber 2016), *Frankfurter Allgemeine Zeitung* (Klein 2015; Schmoll 2014), or the Swiss *Neue Zürcher Zeitung* (Klein 2016). In February 2018, the Rhineland-Palatinate branch of the Konrad-Adenauer-Stiftung, a political foundation closely associated with the Christian Democratic Party, joined antigenderist ranks, organizing a political forum titled "Gender, Instrument of Reeducation? Intentions, Costs, Effects." Drawing on *The Authoritarian Personality*, we can understand antigenderist discourse as more than a surface opinion. Its spread points not only to a certain ideological convergence between the far right and other parts of society. Rather, the stereotypy with which proponents of Anti-Genderismus repeat the same arguments and the rigidity with which they insist the concept of gender denies nature point to deep-rooted psychic anxieties. It is only by accounting for the emotional and psychic qualities of Anti-Genderismus that we can understand the vigor with which detractors currently attack a concept and an academic field.

Following the Frankfurt School in its *socio*-psychological approach, however, the psychic dimensions of authoritarianism must not be considered in isolation. Instead, they have to be discussed in relation to a critical theory of bourgeois society. Yet, in order to understand how Anti-Genderismus relates to the fabric of bourgeois society, the Frankfurt School approach alone does not suffice. Rather, we have to integrate the seminal insights of more recent gender studies, which indicate that the emergence of bourgeois society and the modern nation-state was accompanied by considerable changes in our understanding of gender difference and sexuality. As Andrea Maihofer (1995) points out drawing on historical research in the field of gender studies, while gender had long been conceived of as a gradual difference, from the eighteenth century onward it was increasingly comprehended as a fundamental, binary difference—a difference that more and more became to be understood as rooted in physiological, that is, sex, difference. And whereas earlier times tended to distinguish between acceptable and prohibited sexual practices, sexual orientation gradually became perceived of as a stable part of identity, with heterosexuality representing the hegemonic norm. In other words, from the perspective of a feminist critical theory, the binary, heteronormative concept of gender has to be considered a constitutive part of modern bourgeois society and identity.

Combining this insight with the Frankfurt School's that bourgeois society is not characterized by just one principal contradiction can further contribute to our understanding of Anti-Genderismus. We can then see that Anti-Genderismus is not only about attacking the field of gender studies and defending a binary, heteronormative gender order, but it is also intimately linked to an upholding of a society based on competitive performance and national boundaries. This, in turn, has important consequences for attempts to counter antigenderist positions. From a feminist perspective informed by the Frankfurt School, we cannot limit ourselves to embracing the diversity of gender and sexuality. Rather, confronting *Anti-Genderismus* at the same time requires exploring emancipatory alternatives to a world divided by national boundaries and a neoliberal way of life. It is the utopian perspective of a society beyond borders, capitalism, and a binary, heteronormative gender order that we should seek to advance.

Notes

Parts of this essay were first presented as papers on various occasions. I am grateful for the comments made at those gatherings and particularly indebted to Marc Grimm and Katharina Volk for inspiring personal discussions.

1 The reading I develop is based on the extended discussion in my dissertation, titled "Geschlecht, Familie, Sexualität: Die Entwicklung der Kritischen Theorie aus der Perspektive sozialwissenschaftlicher Geschlechterforschung" ("Gender, Family, Sexuality: The Development of Critical Theory from a Gender Studies Perspective"), which, as of mid-2018, is still unpublished. In it, I draw on a broad variety of authors associated with the Frankfurt School, considering sources that range from the 1930s to the 1970s.

2 The same, of course, is not the case with feminist readings of the Frankfurt School. Since I am concerned here with the dominant reading, however, I cannot go into a detailed discussion of feminist appropriations and criticisms. In general, it can be said that feminists who turned to the Frankfurt School between the late 1970s and the early 1990s, at a time when feminist theory primarily understood itself as women's (not so much gender) studies, were predominantly concerned with how women's experience was represented, whether it was analyzed in its complexity, and whether the necessity for as well as possible avenues toward women's emancipation were discussed. For feminist readings of the Frankfurt School's studies on authoritarianism, see Jessica Benjamin ([1977] 1994a, [1978] 1994b) and Patricia Jagentowicz Mills (1987) in the United States; Regina Becker-Schmidt (1991) or Mechthild Rumpf (1989, 1993) in Germany; and the brief discussion in the third section of this essay.

3 Something similar happens in Martin Jay's influential study, in which the title of the corresponding chapter reads "The Institute's First Studies on Authority" (Jay [1973] 1976: 113). To be fair, one has to add that in the chapter itself Jay's discussion of the family can qualify as quite detailed, at least compared to the marginal attention Rolf Wiggershaus ([1986] 1988) pays to the family in his equally seminal study.

4 See the corresponding sections in Türcke and Bolte (1994: 23–26), Dubiel (1988: 47–49), Jay ([1973] 1976: 124–33), and Wiggershaus ([1986] 1988: 173–77).

5 Unfortunately, until today no English translation of these contributions to the *Studien über Autorität und Familie* is available.

6 On the question of whether a critical theory of bourgeois society still is part of the later study on *The Authoritarian Personality*, see Gordon 2017.

7 A similar argument can be found with the more "homophile" statements by AfD representatives. For example, Alice Weidel, the leader of the party's faction in the federal parliament, who is a lesbian, in a recent interview downplayed the existence of homophobia within the AfD. According to Weidel (2017), these days "the Muslim communities" that react with intolerance to "our way of life" represent the one true threat to homosexuals in Germany. As Weidel would have it, the AfD, by rejecting "Islamization" while all other parties stand idly by, is the only political force defending the sexual tolerance presumably characteristic of German culture.

8 For the increasing radicalization of the AfD, with the extreme right faction gaining strength over the liberal-conservative wing of the party, see Grimm and Kahmann 2017.

9 For a first critical discussion of the recent phenomenon of *Anti-Genderismus*, see the anthology by Sabine Hark and Paula-Irene Villa (2015).

References

Abromeit, John. 2011. *Max Horkheimer and the Foundations of the Frankfurt School*. New York: Cambridge University Press.

Adorno, Theodor W., et al. 1950a. "The Measurement of Implicit Antidemocratic Trends." In *The Authoritarian Personality*, 222–79. New York: Harper and Row.

Adorno, Theodor W., et al. 1950b. "Introduction." In *The Authoritarian Personality*, 1–27. New York: Harper and Row.

Alternative für Deutschland (AfD). 2016. "Manifesto for Germany. The Political Programme of the Alternative for Germany." afd.de/wp-content/uploads/sites/111/2017/04/2017 -04-12_afd-grundsatzprogramm-englisch_web.pdf.

Alternative für Deutschland (AfD). 2017. "Programm Bundestagswahl 2017." www.afd.de /wahlprogramm/.

Becker-Schmidt, Regina. 1991. "Identitätslogik und Gewalt. Zum Verhältnis von Kritischer Theorie und Feminismus." In *Fragmente Kritischer Theorie*, edited by Joachim Müller-Warden and Harald Welzer, 59–78. Tübingen, DE: edition diskord.

Benjamin, Jessica. (1977) 1994a. "The End of Internalization: Adorno's Social Psychology." In *The Frankfurt School: Critical Assessments, Volume III*, edited by Jay Bernstein, 132–53. London: Routledge.

Benjamin, Jessica. (1978) 1994b. "Authority and the Family Revisited: Or, A World without Fathers?" In *The Frankfurt School: Critical Assessments. Volume II*, edited by Jay Bernstein, 299–319. London: Routledge.

Claussen, Detlev. 2003. *Theodor W. Adorno. Ein letztes Genie*. Frankfurt: Fischer Verlag.

Dubiel, Helmut. 1988. *Kritische Theorie der Gesellschaft: Eine einführende Rekonstruktion von den Anfängen im Horkheimer-Kreis bis Habermas*. Weinheim/Munich: Juventa.

Frenkel-Brunswik, Else. 1950. "Sex, People, and Self as Seen through the Interviews." In Adorno et al., *The Authoritarian Personality*, 390–441.

Fromm, Erich. (1936) 1987. "Theoretische Entwürfe über Autorität und Familie. Sozial-psychologischer Teil." In *Studien über Autorität und Familie. Forschungsberichte aus dem Institut für Sozialforschung*, edited by Max Horkheimer et al., 77–135. Lüneburg: Dietrich zu Klampen Verlag.

Gordon, Peter E. 2017. "The Authoritarian Personality Revisited: Reading Adorno in the Age of Trump." *boundary 2* 44, no. 2: 31–56.

Grimm, Marc, and Bodo Kahmann. 2017. "AfD und Judenbild. Eine Partei im Spannungsfeld von Antisemitismus, Schuldabwehr und instrumenteller Israelsolidarität." In *AfD und FPÖ: Antisemitismus, völkischer Nationalismus und Geschlechterbilder*, edited by Stephan Grigat, 41–60. Baden-Baden, DE: Nomos.

Hark, Sabine, and Paula-Irene Villa. 2015. *Anti-Genderismus. Sexualität und Geschlecht als Schauplätze aktueller politischer Auseinandersetzungen*. Bielefeld, DE: transcript Verlag.

Horkheimer, Max. (1931) 2009. "The Present Situation of Social Philosophy and the Tasks of an Institute for Social Research." In *Between Philosophy and Social Science: Selected Early Writings*, 1–14. Cambridge: MIT.

Horkheimer, Max. 1934. Letter to Andries Sternheim. VI 41.112–13, Max Horkheimer Archives, Goethe-Universität, Frankfurt.

Horkheimer, Max. (1936) 2002. "Authority and the Family." In *Critical Theory: Selected Essays*, 47–128. New York: Continuum.

Illing, Sean. 2016. "If You Want to Understand the Age of Trump, Read the Frankfurt School." *Vox*, December 27. www.vox.com/conversations/2016/12/27/14038406/donald-trump -frankfurt-school-brexit-critical-theory.

Institut für Sozialforschung. n.d. "Kollektivarbeit Familie." Archive of the Institute for Social Research, Frankfurt.

Jagentowicz Mills, Patricia. 1987. *Woman, Nature, and Psyche*. New Haven, CT: Yale University Press.

Jay, Martin. (1973) 1976. *The Dialectical Imagination: A History of the Frankfurt School and the Institute of Social Research, 1923–1950*. London: Heinemann.

Kemper, Andreas. 2016. "Foundation of the Nation: How Political Parties and Movements Are Radicalising Others in Favour of Conservative Family Values and against Tolerance, Diversity, and Progressive Gender Politics in Europe." library.fes.de/pdf-files/dialog /12503.pdf.

Klein, Hans Peter. 2015. "Gender-Studien. Heldenhafte Spermien und wachgeküsste Eizellen." *Frankfurter Allgemeine Zeitung*, May 30. www.faz.net/aktuell/politik/inland/gender -studies-genderforschung-auch-in-der-biologie-13603216.html.

Klein, Hans Peter. 2016. "Die Wissenschaft leidet unter dem Diktat der Gender-Studies." *Neue Zürcher Zeitung*, May 5. nzzas.nzz.ch/meinungen/externe-standpunkt-wissenschaft -leidet-unter-diktat-gender-studies-ld.149714?reduced=true.

Knapp, Gudrun-Axeli. 1993. "Der 'weibliche Sozialcharakter'—Mythos oder Realität? Soziologische und sozialpsychologische Aspekte des Sozialcharakter-Konstrukts." In *Was heißt hier eigentlich feministisch? Zur theoretischen Diskussion in den Geistes- und Sozialwissenschaften*, edited by Marlis Krüger, 93–120. Bremen, DE: Donat Verlag.

Konrad-Adenauer-Stiftung. 2018. "Gender, Instrument der Umerziehung? Ziele, Kosten, Wirkung." www.kas.de/wf/doc/kas_24565–1442–1–30.pdf?171213101703.

MacWilliams, Matthew. 2016. "The One Weird Trait That Predicts whether You're a Trump Supporter." *Politico*, January 17. www.politico.com/magazine/story/2016/01/donald -trump-2016-authoritarian-213533.

Maihofer, Andrea. 1995. *Geschlecht als Existenzweise. Macht, Moral, Recht und Geschlechterdifferenz*. Frankfurt am Main: Ulrike Helmer Verlag.

Maihofer, Andrea. 2014. "Familiale Lebensformen zwischen Wandel und Persistenz. Eine zeitdiagnostische Zwischenbetrachtung." In *Wissen—Methode—Geschlecht: Erfassen des fraglos Gegebenen*, edited by Cornelia Behnke et al., 313–34. Wiesbaden, DE: Springer.

Manheim, Ernst. (1936) 1987. "Beiträge zu einer Geschichte der autoritären Familie." In Horkheimer et al., 523–74.

Ross, Alex. 2016. "The Frankfurt School Knew Trump Was Coming." *New Yorker*, December 5. www.newyorker.com/culture/cultural-comment/the-frankfurt-school-knew-trump -was-coming.

Rumpf, Mechthild. 1989. *Spuren des Mütterlichen—Die widersprüchliche Bedeutung der Mutterrolle für die männliche Identitätsbildung in Kritischer Theorie und feministischer Wissenschaft*. Frankfurt am Main: Materialis Verlag.

Rumpf, Mechthild. 1993. "Mystical Aura: Imagination and the Reality of the Maternal in Horkheimer's Writings." In *On Max Horkheimer: New Perspectives*, edited by Seyla Benhabib, Wolfgang Bonss, and John McCole, 309–34. Cambridge: MIT Press.

Schachtel, Ernst. (1936) 1987. "Das Recht der Gegenwart und die Autorität in der Familie." In Horkheimer et al., 587–642.

Schmidt, Carsten. 2009. *Der autoritäre Charakter. Erich Fromms Beitrag zu einer politischen Psychologie des Nationalsozialismus.* Münster, DE: Lit Verlag.

Schmoll, Heike. 2014. "Gender Mainstreaming: Das gute Recht der Eltern." *Frankfurter Allgemeine Zeitung*, November 11. www.faz.net/aktuell/politik/inland/gender-mainstreaming -das-gute-recht-der-eltern-13258831.html.

Schwandt, Michael. 2009. *Kritische Theorie. Eine Einführung.* Stuttgart, DE: Schmetterling Verlag.

Sternheim, Andries. (1936) 1987. "Materialien zur Wirksamkeit ökonomischer Faktoren in der gegenwärtigen Familie." In Horkheimer et al., 575–78.

Strausberg, Hildegard. 2015. "Hurra. Viele neue Jobs durch Gender-Terror." *Die Welt*, March 15. www.welt.de/debatte/kolumnen/die-strenge-stausberg/article138434594/Hurra -Viele-neue-Jobs-durch-Gender-Terror.html.

Türcke, Christoph, and Gerhard Bolte. 1994. *Einführung in die Kritische Theorie.* Darmstadt, DE: Wissenschaftliche Buchgesellschaft.

von Randow, Gero. 2016. "Der Trick mit der Gefühlsbefreiung." *Zeit Online*, November 17. www.zeit.de/2016/48/theodor-w-adorno-faschismus-autoritarismus.

Weber, Christian. 2016. "Mann und Frau und der kleine Unterschied." *Süddeutsche Zeitung*, April 16. www.sueddeutsche.de/wissen/gesellschaft-und-forschung-mann-und-frau -und-der-kleine-unterschied-1.2952490#redirectedFromLandingpage.

Weidel, Alice. 2017. "Interview mit Alice Weidel." *Philosophia Perennis*, September 20. philosophia-perennis.com/2017/09/20/alice-weidel-interview/.

Weiss, Hilde. (1936) 1987. "Materialien zum Verhältnis von Konjunktur und Familie." In Horkheimer et al., 579–81.

Wiggershaus, Rolf. (1986) 1988. *Die Frankfurter Schule: Geschichte. Theoretische Entwicklung. Politische Bedeutung.* Munich/Vienna, DE: Carl Hanser Verlag.

Wittfogel, Karl A. (1936) 1987. "Wirtschaftsgeschichtliche Grundlagen der Entwicklung der Familienautorität." In Horkheimer et al., 473–522.

Christian Thorne

Fulfilling the Fascist Lie: Late Reflections
on *The Authoritarian Personality*

The Authoritarian Personality—I want to use my
allotted pages to explain why I find this admittedly remarkable book to be unpersuasive, why, in
fact, it is a matter of some urgency that we not
accept its arguments. I'm not sure how to come at
the point directly, so permit me to note, by way of
introduction, that anyone who reads widely in the
history of fascism is likely to spot, sooner or later, a
series of antitheses—oppositions, I mean, that
were native to fascism and that historians return
to again and again. If we want to be able to think
clearly about *The Authoritarian Personality*, it will
be enough for us to know about two of them. First,
historians have made the point that fascism proceeded through stages, that, in other words, it
wasn't a single static position, that it was, rather, a
dynamic entity tending to mutate over time. What,
one might ask, were those stages? Broadly, the
scholarship calls attention to fascism as an idea
and an imagining, as an ideological current, therefore, cultivated by intellectuals—a fascism of the
book, if you like—which was then succeeded by
fascism as a mass movement. We need to be able to
distinguish between those two. But then we also
need to be able to distinguish between fascism as a
movement and fascism as a regime—which is to

The South Atlantic Quarterly 117:4, October 2018
DOI 10.1215/00382876-7165959 © 2018 Duke University Press

say, as a *successful* movement, having achieved power or taken hold of the state, a fascism, in short, that governed. The point most commonly made is that fascism in its early stages—a still-ideational fascism—was in certain respects more radical than what came later, or that it was more avant gardist, more likely to strike anticapitalist and antibourgeois poses. The fascists, this is to say, became more conventionally conservative over time, more recognizably a party of the Right, once they felt compelled to make their case to the nonbohemian many and once forced by their very success to make concessions to existing institutions and coalition partners. The stages thus yield an antithesis—at one pole, fascism as dissident counterculture; at the other, fascism as the mainstream run amok, the establishment's protracted revenge against its critics and rivals.[1]

This same antithesis now becomes available in a second, geographical form, via the single, uncomplicated observation that Mussolini's government, unlike Hitler's, did not attempt to monopolize the entire sphere of thought and culture. Historians are keen to point out that there was no Italian *Gleichschaltung*—no effort to bring everyone into line. Within certain parameters, independent intellectuals continued to publish in Italy, which means not that there were still socialists or communists or liberals expressing themselves freely in Florence and Rome—those people really were shut down—but that there remained an outer circle of freelance fascists, the half-fascists or the merely unenrolled, the shirts not of black, but of charcoal and onyx and taupe, who continued to propose hypothetical other fascisms in a scatterplot around the fascism that was actually being implemented. An aestheticist and nonconformist fascism thus remained more visible in Italy throughout the 1920s and 1930s, never wholly subsumed into fascism-as-revanchist-orthodoxy.[2] Early vs. late; Italy vs. Germany—two antitheses that are really one, a fascism with antibourgeois features vs. its snarlingly bourgeois rival.

This compounded antithesis matters because there are a hundred different claims you might wish to make about fascism that will run aground upon it. Arguments about fascism routinely invert or negate themselves, and the reason for this is surprisingly easy to identify. Histories of fascism often posit an A fascism and a B fascism, and even if you think that "A vs. B" sounds too schematic, as it doubtless is, that second term will suffice to undermine one's accustomed sense that fascism was a uniform position— or indeed that it was, to a singular degree, a politics of uniformity, a uniform movement in the pursuit of uniformity. The problem for those of us needing to theorize fascism is that a great many things we will want to say about the

B fascism will not be true of the A fascism. Worse, if we mean to fashion our historical analysis into a politics, then we run the permanent risk of pegging our antifascism to one pole or another of the fascist antithesis, such that by opposing one fascism, we will end up endorsing the other, if only unwittingly, having failed at the outset to so much as recognize this latter as fascist. Our antifascism will be stalked by its fascist twin.

Anyone wanting to come to grips with *The Authoritarian Personality*, then, will need to understand first how basic these transpositions are to the study of fascism. The movement's nearest synonym has always been *national socialism*, in a manner that predates the renaming of the German Workers' Party in 1920. So was national socialism national? Manifestly, you say, nothing is better established than that. Theorists of fascism are fond of the term *ultranationalism*—that's a nationalism made super- and hyper- and arch-. But then what do we say about the swastika, that most recognizable of fascist emblems, incomparably more iconic than any bundle of wooden rods?—the swastika, this hermetic countercrucifix, which, as of 1917, was still associated above all with sites in India and Baluchistan and western Turkey. The point that overfamiliarity makes hard to grasp is that every official building in Nazi Germany was adorned with an Orientalist hex sign. German troops marched under an ankh or dream-catcher, an Aryavartic pentacle that derived its talismanic charisma not from its Germanness—not, that is, from its being indigenous to Silesia or Brandenburg, which it wasn't—but from its near ubiquity across four continents. The word *Aryan*, meanwhile, is not and never was an apt equivalent for *Teutonic* or *Nordic*. Even as a white supremacist term of art, the word has always meant something like *Indo-Germanic*. It's that hyphen we'll want to pay attention to, informing us as it does that doctrines of the Aryan were not premised on yet another nineteenth-century sundering of the West from the non-West, but precisely on their fusing. Of all the ways of naming white people, *Aryan* has got to be the most peculiar—though *Caucasian* is plenty strange and *white* itself mere misdescription. *Aryan*, however, is the only entry on that list that could be suspected of negating whiteness even while exalting it. Aryan—the Eurasian or Occi-oriental (Quinn 1994; Arvidsson and Wichmann 2006).

National socialism, then, was not straightforwardly nationalist. But was it socialist? The historians have a ready answer for that one, which is that even though some Nazi officials were willing to deploy a modified socialist rhetoric, the Nazi regime was quick to dismantle the institutions of the independent and organized working classes, to round up leftists, and to close ranks with IG Farben and Siemens and IBM. No, then, national socialism was not socialist. Not socialist, not national: *Nationalsozialismus* was a capitalism dreaming of two continents.

At this point, there is a question that any antifascist is going to have to ask: What claims can we make about fascism that will escape transposition of this kind? That challenge gives us a few good reasons for endorsing the approach taken by Adorno and his colleagues in *The Authoritarian Personality*. The F-scale, in particular, could be grasped as a solution to this problem, though to say only this is to understate its achievement. Anyone still needing to be convinced of the achievements of Freudianism as a mode of political analysis could do worse than read this book, which turns to psychoanalysis in order to overcome the difficulties that have always weakened other theories, and especially to fix what has been least convincing about attempts to explain fascism in intellectual or ideological terms. To turn to psychoanalysis is to insist that there is no philosophical or merely doctrinal path to fascism—that fascism has never been a matter of the *substance* of one's beliefs. It is akin to a syndrome, hence a way of inhabiting whatever creed or identification a person might have cathected to. There may not be a Protestant path to fascism, which is simply to say that some Protestants turned fascist and some didn't, but there is a fascist way of inhabiting your Protestantism. There may not even be a nationalist path to fascism, but there is a fascist way of libidinizing your nationalism. If that point seems plausible, then the next step is simply to extend it to social history, whose results are similarly inconclusive about such matters. There is no particular social path to fascism, no economic or demographic niche that opens chute-like onto the Far Right—the National Socialists, after all, were a mass party and recruited successfully (if unevenly) from across the regions and classes and professions—but there might be a fascist way of being attached to your social position, *any* social position.

So that's the achievement of the F-scale, and it's worth sticking up for. And yet the theory fails to convince all the same, since the F-scale, no less than rival theories, comes apart upon the fascist antitheses. Maybe the problem is already apparent: Adorno and his colleagues have proposed a series of fixed attributes that they think make up the fascist personality. Here's Adorno summarizing the book's findings at a YMCA in 1948: The protofascist personality type involves "mechanical acceptance of conventional values, blind submission to authority combined with a violently aggressive attitude toward all those who don't belong, anti-introspectiveness, rigid stereotypical thinking, a penchant for superstition, a vilification of human nature, and the habit to ascribe to the out-group the wishes and behavior patterns which one has to deny in oneself" (quoted in Jacobs 2015: 88–89). Anyone alerted to the reversals that occur in the passage from FASCISM to FASCISM′ has got to suspect that we could just as well flip each of these character traits—name its opposite—and still find ourselves sitting across from a fascist. The F-scale describes the personality of a fascist, but then so does the anti-F scale. Handed an antifascist checklist by the Berkeley coauthors of *The Authoritarian Personality*, we should be able to go through and negate each of its terms and thereby find not a nonfascism (the low scorers!), but an alternate path to fascism. Shall we just do it?

1. Conventionalism: Fascists, Adorno tells us, are deeply conformist, the prim creatures of conventional morality, quick to punish anyone who offends against a stupid decency—Victorians in leather trench coats. This observation might be right as far as it goes, but what it omits is that the Babbitt-Nazis of Adorno's description shared the movement with fascist revolutionaries and world-remakers and proclaimers of a New Europe, with those who wanted to de-Christianize Germany, to revive a pre-Frankish religion of runes and Wotan or to forge a *grossdeutscher* Buddhism. Here's Robert Brasillach, writing near the end of the war, not long before he was executed for being one of the most outspoken French Nazis: "Fascism was a spirit. For us it was not a political doctrine, nor was it an economic doctrine. . . . It was first of all an anticonformist, antibourgeois spirit, in which disrespect played its part."[3]

2. Authoritarian submission: The notion that fascists are typically submissive and obedient, meanwhile, is difficult to square with the movement's reliance on mass mobilization—its determination to agitate and unleash the public rather than pacify it. This is often taken to be the characteristic that most obviously distinguishes fascism from a generic authoritarianism. Energy and the deed counter docility and ductility. Enthusiasm counts for as much as compliance.

3. Authoritarian aggression: The troubling sentence is this one: In fascist societies, "hostility that was originally aroused by and directed toward ingroup authorities is displaced onto outgroups" (Adorno et al. 1950: 233). The claim that fascists are aggressive or violence prone is as close to a consensus position as one is likely to find. And yet to say additionally that fascists are the ones who channel their aggression toward an outgroup is drastically to understate the vehemence of their attack on existing institutions (and to skip over the very minor role that anti-Semitism played in fascist Italy for most of its duration). The problem is best grasped as a conceptual one: the fascists came to power only by declaring illegitimate the up-and-sort-of-running institutions of government and by anathematizing entire sectors of

German and Italian society hitherto regarded as normal. They were wholly capable of waging war on the ingroup—or of reclassifying in- as out-. To say that aggression targets the outgroup is to skip all the urgent questions about how the social field gets cleaved and recleaved. Here's another French fascist, Drieu la Rochelle, writing in 1934: "We are against everyone. We fight against everyone. That is what fascism is" (quoted in Sternhell 1995a: 222).

4. Superstition and stereotypy: Superstition and stereotyping have been paired by the Berkeley authors because they both point to the inability of protofascists to think clearly about what is happening in the world at large and why it is happening. People susceptible to fascism are alienated in some properly Left Hegelian sense of the term—unsure of how·events and institutions are produced, mired in the opacity of the social, cognitively thwarted by the complexity of networked causes. But then we have names for people who have been trained, contrariwise, to think carefully about such causes. Some of them we call "historians"; others we call "scientists." To say that fascism thrives where causal understanding collapses is to suggest that there was no protofascist history writing, in the manner, for instance, of Ernst Kantorowicz's (1927) biography of *Frederick the Second*, and no fascist science either. But then, of course, we now have decades of scholarship, much of it Adornian in spirit, documenting the scientific orientation of National Socialism. That fascism requires superstition as its provender can only be maintained by someone who has never heard the term *biopolitics*.

5. Anti-intraception: The Berkeley authors make it hard to so much as register the existence of a fascist science—and then they do the same thing for fascist poetry. Protofascists, we are told, are uncomfortable with inwardness. They would gladly put a taboo on reflection or on the display of inner life or on psychoanalysis itself. But then are we to say nothing about Stefan George and Ezra Pound and Gabriele D'Annunzio and William Butler Yeats? Was there no such thing as a fascist lyric, hence a fascist inwardness? Were the fascist and near fascist poets not fascist *when they wrote poetry*? Did they only become fascist again upon putting down their pens? Are lyric poems written by fascists less lyric than ones written by liberals or socialists? Less inward? Not at all inward? But then what makes them lyric? Did Yeats not write lyric?

6 and 7. Power and "Toughness" + Sex: Then of course there's the idea that protofascists are tough guys with hang-ups about sex. That idea can be dismissed by pointing to a particular person. One of Stefan George's closest associates for a time was Alfred Schuler, a freak classicist of sub-Nietzschean caliber, who wanted nothing more than to resurrect a pagan antiquity and

who thought he could do this mostly by throwing toga parties. Schuler wrote almost nothing; he was more of a counterculture guru than an intellectual; but his central idea seems to have been that European culture was all but permanently rent by a conflict between the male principle and the female principle, to be understood, presumably, along orthodox lines as rationality versus irrationality, logos versus desire, activity versus passivity. Schuler thought that Europe might yet be redeemed if Westerners could agree collectively to abandon settled gender roles and embrace instead a universal androgyny. The Greeks and Romans would point the way in this regard, because they had practiced boy-love; they had been wise enough to worship the she-male. Schuler thought, in other words, that pederasty, by offering a fragile synthesis of male and female or mind and body, might just keep Europe's primal gender conflict in check. This idea had as its extension the idea that everyday life in Europe had been thrown permanently off-kilter when Roman culture went into eclipse; the Roman world had promoted androgyny; the early medieval world had reestablished rigid gender roles. And the culprits behind this almost millennial crime were, of course, the Jews, since they were one of the very few eastern Mediterranean cultures to prohibit male love, which makes of any Christianity that will not spill its seed nothing but a generalized and evangelical Judaism. Christianity, in other words, had merely propagated and enforced the homophobia of the ancient Jews. When love between men thus became taboo, so this line of reasoning ran, the Jewish spirit and its gender orthodoxies went into the ascendancy, and it was this world-historical shift that a sibylline and modernist poetry might yet undo. It matters, then, that Schuler is known to historians mostly as the person who reintroduced into modern European culture the swastika, which was to be the emblem of the Future and Genderless Age. Indeed, Schuler for a time wanted to change his name to the *Hakenkreuz*, a symbol with no spoken equivalent. His reasoning here was roughly like Prince's: the dingbat under which '90s-era Prince released his CDs combined the classic, bathroom-door sign for Mars—hard-on north-north-east—with the classic, incongruously dangling sign for Venus, which makes his just one of several recent transgender riffs on those old gender symbols. The revived swastika, in this sense, was one of the earliest instances of the typesetter's hermaphroditic astrology.[4]

This leaves (8) projectivity as the one item from the F-scale we still need to consider. I would offer that its status is special for anyone still sifting through *The Authoritarian Personality* and that it will require some extra attention. The claim that Adorno and colleagues make is fairly straightforward:

that anyone "ready to think about and to believe in the existence of such phe-nomena as wild erotic excesses, plots and conspiracies, and danger from nat-ural catastrophes" must himself have a rowdy id—he has to believe such things are likely, he must himself feel the pull of sex and destruction (Adorno et al. 1950: 240). Protofascists are the ones ready to see in the world their own most malign impulses. The theory of projection has always been of par-ticular interest because it is psychoanalysis's most obviously dialectical fig-ure, this parody of Hegelian reconciliation, in which the subject rediscovers himself in some other and then, offered the chance for self-communion, declares war on this Other-Self instead, trading in the *bei sich* for a fatuous *gegen sich*. Projection matters to us as readers of Adorno and Co. because it is via its mechanisms that fascism and antifascism are most directly conjoined. The antidemocrat is alarmed at how antidemocratic everything has become. The fascist declares himself worried about fascism. It is here, upon discover-ing that the people we're pretty sure are protofascists are themselves antifas-cist, that caution recommends itself. We will want to pause to at least wonder about the possibility of projection in our own antifascism, and not just in theirs. Are we sure that projection isn't involved in our willingness to believe that other people are fascists, our finding their malignity plausible? Is there perhaps projection in the F-scale itself? Couldn't our diagnosis that other people are given to projection itself involve projection? And if not, why not? Can antifascism itself carry a fascism?

It's at this moment that we'll need to look up from *The Authoritarian Personality* and go back to *The Dialectic of Enlightenment* (Horkheimer and Adorno 1947). It used to be taken as a given that fascism was a movement of the counter-Enlightenment, and if that is no longer the set line—if many of us now take it as given that National Socialism was Enlightenment's apothe-osis and not its negation—then we have Adorno and Horkheimer to thank, in large part, for the revision. It can come as a surprise, then, to realize that Adorno and Horkheimer weren't actually disagreeing with that earlier claim. New readers are going to understand *The Dialectic of Enlightenment* better if they can see that it takes that other, prior point as read. The word that we usually omit when summarizing *The D. of E.* is "also." Adorno and Hork-heimer thought they could show that fascism was *also* an Enlightenment project, that fascism had a disastrous way of getting the Enlightenment and counter-Enlightenment to coincide—or that any organized enlightenment eventually reached a point where it could no longer be distinguished from counter-enlightenment. That's the dialectic in the title—without the word *also* there is no dialectic. The title always has to be heard as *The Dialectic of*

Enlightenment and Counter-Enlightenment, the latter of which, however, the authors mostly call "myth."

The problem, then, is that this very great book almost only gets read as "Enlightenment critique"—indeed, it is often held out as the twentieth century's single greatest entry in that genre. But maybe it's time to admit that "Enlightenment critique" is an intemperate simplification and pretty much a mistake, in which most of Adorno and Horkheimer's argument gets shorn away. Enlightenment critique is *The Dialectic of Enlightenment* de-dialecticized. One forgets the starting point, which was that fascism had presented itself above all as counter-enlightenment. Not in *The Dialectic of Enlightenment* itself, but among its readers, and on the syllabi in which it is excerpted, the counter-enlightenment that is the closest thing that fascism had to an official ideology gets held out as the authentically antifascist option. In this form, *The Dialectic of Enlightenment,* far from being the centerpiece of antifascist philosophy that we need it to be, becomes the vehicle by which a certain protofascist sensibility has been kept alive in the extended postwar era, in which one important version of the fascist temptation survives because it is disguised as its opposite.

Recognizing as much should help us see at last why it is important that we not accept the framework offered by Adorno and the Berkeley team in *The Authoritarian Personality*—because it is in the pages on the F-scale that Adorno signs his name to the nondialectical version of his own dialectical argument. It is in this volume that dialectic gets truncated back to diagnosis. It is finally hard to agree with the West Coast Adorno if we accept that the F-scale was meant to identify protofascists and not just company men. The mind pauses and reflects. Does anyone really think that the fascists were right-thinking squares who always did what they were told and wanted to punch queers in the face? The German catastrophe was an awful lot weirder than that—uncomfortably weird if weird is what you like. A critical theory that preemptively declares itself a *Zona Antifa* gullibly deeds over its stances to the very movement it opposes. Two American thinkers share credit for coining the term *alternative right*: (1) the elderly intellectual historian who gave a speech in 2008 commending the rise of an American *Front National,* a movement less egalitarian than Fox News, the Republican Party, and the Heritage Foundation, welcoming a conservatism willing once again to embrace scientific racism and to stop pretending it admires Martin Luther King; and (2) the young intellectual historian who edited that speech for publication online. The speech in question was Paul Gottfried's "Decline and Rise of the Alternative Right," edited for *Taki's Magazine* by Richard Spencer.

In the 1980s, the older man wrote a book cataloging all the philosophical prizes that Hegelian-Marxist apostates bring with them when they convert to anticommunism (Gottfried 1986). Twenty years later, his fond reminiscences of taking a class with Herbert Marcuse in the early 1960s (Gottfried 2005) are matched by the tributes he writes to Jared Taylor's American Renaissance (Gottfried 2011). First one reads this: "There were . . . Frankfurt School texts that I found instructive, particularly *Dialectic of Enlightenment* and *Negative Dialectics*." And then one reads this: "Which American party stands for the white counterinsurgency? . . . Significantly, the white solidarity that Jared advocates has never really developed in Western history outside of colonial settlements and in the American South." At least one early member of the Frankfurt School spent his later career refunctioning a concept of Marx's, the Asiatic mode of production, into a bludgeon with which to thump the Reds.[6] Frankfurt School accounts of the administered society are now joined by neo-Confederates who define the enemy as "the administrative society" or borderline fascists who can tell you all about the "therapeutic managerial state." The day you first read Guy Debord was the day you should have realized not only that you could practice *détournement*, but also that it could be practiced upon you, that the cultures susceptible to jamming included your antifascist own. In November 2016, that younger intellectual historian addressed a room full of white nationalists. "Hail our people!" he said. "Hail victory!" He'd written his master's thesis on Adorno.[7]

Notes

1   See, paradigmatically, Paxton 2004.

2   For Italy, see Sternhell 1995b, Gentile 2003, and Ben-Ghiat 2004.

3   Brasillach is quoted in Sternhell 1995a: 247. Evidence for this point is so abundant that Adorno's oversight seems genuinely hard to explain. One way to come at this is to consider the scholarship on fascism, which refers to the nonconformist features of the movement over and over again. A taste: the first section of Richard Evans's chapter on "The Rise of Nazism" is called "Bohemian Revolutionaries" (Evans 2004: 156–75). Evans again: "Unable to come to terms with his failure to get into the Academy, Hitler conceived a violent hatred for bourgeois convention, the establishment, rules and regulations" (164). Evans quotes Röhm: "Since I am an immature and wicked person, war and unrest appeal to me more than well-behaved bourgeois order" (183). Alternately, one might consult Leonard Zeskind's (2009) history of white supremacy since the 1980s. Describing the rapid growth of the racist Right in the late twentieth century, Zeskind writes, "Some of [the new organizations] eschewed the trappings of middle-class mainstream society and opted instead for an alternative lifestyle" (59). Of William Pierce, author of *The Turner Diaries*, he remarks, "The bookish physics professor step by step exited conventional society" (18). Such quotations could be multiplied at will.

4   On Schuler, see Norton 2002: 294–98.
5   The speech in question was Paul Gottfried's "Decline and Rise of the Alternative Right," edited for *Taki's Magazine* by Richard Spencer.
6 ·   That would be Karl Wittfogel. See Gottfried 1986.
7   Richard Spencer's master's thesis is routinely mentioned in profiles. I first learned of it from Harkinson 2016.

References

Adorno, Theodor W., Else Frenkel-Brunswik, Daniel J. Levinson, and R. Nevitt Sanford. 1950. *The Authoritarian Personality*. New York: Harper and Row.

Arvidsson, Stefan, and Sonia Wichmann. 2006. *Aryan Idols: Indo-European Mythology as Ideology and Science*. Chicago: University of Chicago Press.

Ben-Ghiat, Ruth. 2004. *Fascist Modernities: Italy, 1922–1945*. Berkeley: University of California Press.

Evans, Richard. 2004. *The Coming of the Third Reich*. New York: Penguin.

Gentile, Emilio. 2003. *Struggle for Modernity: Nationalism, Futurism, and Fascism*. Westport, CT: Praeger.

Goldstein, Joseph. 2016. "US Alt-Right Gathering Exults in Trump Election with Nazi-Era Salute." *New York Times*, November 20.

Gottfried, Paul. 1986. *The Search for Historical Meaning: Hegel and the Postwar American Right*. Dekalb: Northern Illinois University Press.

Gottfried, Paul. 2005. "The Marcuse Factor." *Modern Age* 47, no. 2: 113–20.

Gottfried, Paul. 2008. "Decline and Rise of the Alternative Right." *Taki's Magazine*, December 1. takimag.com/article/the_decline_and_rise_of_the_alternative_right#axzz4 ZoqxSxpB.

Gottfried, Paul. 2011. "Right but Doomed." *Taki's Magazine*, May 17. takimag.com/article/right _but_doomed/print#axzz4ZoqxSxpB.

Harkinson, Josh. 2016. "Meet the White Nationalist Trying to Ride the Trump Train to Lasting Power." *Mother Jones*, October 27. www.motherjones.com/politics/2016/10/richard -spencer-trump-alt-right-white-nationalist.

Horkheimer, Max, and Theodor Adorno. 1947. *Dialektik der Aufklärung* (*The Dialectic of Enlightenment*). Amsterdam: Querido.

Jacobs, Jack. 2015. *Frankfurt School, Jewish Lives, and Anti-Semitism*. Cambridge: Cambridge University Press.

Kantorowicz, Ernst. 1927. *Kaiser Friedrich der Zweite*. Berlin: Georg Bondi.

Norton, Robert. 2002. *Secret Germany: Stefan George and His Circle*. Ithaca, NY: Cornell University Press.

Paxton, Robert. 2004. *Anatomy of Fascism*. London: Penguin.

Quinn, Malcolm. 1994. *The Swastika: Constructing the Symbol*. London: Routledge.

Sternhell, Zeev. 1995a. *Neither Left nor Right: Fascist Ideology in France*. Translated by David Maisel. Berkeley: University of California Press.

Sternhell, Zeev. 1995b. *Birth of Fascist Ideology: From Cultural Rebellion to Political Revolution*. Princeton, NJ: Princeton University Press.

Zeskind, Leonard. 2009. *Blood and Politics*. New York: Farrar, Straus and Giroux.

City Plaza: The Best Hotel in Europe

Loukia Kotronaki and Olga Lafazani, Editors

**Loukia Kotronaki, Olga Lafazani,
and Giorgos Maniatis**

Living Resistance: Experiences from
Refugee Housing Squats in Athens

The signing of the EU-Turkey deal on March 2016 ended the "long summer of migration," which had erupted in 2015, leaving behind a series of
control mechanisms, including border fences, hot spots, and border
patrols to block the movement of migrants. The tens of thousands of refugees who were about to cross the Greek-Macedonian borders found themselves trapped in Greece, homeless or "semi-housed," crowded into awful
conditions, in camps, athletic fields, airports, and ports, and facing extreme
poverty and a lack of basic amenities. Even worse was the situation for the
newcomers, who were trapped in the Aegean islands, which had been transformed into a buffer zone between Greece and Turkey.

Migrants, who during the summer of 2015 reclaimed the right to
move from one place to the other, fighting for a life with safety and rights,
became objects of the European biopolitics of segregation and selective
attribution of rights. But they were also subject to the applied disciplinary
politics and exemplary violence of the EU repressive apparatus. The new
Europeanized "reception and identification center," the hot spots, became
the symbol of the state's organized impoverishment, functioning as
mechanisms of exemplary punishment for discouraging future refugees
from entering EU territory.

Within these circumstances, the Solidarity Initiative for Economic
and Political Refugees, which comprised four groups of the radical Left in

The South Atlantic Quarterly 117:4, October 2018
DOI 10.1215/00382876-7166031 © 2018 Duke University Press

Athens, took the initiative to squat City Plaza, an eight-floor abandoned hotel with one hundred twenty rooms in the center of Athens.

The squat of City Plaza had a double scope: On the one hand, its aim was to provide safe housing for refugees in dignified conditions in the center of the city. On the other hand, it sought to become a center of struggle against the European border and migration policies. However, the Plaza squat also intervened in several other sociopolitical issues. The hotel was a symbol of the economic crisis: after closing and filing for bankruptcy in 2010, it left dozens of employees jobless and unpaid for several months. The neighborhood where the hotel is located, Victoria Square, is a "migrant's neighborhood," which is the main reason why after the closing of the borders it was transformed into a peculiar public dormitory for hundreds of homeless refugees. At the same time, this neighborhood was the main stage of the neo-Nazi party Golden Dawn, which conducted innumerable attacks against migrants, especially from 2009 to 2013.

In this spatio-temporal conjuncture, the City Plaza project aimed to thread together those different facets of the multiple crises as they were manifested in the urban landscape. Highlighting the new political content accrued by social needs at risk was a promising starting point. From a narrow perspective, City Plaza was a political challenge limited to a specific area and related to a small number of people. From a broader perspective, City Plaza has been a materialized proposal for new forms of social coexistence and interaction in the European cities, a proposal stressing the practical dimension of the rights, freedoms, and constitutive power of solidarity. It has emphasized that locals and migrants can reappropriate rights from which they have been excluded through common action and the emergence of spaces of freedom and collective practices.

The City Plaza community believed that the reappropriation of rights and freedoms could not be accomplished within one or several "niches of freedom" beyond state and market control. Rather, it insisted on the importance of concrete struggles and their material outcomes at local and transnational levels, arguing that small victories can shape social coalitions, enhance the self-confidence of the oppressed, and broaden possibilities for social change—sometimes by overcoming the original aims and expectations of subjects of the struggles. Such an approach was of great importance, especially during a period characterized by a diffuse mood of disappointment and demobilization manifested and proliferated within the lines of the Left. It was particularly important for the organization of social movements in the fallout from the collapse of the political plan of Syriza, especially after that government overturned the referendum of July 5, 2015, in which the Greek people had voted to reject the austerity measures imposed by the International Monetary Fund, the European Commission, and the European Central Bank. Finally, Syriza had subordinated hope to the Thatcher-era slogan and doctrine of neoliberal rationality, "There is no alternative" (TINA).

In this context, the Solidarity Initiative for Economic and Political Refugees squatted the bankrupted three-star hotel in April 22, 2016, and transformed it into a housing project. With its one hundred and twenty-six rooms, City Plaza became one of the largest refugee accommodation squats in Athens, with a capacity of hosting between three hundred fifty and four hundred people. Among the new residents of the hotel were many migrant families from about ten different countries. About one-third of the population were children. There were also many single-parent families, single women, and single men. And let us not forget the dozens of local and international activists.

City Plaza's everyday life has followed principles of self-organization and political autonomy. There has been no official funding, either from the state or from nongovernmental organizations, and no one has been paid for their work on the project. Different working groups, which have answered to regular assemblies and coordination meetings, have been responsible for the Plaza's operations, including cleaning, cooking, security, logistics, education and childcare, medical care, reception, and other tasks.

The four essays in this special section of *South Atlantic Quarterly* are written by people who have been involved in the City Plaza project from day one and who have been active for many years in the antiracist and emancipatory movements in Greece and in Europe. These contributions address different aspects, debates, and analyses that have emerged over the course of the two-year experience of European refugee management and the City Plaza "living resistance" project and that concern many other refugee solidarity projects at both local and transnational levels.

In the two years City Plaza has been operating as a squat, it has housed more than twenty-five hundred people and has been engaged in numerous mobilizations and struggles. It has become not only a counterexample of migrant housing but also a radical alternative to the European Union's policies of bordering, repression, and migration management. At the same time, City Plaza has been an open-ended project that has created a heterogeneous and transit community, kept alive also in the diaspora, that is, in different European cities where former residents of City Plaza now live.

Olga Lafazani

Homeplace Plaza: Challenging the Border between Host and Hosted

In the first day of our squat in the narrow Katrivanou Street where City Plaza's entrance is, it was chaos. Many neighbors, along with the owner of the building and her friends, had gathered outside and were swearing at us, threatening to call the police and members of the neo-Nazi party Golden Dawn, demanding that we leave immediately. At the next corner, there was a group of migrants who had previously stayed at the Camp of Hellinicon and had just arrived. Because of the whole mess, they could not reach the door and get into the hotel. After a while, since we did not have any other solution, we formed a human chain to help the migrants to get into the building. At the time I thought—a recurring thought I had on different occasions—that the migrants must have felt deeply insecure that day since they were in the middle of a fight between locals who spoke a language totally unfamiliar to them in unprecedented conditions. Several months later, I read an interview by K., a woman from Afghanistan who said, referring to the same incident: "I scarcely knew those people. But from day one, when they used their own bodies to protect us, I had a real sense of safety and trust" (City Plaza Collective 2018). This article approaches these different ways of understanding a common action, the multiple contradictions, and the different experiences of everyday life in City Plaza, along with the consequent problems.

From the solidarity movement's point of view, the organization of the City Plaza project is really compound and complex but is also a really interesting experience. From the start, we aimed to make City Plaza a counterexample to the dominant migration policies. City Plaza is not just a housing occu-

The South Atlantic Quarterly 117:3, October 2018
DOI 10.1215/00382876-7166043 © 2018 Duke University Press

pation but a political project at many levels: from collectively organizing social production in everyday life, to resistance in the face of policies that aim to control and subjugate migrants.

In spite of all the planning before the squat, the experience of City Plaza challenged us in many ways. It is a deeply transformative project for probably everyone who lives there. City Plaza's everydayness is based on encounters among people who come from totally different backgrounds with different social, political, and cultural references, with different needs, strategies, and plans, and who happen to coexist for a shorter or longer period of time.

These encounters reveal some inherent contradictions, and the project overall entails many difficulties because it demands a highly scaled organization that often conflicts with basic principles and values of the solidarity movement. In this essay, I examine some of those contradictions. Rather than praise the project and show off its achievements, I wish to discuss its difficulties, the ways in which we coped with them, the ways in which we failed to cope with them. The aim is not to present a best practices handbook but to open a debate about the contradictions and the problems of similar projects, in contrast with the prevailing ways of managing migration and the tendency to romanticize both solidarity projects and the migrants themselves.

City Plaza's Door: A Stiff Border

As early as the first day of the squat, the process of deciding who would stay at City Plaza became one of the most difficult problems because it required a process of choice and hierarchization that is directly counter to our basic principles. While we fight for a world without borders and discrimination, where everyone has the right to decent housing—and for us, City Plaza is a small part of this struggle, dozens of migrants who would like to live in City Plaza are excluded. To give a sense of scale, the waiting list is thirteen hundred registrations long, and every registration is either a single man, single woman, or large family.

However, City Plaza's rigid door policy is the result of a certain political choice: City Plaza strives not to solve the housing problem of migrants in toto or to house as many people as possible but to become a counterexample of coexistence. As such, City Plaza aims to create conditions of decent standards of living for as many as the building can house securely with common areas and basic private spaces. City Plaza's door policy has often been a point of conflict with solidarity activists, especially those from abroad; it has also, naturally, caused virtually daily tension as people knock on the door looking for a place to stay, begging to sleep in the dining room or the corridors.

Nevertheless, although City Plaza's door is for many a rigid border, it has never followed the rules and requirements of the prevailing migration policies. The choice as to who stays was never based on the legal status (refugees or irregular immigrants, asylum seekers, possessing documents or not), and it was never based on the nationality (this is why City Plaza houses more or less ten different nationalities); up to a point, we have also tried to avoid granting housing to the "most vulnerable cases" (from day one, City Plaza housed also "very healthy" single men and women). We did not endorse the prevailing management of "migration flows" because we believe that all these statuses—the immigrant, the refugee, the transit, and so on— are legal statuses and do not really describe the paths of migration or the needs of the subjects that migrate (De Genova 2002). They describe, rather, the need of the host states to control and manage the bodies and the labor they bear (see also Neilson and Mezzadra 2013).

Residents are selected by the reception working group. Each time that a room becomes free, we discuss the current issues and try to balance the needs of migrants with those of the project. For instance, we try to avoid allowing a single nationality to dominate the population, maintain a gender balance, and include people who can sustain the basic operations of the project (translators, cooks, etc.). But we have admitted, through often exhausting collective procedures, that we cannot be "fair," cannot pose some neutral criteria that validate the needs of those who reach City Plaza's doorstep asking for a room. We have admitted that every system of division and selection is unjust and that, under the particular circumstances, the rooms shall be given to those who more or less have an immediate need for shelter.

"This Place Looks Like a Hotel but It Is Not a Hotel"

These are the first words of the detailed introduction given by the reception team before someone gets a room at City Plaza. This introduction attempts to describe City Plaza in the simplest terms: it is an occupied place and not a housing institution that belongs to the state or to any nongovernmental organizations, that none of us works at City Plaza, that we participate because it is part of a broader political struggle, that all the money and supplies are donations from individuals or collectivities and not from official bodies, and that the project is self-organized and everyone can participate in the procedures of organizing and decision making. That information may seem simple and understandable to people who participate in Europe's antagonistic movement but it is not simple for those who come from totally different social and political backgrounds. This is so not only because these things cannot be explained or translated but because in reality they cannot be translated into relevant or similar experiences and forms of social and political struggles. Thus, for example, someone may have never heard the words *self-organization* or *squat*, or these words might mean something rather different to them. Similarly, the fact that we spend so much time and effort on a project without getting paid seems absurd or unbelievable not only to the migrants but also to the locals who are not involved in the movement. Besides, in societies characterized by individualism and neoliberalism, it may make sense for people to stand in solidarity with their close relatives or close friends but not with those they have never met. Therefore, the difference between a squat and a state institution, the fact that we do not accept money from the European Union or other official bodies for running City Plaza, as well as the fact that we do not demand any given that "we do such a hard work for the refugees" seem incomprehensible. Finally, the majority of those who come to stay at City Plaza are accustomed to societies with strict hierarchies; they seek the "person in charge," the "manager," the "director," in order to address their claims. Of course, this is a broad generalization and does not apply to everyone. For instance, the Kurds of Rojava or Turkey or the politicized Turkish refugees who have had similar experiences understand the project of City Plaza much better.

We partly overcome this lack of mutual understanding through common everyday experiences: mundane actions and ways of coexisting, strategies for coping with common problems, and the everyday codes. For instance, they will see those whom they consider "managers" mop the stairs, carry the dirty blankets and food supplies, or queue up for dinner. In these everyday moments, in a much more convincing way than words could convey, given apperceptions are destabilized and the limits of understanding as to what City Plaza is become broader. Moreover, moments of common struggle, whether they concern broader political claims or City Plaza, form totally different relations for its inhabitants. For instance, when we organize large campaigns, as we did on March 18, 2017, against the agreement between Turkey and the European Union, it is obvious that we all stand together against the prevailing policies. Much more so, the morning that we went down the street to prevent the water from being cut, while we guarded the electrical supply of Public Power Corporation-DEH because they kept cutting off electricity in the hotel, and when we had to organize City Plaza's picket lines against possible fascist attacks: during those days and nights, it became obvious that City Plaza is not a hostel funded by official bodies or run by a manager. It is a different "home" for which we must all fight together and take a stand.

"Here We Cook Together and Eat Together"

During the first days of the squat, participation in day-to-day chores (cleaning, cooking, dishwashing, etc.) was voluntary. Gradually, as the Plaza population grew, there were complaints, namely, that some people worked more than others who would not contribute at all to the common tasks. Thus, the reception group began reflecting on how to organize a system to divide these tasks. Through trial and error and after several debates during house assemblies, we ended up with a system according to which the adults of each room had to take a shift of either kitchen work or cleaning work once a week. At the same time, an internal division of this everyday labor started, according to the principle "to each according to their needs, from each according to their abilities": for example, cleaning and building maintenance, which is a heavier task, is undertaken by men's rooms, while the breakfast shift, which is relatively short and easy to do, is taken up by single mothers. Certain elderly people or mothers with newborn children are excluded from shifts.

Similarly, one of the many problems we faced in this initial period was the huge line that formed at mealtimes. People who had lived for many months in miserable conditions at poorly organized camps like Edomeni always felt that there would not be enough food for everyone; one or two hours before food was to be served, they would line up by the dozens—sometimes the line would reach the first-floor staircase. After many attempts to avoid this problem, for instance, serving food to different floors at different times, which turned out to be in vain, we came up with a solution following a suggestion made at the house assembly: we would distribute a food card to each room. Thus, one adult from each room would be given all the food portions allocated for the room. This reduced the line, yet it did not make it go away. What did eliminate the waiting line was not a technical solution, but rather the feeling of trust, built over the course of several months; in time, the residents developed an understanding that food would always be sufficient for everyone.

Engaging everyone in the project is not just a practical decision to ensure that tasks are completed. It is first and foremost a political choice against the relationships of dependency created in most institutional structures, where migrants are conditioned to be passive and simply expect food, clothing, and all other bare necessities to be provided for them. Taking part in the chores of City Plaza means that refugees are not just treated as helpless victims but as members of a community with responsibilities and obligations. In a similar vein, the participation of everyone in the project signals the creation of a self-organized community that does not solely rely on the solidarity group. Finally, engaging everyone in everyday tasks fosters substantive encounters between different people—in terms of age, ethnicity, gender, and class—who could otherwise just coexist as neighbors without any further contact. For instance, the kitchen has hosted the strongest friendships as well as the biggest confrontations. This meaningful participation and coexistence creates conditions in which people stop feeling helpless, vulnerable, or victimized; they are capable of helping others, they undertake various responsibilities, and they take care of their space. Henri Lefebvre (1971) wrote that everyday life is not only about tedious tasks and preoccupations with the bare necessities but also about the coincidence of need with satisfaction and pleasure, the extraordinary in the very ordinary, the feeling of fulfillment. For the residents of City Plaza this process of participation and sharing responsibility is in some ways that of political and social emancipation within the realm of everyday life. Relationships of dependence are, in a sense, transformed into relationships of interdependence and cooperation within a community.

House Assembly

Since the very beginning, we did not want to limit participation to everyday tasks; we also wanted to involve residents in decision making. So, from the start, we would hold a house assembly, an assembly that included all residents and solidarity activists who lived on the premises and were involved in the project. Of course, over time, we have often had to challenge our choice—without ever changing it.

Although the assembly is, for us, the most direct democratic procedure, it actually involves multiple exclusions and hierarchies. House assembly in City Plaza brings a turnout of one hundred and fifty people. Most of them, and women in particular, are not accustomed to similar procedures and find it difficult to speak before a large audience, especially if they are going to disagree or argue with a neighbor, friend, relative, or people from the solidarity group. At the same time, certain issues, such as who is to occupy a vacant room, can hardly be decided at the squat assembly because whenever we have tried raising them, the residents have always ended up confronting each other. Each resident vehemently claimed a room for relatives or friends who were homeless or staying in camps. Occasionally, they suggested having secret ballots to decide on difficult issues. This proposed method, being foreign to our own sociopolitical codes, was never tried. However, perhaps for people who were never really involved in participatory political procedures, it might have been a more democratic and participatory manner of expressing their opinion, compared to the squat assembly. We did try forming smaller working groups, such as the kitchen group, café, reception, the women's group, kindergarten, school, and guardianship. These groups reinforced participation because they were tasked with solving more specific and practical issues; their significantly smaller size made discussion and cooperation easier as well.

Solidarity activists often wonder why more people do not participate in the assembly and the decision-making processes. There are some obvious reasons, including lacking similar political experiences, as mentioned above. Moreover, most of them are in a transitory period of their lives; rather than setting up house in Greece and becoming active members of a local community, they are interested in resuming their journey to northern Europe, toward a final destination and place of settlement. There are also some less visible reasons. As Balibar (2009: 203) has noted, the European border regime transforms migrants into subjects of fear: "This is supposed to make sure that they will not become integrated into the political 'constituency,' in particular through their participation in common social struggles, in the end becoming 'citizens' in the active sense, with or without a European passport." Many, perhaps due to the sociopolitical structure of their countries of origin and through the process of crossing the European borders, carry a sense of subalternity face-to-face with the local population or toward European solidarity activists. They do not perceive themselves as equal interlocutors who can be involved in decision-making processes. Likewise, some of the solidarity activists, despite contesting European superiority, have been nurtured in it and thus, in many cases, unconsciously reproduce a relationship of pity and charity toward migrants.

Power Relations

Power relations abound in projects like this. First, it should be noted that objectively we are not all equal. We cannot be equal just because we wish to be, believe we are, or want to be. A poor Afghani woman with two children who finds herself without papers in Athens has, as a matter of fact, an inferior legal, economic, political, and social status compared to a young German student who comes to Athens for few months in order to support solidarity projects for refugees. These structural differences cannot be overcome ideologically or by will because they ultimately tend to shape the present and future of the subjects.

Likewise, in different ways, there are multiple hierarchies among refugees. They either express gender, class, ethnicity, and other social roles previously established in their countries of origin, or they are fashioned upon arriving on European soil. The distinction, for example, between "real" refugees from Syria and the not-so-genuine Afghan refugees has been translated into different allocations of rights in the European legal context; perhaps the most characteristic example is the right to legal transport through relocation programs within Europe to which Syrians are entitled and Afghans are not. These differences frequently take the form of ethnic rivalries among migrants, while, in fact, they disguise the serious discriminations and hierarchies imposed by the differential status of European border policies.

There are also different types of power relations within City Plaza. For example, the local solidarity group, which took the initiative to occupy the space and still takes primary responsibility for its functioning, has a stronger influence on issues than, for example, international solidarity activists who come to support the project for a few weeks or months. This power does not arise from a strict and established hierarchy but, rather, from our position of knowledge of the local context and networks, responsibility, and commitment to the project.

Still, lack of political experience in self-organization and horizontal structures among both refugees and solidarity activists often links their contribution to claiming greater or lesser privilege. For example, when M., a cook from Damascus, would finish cooking the meal for everyone in the common kitchen, he would make something special for his own family with ingredients he had purchased for himself. He was offended when it was explained that he cannot cook something personal in a kitchen which is only for cooking the collective food; he thought we did not appreciate his contribution to the project: "I work here for hours without pay. Don't I have the right to use the kitchen for ten minutes?" Thus, the migrant who holds the keys to the kitchen, or a small solidarity fund that covers daily expenses, the one who does warehouse shifts, or the one who translates, all acquire or claim better status in relation to others. Such a position is challenged by other migrants, more than that of a European solidarity activist who as a "host" seems to have the undeniable power to set cohabitation rules, unlike the refugee who is "one of them."

Thus, the City Plaza experience proves that inequalities and hierarchies cannot be eliminated in "laboratory" conditions. It has, however, also proved that it is a really meaningful social and political process to challenge established hierarchies, to subvert the boundaries between host and hosted, to try to manufacture, through a community of everyday life, a leveling process.

A Project of Cohabitation and Struggle in Difficult Times

Despite the problems, difficulties, and contradictions, or perhaps because of them, the City Plaza experience is invaluable. For those of us involved, it is an experience that redefines our political thought and practice and makes us reflect on the power relations in everyday life, on cohabitation and its limits, on the sites and means of common struggle. My essay aspires to offer fragments of this reflective process.

Despite the hardships, City Plaza, through what have often been arduous procedures, has in practice challenged the dominant border policies, the ways of managing and ranking migrants, and the camp model. At the same time, our common everyday experiences have offered everyone the experience of organizing a different life, a very different type of cohabitation: the power and the optimism of a community.

One of the greatest accomplishments of the project has been that, for hundreds of people, it has transformed what is a transitory period of their lives—an intermediate period of uncertainty, loneliness, intense insecurity, anxiety, and worry—into a time that also offers a sense of community, creativity, security, joy, and optimism. To illustrate my point, when most families or individuals are to leave City Plaza—when, for example, their application has been approved and they will be reunited with their family in Germany—they cry for City Plaza and promise to come back. Keys to City Plaza rooms are currently all over Europe; they are the keys that residents insisted on holding, or "forgot" to return; they are the keys that one day will bring them "home." For City Plaza is a peculiar home, a temporary one and yet so enduring.

References

Balibar, Étienne. 2009. "Europe as Borderland." *Environment and Planning D: Society and Space* 27, no. 2: 190–215.

City Plaza Collective. 2018. *Two Years of City Plaza: Living Resistance.* Athens: City Plaza Collective.

De Genova, Nicholas. 2002. "Migrant 'Illegality' and Deportability in Everyday Life." *Annual Review of Anthropology* 31: 419–47.

Lefebvre, Henri. 1971. *Everyday Life in the Modern World.* New York: Harper and Row.

Neilson, Brett, and Sandro Mezzadra. 2013. *Border as a Method, or, the Multiplication of Labor.* Durham, NC: Duke University Press.

Giorgos Maniatis

From a Crisis of Management to Humanitarian Crisis Management

In late June 2015, the United Nations High Commissioner for Refugees (UNHCR) declared a refugee emergency situation in the Eastern Aegean Islands. At the time, the number of arrivals to the islands amounted to one thousand per day, and the "reception"/detention system had completely collapsed. In the absence of state-organized reception, the passage to the islands of the Eastern Aegean Sea was developing, according to the UN, into a potential humanitarian crisis. Amid the dense political developments of the time—peaking with the "no" result of the July 5 referendum, in which Greek voters rejected the austerity conditions dictated by the Juncker Commission, and its overturning a week later—the UN's decision introduced a sort of humanitarian intervention on EU ground for the first time.

This decision attracted a multitude of actors from so-called civil society and the international media, as well as experts on migration policy. These actors intervened in the contested geographies of the Aegean borders, where illegalized migration movement intersects with the tourism industry and Greek-Turkish antagonism.

Given these circumstances, the intervention on the part of international humanitarian organizations assumed certain characteristics. The collapse of the reception/detention system and the apparent lack of coordinated intervention by no means meant the "absence of the state," an expression that dominated public discourse from the Right to humanitarian and anti-racist organizations. On the contrary, "humanitarian intervention" took place

The South Atlantic Quarterly 117:3, October 2018
DOI 10.1215/00382876-7166068 © 2018 Duke University Press

in an already politicized space and complemented the state and European apparatuses taking on a crucial role in European migration management.

The UNHCR and the cooperating international and domestic nongovernmental organizations (NGOs) undertook to organize from scratch the registration and temporary housing of new entrants to the islands. The existing detention centers and other facilities were turned into registration centers, and camps were set up to accommodate the short-term transit stay of refugees. NGOs also played a key role in organizing coordination among local authorities, ministries, national and European services, and international humanitarian organizations, which are implicated on different levels in the management of migration. This type of NGOized migration governance function manifested clearly at the eastern Aegean Islands was also the case at the informal camp at Idomeni at the Greek-Macedonian border. In Idomeni, on account of the state refusal to assume responsibility for the transit camp right on its borders, international NGOs virtually substituted for the state, while the UNHCR, along with the authorities of the Republic of Macedonia, organized and handled registration and identification paperwork for border crossings, and implemented nationality restrictions after October 2015.

The declaration of refugee emergency in Greece was justified by pointing out both the potential risk to life posed by the informal crossing of the sea borders and the Greek state's inability to organize the reception of increasing numbers of migrants. Furthermore, at the moment of the declaration, the crisis of migration control had already reached Macedonia and was already continuing to the Balkans. However, in the same conjuncture, a risk to the security of the transit migrants implied also the possibility of migrants to reclaim their right to mobility. Awareness of this potential is what made migration appear as what it really is: a social movement, which in its presence and through its practice posed a relentless dilemma for the European governments in 2015. It was always a question whether they would react in a humanitarian way or deploy military forces against the migrants.

The Balkan Route as Humanitarian Corridor

The "Balkan Route" emerged as a state-regulated corridor on the way to central and western Europe, due to the inability of states in the western Balkans to control the massive migration movement. Such control would require extreme, nonlegitimate violence against refugees, and of course it would mean insurmountable administrative barriers and political cost for governments. Thus, the Balkan states opted for a stance of tolerance, which in turn developed into the promotion and supervision of the transit movement toward the next borders.

In Greece, the newly elected Syriza-ANEL government implemented a policy of partial "humanitarianization" of the borders. It terminated the coastguard's illegal practices of pushing migrants back at the sea borders, reduced administrative detention time, and limited police repression. It thus applied a passive humanitarian policy by withdrawing the state from practices that violated human rights. This policy was by no means part of a coherent immigration policy, let alone an alternative. It remained a temporary change in practices and did not lead to deeper institutional changes but anticipated a return to repressive policies.

At the EU level, the creation of the "Balkan Route" has again, for the first time since the expansion of the Schengen Zone and the EU enlargement to the east, brought back the tensions of the "external borders" of the EU to the center of Europe. By the end of August, when refugee caravans had crossed the border between Austria and Germany, the crisis had escalated, and the dilemma of whether to pursue humanitarian or repressive treatment of migration was posed once again, this time to the governments of the EU's core states. When Austria aligned with Viktor Orban's Hungary and the Visegrad countries in favor of a repressive "national solution" and border militarization, Germany made the political decision to act as a "last resort" host country for the whole of the EU: they opened borders and, by suspending the Dublin Regulation, allowed access to asylum for the vast majority of those on the Balkan Route.

This groundbreaking decision prevented both the creation of a "refugee crisis" at the German border and a further escalation of the political crisis within the EU that would have led to the abolition of the Schengen Agreement. Yet, at the same time, arrivals to the Aegean Islands reached ten thousand, and migration movement was for the first time decriminalized, and handled through public transport fares from the Aegean Sea to Germany.

Refugees Welcome?

Migration movement imposed itself and triggered an unprecedented solidarity movement. "Refugees welcome" became the slogan that spread along the Balkan route. Welcoming refugees involved quite contradictory and ambivalent practices. The attention of international media turned the island of Lesbos and the small village of Idomeni into global points of interest. In the (social) media, the representations of migration and humanitarian aid turned often into a spectacle and a narcissistic self-portrayal of the supposedly tolerant and charitable Western societies. Nevertheless, lots of actors, ranging from the big international NGOs to inhabitants of small villages, and from tourists to international antiracist activists and local leftist groups, were active in the field and functioned as a shield against repressive policies and the public intervention of the extreme right.

Self-organized and improvised "reception" structures were built on shores where migrants' flimsy boats were arriving, as well as transport caravans organized to convey migrants to the registration centers. From the islands to the Greek-Macedonian borders, in parks and squares, in fields and parking lots, volunteers provided kitchens, children's groups, makeshift clinics, mobile charging stations, clothing, and travel supplies. The refugee camps, official and informal, were also assisted by hundreds of people on a daily basis. As a result, solidarity projects, which were largely spontaneous, self-organized, and transnational, have managed to produce spaces of security, communication, and networking, and, at times, of substantial solidarity and joint struggle with migrants in transit.

Solidarity Unwanted

The subsequent border closures in March 2016 as well as the creation of the hot spots[1] and the implementation of the EU-Turkey deal, were moments of the state reclaiming its monopoly on the violence. This meant the creation of exclusively state-regulated zones, depoliticized management areas where refugees in transit would be subject to state authority. At the maritime borders, NGOs that had developed rescue and assistance operations in international waters were initially ousted, through the exemplary persecution of rescuers under the serious charge of "human trafficking." A key concern of the Ministry of Migration policy was the removal from refugee camps and the hot spots of all volunteers and organizations whose presence was considered an obstacle to the implementation of detention, restriction of movement, and deportations to Turkey. Therefore, a strict process of registration of "recognized NGOs" was implemented, excluding all independent volunteers and antiracist groups from the field, while at the same time a number of NGOs were coopted in the hot spot system.

After months of having praised "Greek hospitality" and humanitarianism, the government and the media now spoke of "instigators" and "exploiters of the refugees." At the same time, protests, mobilization, and upheavals in hot spots faced harsh repression, arrests, heavy charges, and imprison-ment. Divesting the refugees of political agency was, and still remains, a necessity in order to transform them into objects of management, which will be subject to biopolitical administrative techniques and selective rights.

NGOization of Migration Management

The involvement of the "civil society" of the NGOs in the hot spot system is a new element of the border regime. Integrating humanitarian organizations in migration management can be seen as the EU Commission's attempt to stem the criticisms and litigation campaigns concerning human rights violations and exclusion from asylum at the Greek reception and detention centers. These led to the exclusion of Greece from the Dublin returns in 2011.

The new roles that NGOs undertook in the administrative function of the hot spots have been criticized as attempts to coopt them in policies that restrain international humanitarian law. Indeed, due to the implementation of the EU-Turkey deal and the "safe third country" clause, the Greek and European asylum agencies at the hot spots do not examine asylum applica-tions, but merely conduct a fast track inadmissibility and readmission check. Such subordination of the international humanitarian law to the ends of EU migration control policies corresponds also to the "war against migrant smuggling." This effectively restricts the international law of the sea, hin-ders and discourages search and rescue operations, and is used to criminal-ize rescuing NGOs.

Another field in which NGOs have expanded drastically since the clo-sure of the borders is that of integration and social policies. The European Union and UNHCR developed programs concerning health, education, accommodation, and social welfare allowances, addressing special target groups and time-limited actions. Thus, in Greece, amid the financial crisis, European funds poured into domestic and international NGOs, which became major employers for professions facing mass unemployment, such as social scientists, lawyers, doctors, and interpreters. A new branch of "migration professionals" was created in this field, employing among others a number of sensitized and progressive people, as well as immigrants, who were already involved in solidarity networks and were recruited as interpret-ers, "cultural facilitators," and "community leaders."

The NGOization of social policies legitimated itself with respect to the particularity and special needs of the refugees as matters to which the public social services cannot adjust. This apparently reasonable point—given the collapse of the welfare state during the financial crisis—became an excuse for the promotion of a neoliberal governance, whose primary goal is to avoid the establishment of new social rights and face social issues as states of emergency. This privatized relation is reproduced at every level: entrepreneurial hierarchical organization, precarious working conditions, huge pay gaps between managers and employees, and lack of control over the conditions of work and the content and objectives of the services provided, not as citizens entitled to certain rights, but as "recipients," not as equals but as vulnerable beneficiaries.

City Plaza and Practical Critique of NGOization

The end of the "long summer of migration" brought with it a new spatial and temporal order. National and European institutions took control of spaces and procedures, restricting radically the field of practical solidarity. Thus, in the spring of 2016, new questions were raised for the antiracist movement. Could there exist a continuation of the solidarity movement that had emerged in recent years? Or were the more spontaneous initiatives bound to retreat? How could solidarity initiatives overcome the spatial segregation and the subjection of migrants to depoliticized technologies of migration management? How should the antiracist movement respond to the increasing racism and criminalization of migration, and how could it deal with the strategies of invisibility adopted by a large number of transit migrants?

In the summer of 2015, migration became a protagonistic social force presenting the European states with the dilemma of choosing either a repressive or a humanitarian reaction. In this peculiar conjuncture, the "humanitarianization of the borders" and humanitarian aid to migrants was effectively facilitating their mobility. This convergence of humanitarianism with the struggles of migrants for the right of movement created a unique moment of unity in struggle, which managed not only to change the discourses on migration but also provoked a temporary shift in the balance of power in the European Union.

This particular conjuncture ceased to exist after the closing of the borders and the implementation of the EU-Turkey deal and the hot spot approach in March 2016. In the process of restabilizing the border regime, the hegemonic powers of the European Union, represented mainly by the European Commission and Germany, disengaged the right of movement from the humanitarian aid and reformulated the dilemma posed by migration to an existential question about the EU project: either a Europeanized neoliberal migration management or the authoritarian renationalization and disintegration of Europe. The reelected Syriza-ANEL government aligned itself with this hegemonic discourse. By using the term *pragmatic humanitarianism* it tried to justify the implementation of the EU-Turkey deal. According to this term, the only "humanitarianism" possible is the one subordinated to the ends of Europeanism: a concept of a narrow, depoliticized and NGOized humanitarian intervention.

The paradigm of NGOization combines charity and technocratic management by taking advantage of skills and knowledge developed within the solidarity movement. People recruited from among solidarity initiatives have, however, a restricted field of autonomy of action, almost exclusively on the level of individual help, which is moreover bound to the rationalities of migration management.[2] Furthermore, precarious working conditions discourage the organization of trade unions and prevent them from intervening as to the objectives and the content of the services provided.

The groups who squatted the bankrupt City Plaza Hotel and turned it into a housing project for migrants shared such a left critique of NGOization of migration and social policies. The project itself has aimed to respond to the urgent needs of migrants for conditions of dignity and security, and to do it in a way that constitutes a radical alternative to and a practical critique of NGOization. In contrast to a conception of providing services to "vulnerables" that relies on the work of "experts" and professionals, City Plaza has been a political and financially autonomous project supported exclusively by contributions of volunteer time and passion and the individual and collective knowledges of hundreds of people. This approach demanded an enormous amount of effort to cope with practical issues and, at the same time, build up self-organized structures, to promote mutual responsibility, and to experiment with processes of collective decision making. It was even more challenging to try to reflect on the multiple inequalities that undermine and affect all the relations within the project: locality, class, gender, language, education, to name a few.

From this perspective, City Plaza distanced itself from the common sense of migration management and challenged some of its central concepts, even if it was impossible to totally overcome them. For example, nationality or the residence status was not a criteria of granting or denying a person accommodation. Additionally, City Plaza refused to pose as a criterion the reasons for immigration—this constant and repeatable torment for migrants that was such a basic means of disciplining and selection. Following the same logic, the concept of vulnerability was also put in question, since it has become a perverse category of the exclusion.

City Plaza saw itself as a means to an end within a larger field of struggle. It saw itself not as an end in itself but as a part of a broader struggle for equality and freedom. It did not pretend to be an "island of freedom," overlooking inequalities and power relations. On the contrary, it tried to examine and improvise new ways of coming together, sharing everyday life, and organizing common struggles, and at the same time acknowledging different needs, desires, life experiences, and perspectives.

City Plaza attempted to constitute a common, a space of security, equality, and freedom, open to encounters and the development of social relations, a space which promotes transnational cooperation and networking, as well as a space of sharing information and practical knowledge to the newcomer migrants. City Plaza did not, however, intend to replace the state in its responsibility to guarantee social rights to migrants. It tried, instead, to claim those rights together with the migrants and to help express the demand for social and political rights for all. This conception of common struggle is expressed through the founding moment of the project, the occupation of private property. Contrary to neoliberal migration management and left nationalist approaches, City Plaza conceived the needs of migrants not as particularities but as social needs, as the needs of society as a whole, and, therefore, conceived of migration as an integral part of the social question.

However, City Plaza had to confront its limits and contradictions from its founding moment. Having emerged in the background of the border closing and the implementation of the EU-Turkey deal, City Plaza expressed the will of thousands of people to continue struggling, maintaining the momentum of the Long Summer of Migration. City Plaza inspired thousands of people, became an international symbol of struggle against the racist migration regime of the European Union, and offered hospitality to over twenty-two hundred migrants, while radically critiquing NGOization. But from its inception, it was bound to remain incomplete, as it depended on the subjective capacities and potentials of both the political groups that supported it and its very residents, with their hearts, minds, and nerves.

City Plaza has been a great struggle, and as such cannot be evaluated in a simple and clear-cut way. Undoubtedly, it has been one of the most interesting projects of antiracism and self-organization in Greece. And for sure it has seen an unprecedented mixture of subjectivities, needs, genders, ages, and cultural, social, and political experiences. City Plaza, as with every mixture, will take some time to separate and sediment within our personal and collective experiences. It may be a fertile ground for new resistances, struggles, and human relations to grow in dignity and solidarity—whether in

Athens or in the other cities that City Plaza residents have reached and might manage to reach.

Notes

1   The term *hot spot* refers to new types of reception and identification centers in Greece and Italy established by the EU Commission in May 2015. They can be described as multifunctional reception centers, which unify and Europeanize the procedures of identification, fingerprinting, registration, asylum, and relocation/deportation. The novelty of the hot spot approach is the active cooperation of national police and administrative authorities with the EU agencies, as well as the coopting of the UNHCR, International Organization for Migration, and NGOs in different fields to foster unified procedures. In Greece, hot spots exist on the islands of Lesbos, Chios, Leros, Kos, and Samos and are bound up with the implementation of the EU-Turkey deal.

2   A case in point is the assessment on "vulnerability" that NGOs conduct in the hot spots and that can suspend the geographical restriction and give the right of access to the normal asylum system.

Loukia Kotronaki

Outside the Doors: Refugee Accommodation Squats and Heterotopy Politics

"There is a big difference between City Plaza and the camps. Here we have a room, we have privacy. We have a shower, a toilet, our own space. It's a home here. In camps there are big problems between the people, there's a lot of violence. Here, ok there are problems like in every family, but at least we are safe. When we were in the camps the conditions were for animals. Here it is clean and we are treated as humans, living together in a home. . . .

City Plaza means love, sharing, fun. . . . I think about leaving City Plaza a lot. It will be a sad day. It breaks my heart to think about leaving here, leaving my friends and my City Plaza family. We have so many memories here. I know I will cry. When I speak with the families who are now living in Europe they say they miss City Plaza every day and I know it will be the same for me.
—Moustafa Haj Rashid, *A Day in the Life of City Plaza*

Henri Lefebvre argues that one of the defining properties of heterotopias is their capacity to create "differential realities" with a transformative potential. Both excluded from and interwoven with the urban space, these "spaces of difference" do not necessarily arise out of a conscious plan, but rather, simply, out of what people do, feel, sense, and come to articulate together as they seek meaning in their daily lives (Lefebvre 2003; Harvey 2012).

    The self-organized refugee squats that emerged in the center of Athens during the long "summer of migration" as "alternative spaces" differ drastically from the limbo accommodation zones of the refugee camps.[1] Can they, then, be portrayed as potential collective vehicles challenging the ratio-

The South Atlantic Quarterly 117:3, October 2018
DOI 10.1215/00382876-7166080 © 2018 Duke University Press

nalized spatial order of neoliberalism and the state (isotopy) in the continuum of crisis regimes in Greece?

Returning to the essay's epigraph, what did Rashid, a thirty-eight-year-old old Syrian and former resident of City Plaza, mean by "a big difference between City Plaza and the camps"? How—under which circumstances and through which practices—can emotional energies (such as love, sharing, and day-to-day fun) trigger contentious dynamics of social change on a multilevel scale?

I will attempt to shed light on these questions by focusing on the refugee accommodation and solidarity space known as City Plaza. I map and classify protest events and public performances as they were invented, orchestrated, and interpreted from the "House" (formerly the City Plaza Hotel), from the inaugural action of squatting up through the present time (April 2018). I will assume that, in many cases, communities of struggle for dignified refugee housing can perform the constitutive functions of heterotopy at the micro, meso, and macro levels, by setting in motion three concatenated processes: changing forms of urban interactions and therefore introducing new patterns of citizenship; shaping and/or extending collective identities and the boundaries of local collective action; and mobilizing new cultural frames of solidarity and meanings of struggle at the transnational level.

Changing Urban Anthropogeographies—Reinventing CitYzenship

In 2010, the City Plaza Hotel went bankrupt, leaving dozens of workers without compensation, and it remained abandoned for several years. The hotel is situated between Victoria Square and Acharnon Street, in the "innermost-outermost" region of the city. It is in the innermost region in the sense that it belongs to the broader area of the city's trade and political center (Omonoia-Syntagma); but it is also in the outermost region in the sense that, for many years, media and mainstream political narratives have depicted the neighborhood as a migrant ghetto from which the public eye deliberately looked away. It is a part of the city that would appear particularly inhospitable to a squatted migrant hospitality project. Neo-Nazi gangs of the political party Golden Dawn (GD) (*Chrysi Avgi*), beginning in 2004, claimed terrestrial and ideological control of the area by undertaking action for protection (of the locals) and punishment (of the migrants). This included, among other things, stabbings, vandalizing of small shops owned by immigrants, and everyday brawls that often ended in injury.

Between 2004 and 2009, the assault groups of GD gained so much organizational and political strength that it is reasonable to claim that they were transformed from violent gangs of roughs engaging in late-night attacks into a countermovement structure (Zald and Useem 1987; Meyer and Staggenborg 1996). GD took on the accompanying characteristics of a countermovement: reactive and backward-looking normative frames; de-democratization claims (demanding contraction of the public sphere and of social categories having access to it); exclusive (versus inclusive) forms of political participation; and close attachment to elite and state apparatus mechanisms for the acquisition of mobilizational resources (Seferiades and Kotronaki 2015).

Crucial factors explaining the growth of neo-Nazi organizational and political prowess (also reflected on an institutional level during the local elections of 2010, when they polled 5.9 percent of votes in the municipality of Athens) were a defensive "law and order" coalition appearing in response to the salience of the militant wave that had emerged in December 2008 after the murder of fifteen-year-old Alexandros Grigoropoulos in Exarheia by riot police: the financial crisis leading to the further devaluation of the social and economic conditions of the urban population (loss of jobs, health care, and housing rights), and the simultaneous political crisis and crisis of representation reflected in the collapse of the two-party system in 2012, including the evaporation of political forces, such as the neo-orthodox-populist party Popular Orthodox Alarm (*LAOS*), which, having participated with the ex-social democratic PASOK and the conservative party "New Democracy" in the three-party coalitional government in the name of the vote of the second memorandum in 2010 (the bailout package), saw its voters move to GD.

In this combination of critical (con)junctures, the assault groups that used to operate illegally acquired an organizational and institutional status—especially in the broader area of the metropolitan center, where the quotidian was further degraded by austerity policies. At first by organizing the informal committees of "Indignant Citizens" and then the "Citizen Committees of Saint Panteleimon," they took it upon themselves to "reoccupy" the public area from the "unwanted": the migrants, stigmatized as the ones to blame for the everyday suffering, and the radical political groups of the nearby Exarcheia neighborhood. In all these attempts to deter "dangerous citizens" from the use of public services (local playgrounds, public markets, and so on), the assault groups disguised as "Citizen Committees" had either the overt support or the friendly tolerance of the local police. In any case, the police were GD's most powerful institutionalized ally, providing material and symbolic resources to the organization, thereby supporting its criminal activity. This seems to have been halted in September of 2013 when the leading team of GD was prosecuted for the murder of the antifascist rapper Pavlos Fysas in another economically disadvantaged area of Athens, Keratsini.

All things considered, it is clear that the geographical and sociopolitical territory where City Plaza is located was hardly an ideal setting for the development of spaces of solidarity and accommodation for the refugees who arrived in Athens during the summer of 2015. Nevertheless, as pointed out by Paasi (2003), "spaces or—in their use—territories are not frozen frameworks . . . rather they are made, given meaning and destroyed in social and individual action. Hence, they are typically contested and actively negotiated."

The operation of City Plaza not just as "a counterexample of how the refugee housing issue needs to be addressed by the movement and society . . . but also as an initiative of self-organization of everyday life and of common struggle for locals and refugees [as well as] . . . a center of struggle for creating a wide network with unions, schools, hospitals and social spaces, to organise solidarity to the trapped refugees and . . . to carry outward facing actions for claiming the social and political rights of refugees has been transmuted into a crucial urban spatial agency (City Plaza 2016). It has established—among other things—new spatial routines, new figures of urban personas having access to public services, and new channels of interaction between locals, former groups of migrants, and the City Plaza community. How did it achieve that?

First and foremost, City Plaza evolved into such a space by inaugurating a cycle of everyday commercial activities with the local market. The bread, the gas, the laundry, a series of goods necessary for the everyday functioning of the squat, and for the needs of "solidarians" demanded everyday transactions with the small traders of the area. This intensification of economic exchanges may not have established links of mutual trust between locals and refugees, but it led partially to the familiarization of the "rooted us" with the "transitory other." This "other" was no longer an individualized unit in an inhospitable city, but a member of a mixed community of refugees, locals, and international solidarity groups embedded in the economic everydayness.

Second, City Plaza evolved *by* disrupting the quotidian of the public time-space. With the master frame "We live together, we fight together, we celebrate together," the community of City Plaza sometimes initiated public celebrations and artistic performances in Victoria Square and the surrounding areas (see Table 1, Public Displays), and at other times it responded to the invitation of other social actors and participated in festivities and celebrations prescribed by the "national calendar" (anniversary of the student uprising of the Polytechnic School, Christmas, Clean Monday). By contesting the normalities of the spatiotemporal continuum of the square, but also the "nationally homogenized" character of the acknowledged participant to the official celebrations, the City Plaza experiment attributed new meaning to the uses of the space as well as the users of public initiatives. Victoria Square was not just a decadent urban spot where deprived refugees would gather patiently waiting for "something to happen," but it was also a place of celebration, coexistence, and osmosis between "old" and "new" residents. National celebrations were no longer special moments of nostalgia or euphoria for loyal Greek citizens, but occasions of dense interaction, sociability, and knowledge for an extended urban, multicultural public.

Undoubtedly, all of these practices—conceived as molecular attempts to forge new representations of "citYzenship" at the micro level—triggered broader dynamics when they were transformed into claims for the social inclusion of refugees through access to education and health care structures. In the background of the state's unwillingness to recognize the refugees as full citizens, and even though their stay in Athens is temporary, one of the main aims of City Plaza was the integration of refugee children into classes starting at the beginning of the school year. This required mobilization and networking with the existing teachers' trade unions, as well as with the school staff. By putting pressure on school principals objecting to the registration of refugee children to classes (either for bureaucratic reasons or claiming that this would disturb the "internal school balance"), the City Plaza education group, in collaboration with teachers' Union "Aristotle," managed to enroll more than one hundred children hosted at City Plaza in the local schools. A similar initiative was made by the health team that had already been formed to procure basic health services to City Plaza residents and coordinate their access to public hospital primary structures.

Demanding the democratization of the public space and minimum social inclusion rights for transit citizens was of high importance for the promotion of an extended form of CitYzenship, especially if we consider that (a) economic crisis meant that more and more citizens had lost access to basic welfare structures; (b) formal regulation for the "education" for refugee children provided either in sloppy classrooms in the detention centers, or learning the Greek language in evening classes, outside of the locals' timetable; and (c) primary health care in the camps was virtually absent.

In the majority of camps, not even interpreters existed capable of translating the pain.

Shaping Collective Identities, Creating Transnational Communities

That social movements increasingly operate in a realm between the public and the private sphere is commonplace in the study of collective action (Melucci

Table 1. Forms of Action

	City Plaza's Repertoire of Collective Action		
By Year	**Public Displays**	**Protest Events**	**International Campaigns (6+month duration)**
2016 (2nd semester)	OA (CP), OA (CP), OA (CP), OA (CP), OA (CP), OD (Health and Education Groups, CP), F (Victoria Sq.), OA (Camps Groups, CP), C (debates/ concerts/ assemblies, CP), PG (National Day— Polytechnic School revolt, Athens), CC (Fiadelfia Municipality), CC (High School, Victoria Sq.)	R (right to urban and educational inclusion), SD (open borders/ urban housing), SD (against fascist attacks to Notara Squat), SD (against police violence), D (civil disobedience/ open borders)	"The Best Hotel in Europe" (Germany), #Welcome2stay (Germany), "Solidarité avec le people grec" (Lyon, France), "SoliGrèce" (Nîmes, France), "Un convoi pour la Grèce" (Paris, France)
2017 (1st semester)	OA (#18M coordination, CP), OD (Open Borders, CP), F (Victoria Sq.), F (National Holiday, Exarcheia), F (Victoria Sq.), OA (#18M coordination, CP), OA (European Refugees Politics, CP), C (concerts, debates, CP)	D (civil disobedience/against Fortress Europe), D (protest for the deaths at the hot spots), D (International Women's Day), PRC (#18M/ against EU-Turkey agreement), D/ GAD (#18M against EU-Turkey agreement), D (May Day), D/GAD (#Hands OffSquats/against squat's evictions, Athens/Berlin)	"Keep City Plaza Open"/youcaring .com (Friends of CP, UK), "A day in the life of City Plaza"/ youcaring.com (Friends of CP)

Table 1. Forms of Action (*continued*)

By Year	Public Displays	Protest Events	International Campaigns (6+month duration)
	City Plaza's Repertoire of Collective Action		
2017 (2nd semester)	C (concerts, debates, CP), PG (National Day—Polytechnic School revolt, Athens), OA (Pan-Hellenic Networking of antiracist and refugee organizations)	D(#We'llCome United/Antiracist Parade, Berlin), D (in memoriam of the rapper murdered by the fascist political party Golden Dawn), R (family reunification), D (against fascist attacks on Afghan refugees), R (family reunification), D (against fascism and transphobia), PC (refugees' hunger strike/family reunification), PRC (refugees' hunger strike/family reunification), D (family reunification, Athens/Berlin), D (International Day against Women's Violence), PRC (family reunification), D (#Stop EuropeFunding Libya)	"Swarming Solidarity" (Ex-Residents of CP, Germany), "Keep City Plaza Open" (Germany), "Ados sans Frontières" (Nîmes, France), "Eclaireurs de France" (Lyon, France)
2018 (1st semester)	OD (Mediterranean Borders), OA (#17MActionDay against EU-Turkey agreement), OD (#FreeTheMoria 35Refugees), C (concerts)	SS (against the nationalistic march for the name of Macedonia), D (International Women's Day), D/GAD (#17MAction Day against EU-Turkey agreement), D (#FreeTheMoria35 Refugees)	"Comment aider ceux qui aident" (Narbonne, France)

C: Celebration, CC: Christmas Celebration, CP: City Plaza, D: Demonstration, F: Festivities, GAD: Global Action Day, HS: Hunger Strike, SD: Squats' Demonstration, OA: Open Assembly—House, OD: Open Debate, PC: Public Camping, PG: Public Gathering, PRC: Press Conference, R: Rally, SS: Squats' Safeguarding

1989; Taylor 1989; Johnston 2011). Through practices that belong to an intermediate sphere between "private" pursuits and concerns, on the one hand, and an institutional, state-sanctioned mode of politics, on the other, they seek to politicize the institutions of civil society, reconstituting it as a sphere no longer in need of increasing regulation, control, or intervention (Offe 1985).

The key term here is *intermediate sphere*. The dynamics of *heterotopy* can emerge precisely in this interplay, where oppositional frames and collective identities are constructed.

If we take a closer look at the canvas of actions and performances composing the City Plaza "repertoire of action" (Tilly 1986) as depicted in Table 1, it is clear that this intermediate sphere is the "House" for at least three reasons: first, because the "House" becomes the place and the content for the primary politicization of transitory people carrying extremely different cultural, ethnic, and political baggage; second, because the "House" often takes to the streets, becoming a contentious issue for collective actors with similar previous experiences; and third, because the "House" becomes a reference point for the transnational networking and campaigning process.

Let us get things in the right order. Concerning the residents of City Plaza, the consciousness of the political thread connecting them with the City Plaza political project—a normative glue distinct from charity—bringing together refugees and European locals, would have never been accomplished without everyday practices and principles of spatial organization (working groups, chore shifts, rules for coexistence, etc.). These performativities, however cognitively important, are not sufficient to put in motion the "cognitive liberation" process, or, "a common definition of their situation as unjust and subject to change through collective action" (McAdam [1982] 1999). It is estimated that the organization of open assemblies and open debates that focused on the refugee issue, European policies, and the borders regime, but especially on the participation of the "House" in protest events, served as a catalyst for this critical process of the political (re)activation of the refugees in their transit condition. The original—but hardly surprising—element in the mobilization of the residents of City Plaza is that this motivation to collective action frame remained mainly "domestic." With the exception of "Azadi" (Freedom), the main slogans shouted during demonstrations were "City Plaza, City Plaza!," and "We are City Plaza." Even in cases of protest against police violence at police stations, or against the deplorable conditions at the camps and deaths at the Mediterranean Sea, "City Plaza" was the omnipresent constitutive piece of their new "collective we."

But the "House," from its very beginning, bears the characteristics that we find in "submerged networks," which Melucci (1989: 60–72) defines as "networks composed of a multiplicity of groups that are dispersed, fragmented, and submerged in everyday life, and which act as cultural laboratories for the experimentation and practices of new cultural models, forms of relationships and alternative perceptions and meanings of the world."

In other words, City Plaza was not only a space of "accommodation" for the refugees, but also a new political house for many Greek activists who had either participated in the Left party Syriza and were politically disengaged and disaffected after the swindling of the results of the 2015 Referendum by the Syriza government, or joined organizations of the extraparliamentary Left and found themselves at a strategic dead end after a long and stormy epoch of anti-austerity struggles (2008–15). Besides those disjointed and/or reoriented political groups, there were dozens of solidarity initiatives involved in City Plaza by fueling the House with necessary consumable items. The majority of them had previously animated the structures of social solidarity that had spread all over Greece during the second phase of the anti-austerity contentious cycle (2012–15), when the huge confrontational demonstrations had subsided and the protest was on the road to *parliamentarization* (Kotronaki 2018). This "human yeast," which formed by creating coalitions with antiauthoritarian groups, and a new political figure that flourished with the outbreak of the refugees' tragedy, *the volunteer,* searched new codes and rituals of interaction and was coarticulated to submerged networks. The master frame "You can't evict a movement!" illustrates the new dynamics that emerged from the merging of the street with the House and the coming together of "old" with "new" social movement actors into new submerged networks. These latent movement infrastructures became visible once they became engaged in overt political conflict and initiated protest events around issues such as the threat of evictions, fascist attacks, nationalistic parades, the Greek government's (anti)refugee polices, EU agreements with Turkey/Libya, and so on. This meeting between the "new" and the "old," however, did not take place only at the local political scene. It also pervaded the political ethos of transnational solidarity and the forms in which it was manifested.

The international publicity and the expressed solidarity to the City Plaza example was of such a magnitude that it merits a full discussion elsewhere. Nevertheless, it is possible to discern two major forms of transnational solidarity that played a pivotal role in its survival: the hundreds of volunteers who, since April 2016, have been coming to the House, remained there for months, and staffed the shifts and the organization of the working groups (English classes, women's space, cultural activities); and the international campaigns of political and economic support.

Concerning the international campaigns (traditionally, the most effective instrument of connectiveness between otherwise isolated groups engaged in a common cause), the main veins of sociogeographical diffusion of political energies were: (a) former strong bonds of mutual respect and trust between City Plaza members and transnational networks of militants built in the course of previous common contentious experiences (antiglobalization movement/"Medico International," No Border European network of antiracist groups/"Welcome2Europe," and the pan-European platform against European austerity policies "Blockupy"); (b) the international solidarity groups or individuals ("the solidarians") who, having voluntarily invested in the City Plaza project, became "City Plaza missionaries" when they returned to their local bases ("Friends of City Plaza"); (c) solidarity to "Greek people" as a political injunction enormously widespread during the previous anti-austerity protest cycle; (d) the ex-residents of City Plaza (especially those who moved to Germany) and who, even after leaving "the House," continued to consider City Plaza their primary sociopolitical community on their way to Europe, also communicating this experience in the social media community: "City Plaza around the World" /"City Plaza is still our home."

In the above patchwork, it is possible to discern the main transnational networks of solidarity of City Plaza, which, in turn, and through other, unexpected procedures and contentious events, can be transmuted to new international communities of struggle beyond the case of City Plaza, for the advance of social emancipation.

Conclusion

Refugee accommodation squats such as City Plaza challenge the urban rationality of the current crisis regimes and can be prominent spatial agents that establish new forms of everyday interaction, change local anthropogeographies, and promote new patterns of citizenship. These contentious spaces, along with their latent social-movement infrastructures, can moreover be transformed into laboratories of new meaning and collective identity, generating the structure of social conflict at the transnational scale. Such sustainable collective action, however, presupposes robust collective identities and long-term perspectives of action. The permanent transit status of the refugees, the temporal uncertainty of submerged contentious networks supposing to act as welfare-state actors, and the fragile forms of voluntary engagement put some important limits in their transformative dynamics.

Note

1   Beginning in September 2015 with the closure of the Balkan route, several groups, especially those identified with the antiauthoritarian and Left-libertarian movement, occupied empty buildings for the purpose of transforming them into housing spaces for refugees. Mostly located in the alternative neighborhood of Exarcheia, and in the "migrants' center" of the Athenian center (the area surrounding Victoria Square), these squats host around 150 to 200 persons each, and are the only accommodation structures for refugees fit for inhabitation. Today there exist nine self-organized squats (City Plaza, Squat Notara 26 St.; Arachovis 44 St. / Single Men Squat; Kaniggos 22 St.; Spyrou Trikoupi 17 St.; Themistokleous 58 St.; Acharnon 22 St.; Hotel Oniro; 5th School), with City Plaza probably being the most prominent among them. Since April 22, 2016, City Plaza has become the home, but also the solidarity nest, for more than two thousand migrants originating from nine different countries, and it operates as a coordination center for migrants' and refugees' struggles.

References

A Day in the Life of City Plaza (blog). 2017. "10 Questions," January 17. adayinthelifeatcityplaza .wordpress.com/2017/01/17/170117.

City Plaza. 2016. "What Is City Plaza?" (leaflet), June 14. solidarity2refugees.gr/city-plaza-leaflet.

Harvey, David. 2012. *Rebel Cities: From the Right to the City to Urban Revolution*. London: Verso.

Johnston, Hank. 2011. *States and Social Movements*. Cambridge: Polity Press.

Kotronaki, Loukia. 2018. "From the Streets to the Parliament: Topographies of Protest and SYRIZA in Times of Crisis, 2009–2015." In *Facets of the Greek Crisis: Contentious Cycle of Protest and Institutional Outcomes*, edited by Nikos Serntedakis and Stavros Tompazos, 135–76. Athens: Gutenberg [in Greek].

Lefebvre, Henri. 2003. *The Urban Revolution*. Minneapolis: University of Minnesota Press.

McAdam, Doug. [1982] 1999. *Political Process and the Development of Black Insurgency, 1930–1970*. Chicago: University of Chicago Press.

Melucci, Alberto. 1989. *Nomads of the Present*. London: Hutchinson Radius.

Meyer, David S., and Suzanne Staggenborg. 1996. "Movements, Countermovements, and the Structure of Political Opportunity." *American Journal of Sociology* 101, no. 6: 1628–60.

Offe, Claus. 1985. "New Social Movements: Challenging the Boundaries of Institutional Politics." *Social Research* 52, no. 4: 817–68.

Paasi, Anssi. 2003. "Territory." In *A Companion to Political Geography*, edited by John Agnew, Katharyne Mitchell, and Gerard Toal, 109–22. Oxford: Blackwell.

Seferiades, Seraphim, and Loukia Kotronaki. 2015. "Fascism as a Mass Phenomenon: Should We Be Calling It a Movement?" Paper presented at the conference Fascisms across Borders. Hyman Center. Columbia University.

Taylor, Verta. 1989. "Social Movement Continuity: The Women's Movement in Abeyance." *American Sociological Review* 54, no. 5: 761–75.

Tilly, Charles. 1986. *The Contentious French: Four Centuries of Popular Struggle*. Cambridge, MA: Harvard University Press.

Zald, Mayer N., and Bert Useem. 1987. "Movement and Countermovement Interaction: Mobilization, Tactics, and State Involvement." In *Social Movement in an Organizational Society*, edited by Mayer N. Zald and John D. McCarthy, 247–72. New Brunswick, NJ: Transaction.

Sandro Mezzadra

In the Wake of the Greek Spring and the Summer of Migration

It was spring in Athens. Can you remember that? Somebody would say that the spring started on a Sunday, in January 2015, with the victory of Syriza at the national elections. A new "radical left coalition" party founded in 2004, Syriza, and its young leader, Alexis Tsipras, had been able to catalyze the imagination and hopes of the Left throughout Europe in the previous years, positioning themselves at the forefront in struggles against "austerity" in the wake of the "sovereign debt crisis," the specific form in which the financial crisis of 2007/8 hit Europe in 2010. But the Greek spring also had different histories and temporalities. One could say that it started with the uprising and riots after two special police officers killed a fifteen-year-old student, Alexis Grigoroupolos, on December 6, 2008, in the Exarchia district of Athens. Yet another starting point was the occupation of the central Syntagma square in 2011, the Greek manifestation of the Occupy movement. And how many general strikes took place in those years? How often were high schools and universities occupied? How many times did demonstrators violently clash with riot police in front of Parliament to protest the vote to accept the European Union's austerity requirements?

Here are just a couple of snapshots, which could be easily multiplied: Greece was for several years center stage in a radical clash surrounding European austerity policies, living through a deep economic crisis, and under attack from the so-called Troika (European Commission, European Central Bank, International Monetary Fund). But it was above all a space of rebellious and constituent politics, driven by a heterogeneous social composition, capable

The South Atlantic Quarterly 117:3, October 2018
DOI 10.1215/00382876-7166092 © 2018 Duke University Press

of combining different forms of action and reassembling political cultures of the Left rooted in a long history of struggles and dissensions (see, e.g., Nasioka 2014; Arampatzi 2017; Cappuccini 2017). Behind and beyond the surge of Syriza's electoral power since 2012, a tumult of struggles and self-organization has ensued that has resulted in, among other things, the taking over of productive structures, the establishment of autonomous hospitals, popular kitchens, and schools, as well as the spread of new forms of solidarity across society. Activists visited Greece from all over Europe and elsewhere in the world to be inspired, while the Greeks were a driving force behind various important European campaigns such as Blockupy, an anti-austerity alliance of social movements, unions, nongovernmental organizations (NGOs), and left-wing parties that organized huge demonstrations against the European Central Bank in Frankfurt in 2012, 2013, and 2015.

So many beginnings for a tumultuous spring, which in fact lasted several years. What is clear is that the spring ended just after its peak, in the night of July 5, 2015, when an astonishing 61 percent of Greek citizens voted OXI (NO) on a referendum on the new "memorandum of understanding" proposed by the "troika." It was a night of dancing and toasting in the streets, red and Greek flags waving, preparations for an even stronger resistance in the months to come. But the resistance of the Greek left-wing government was broken a week later, when Tsipras accepted the "memorandum of understanding" at a seventeen-hour meeting of the so-called Eurosummit, after what a senior EU official described as an "exercise in extensive mental waterboarding" (Traynor, Rankin, and Smith 2015). It was the triumph of German finance minister Wolfgang Schäuble and yet another defeat of the Left in Europe. It was above all a shock for a whole generation of Greek activists, who had become politicized in the previous years and suddenly found themselves disoriented and deprived of what had been, particularly in the first half of 2015, a crucial plane of convergence for myriad struggles and forms of self-organizing. What followed, with splits and accusations within and beyond Syriza, could not rebuild such a plane of convergence.

It was necessary to start with some references to what has been widely described as the "Greek crisis" in the first half of 2015 to shed light on the background of the experience of the City Plaza Hotel in Athens. Movements and struggles of migration had been a defining feature of the social and political landscape in Greece at least since the late 1990s, supported by such organizations as DIKTIO, the Network for Social and Political Rights, which plays a pivotal role also in the City Plaza Hotel. During the Greek spring those movements and struggles had continued to develop, often intertwining with other forms of political action—from antifascist resistance to occupation of houses and public spaces. The first steps of Tsipras's government after the election in January 2015 led many of us, in Greece and elsewhere, to think that advanced political experimentations in the field of migration, including a stop to deportations and a steady dismantling of detention structures in the country, were possible. The "deal" of July and the ensuing conclusion of the Greek spring abruptly put an end to those expectations.

The Long Summer of Migration

Even as the European establishment was celebrating its supposed triumph over Greece and the continuity of neoliberal austerity management, a new "crisis" was looming on the horizon. Again, Greece would be at the front line. After months marked by a tragic series of lethal shipwrecks off the Libyan and Sicilian coasts, a shift in migrants' routes from the central to the eastern Mediterranean as of May 2015 made the crossing of the European maritime "external borders . . . significantly safer for the first time in the recent history of trans-Mediterranean migration" (Heller and Pezzani 2016). Needless to say, this does not mean that there would be no deaths at sea in the following months. But thousands of migrants were able to get to European shores on the Greek islands and to continue their travel farther north across the "Balkan route." What followed was called by activists and critical migration and border scholars in Europe the "long summer of migration" (Hess et al. 2017). The multiplication of border fences and walls from Macedonia to Hungary could not stop the tens of thousands of women, men, and children on the move, who at least for a moment seemed uncontainable and capable of radically challenging the European border regime. At moments, in particular during the so-called march of hope from Budapest to the Austrian border on September 4, 2015, the movement of migrants took on explicitly political characteristics, claiming the right to enter European space (Kasparek and Speer 2015).

The challenge posited to the European Union by the "long summer of migration" was not met in any democratic or progressive way. Rather a process of disarticulation of the geographical coordinates of the process of European integration ensued, with the further entrenchment of an East/West divide superimposed on the North/South cleavage that had shaped the development of the "Greek crisis." Processes of renationalization of politics in

Europe, underway since the beginning of the decade, became even more pronounced in the framework of what was immediately defined as a "migration" or "refugee crisis." At the same time, old and new forces of the Right started to grow in several European countries, addressing impoverished sectors of the population with an aggressive anti-immigration rhetoric (and often targeting migrants with racist violence). These processes of renationalization of politics set the stage (as well as the limits) for the effort undertaken by the European Commission to tackle the *real crisis* made apparent by the "long summer of migration," which means the crisis of the European border and migration regime (Bojadžijev and Mezzadra 2015). One can say that the so-called hot spot approach put forward by the European Commission corresponds to an attempt to reorganize that regime according to a "logistical" rationality of filtering migration "flows" into Europe in a differentiated and hierarchical way (see Altenried et al. 2018). Nevertheless, the tensions and frictions between the "hot spot approach" and the ongoing processes of renationalization of politics (and border controls) have led to a situation in which a kind of fatal "double pincer" radically limits the mobility both of migrants and refugees already in Europe and, more generally, of people actually or potentially on the move toward Europe (see for instance Garelli and Tazzioli 2016).

While the border regime in Europe had worked for years as a device of differential and hierarchical inclusion and exclusion (see Mezzadra and Neilson 2013: 131–65), the only currently active side is the attempt to stop movements of migration and to militarize the control of migratory routes through the multiplication of agreements with "third countries" and through a further entrenchment of the process of "externalization" of border control that has been underway in Europe since the 1990s. It was again in Greece, along the border with Macedonia (in Idomeni), that the "crisis" took yet another dramatic twist in February 2016, when clashes between migrants and police led to the closure of the border, the first step of what became within a few days the de facto closure of the "Balkan route." The EU-Turkey deal, signed in March 2016 to speed up deportations from Europe to Turkey and to counter migrants' crossing of the Aegean Sea, was the crowning of those developments. And while migratory routes began to shift again toward the West, making passage of the Mediterranean even more dangerous and lethal, thousands of migrants remained stuck in Greece, living in camps (in particular although not exclusively on the islands) in conditions of deprivation and destitution that have been denounced by several NGOs and international media reports.

Migration as a Field of Struggle

Those camps, managed by a government led by the same Alexis Tsipras who one year back had embodied the challenge to austerity and the hope for a new democratic Europe, are the mirror of a wider process of disintegration of the European Union—or, maybe more accurately, of a conservative and technocratic stabilization of its policies in a way that is consistent with the ongoing renationalization of politics. While economic and social inequality is expanding well beyond the southern region of the continent and the dismantling of the welfare state and social citizenship is prompted by the continuity of neoliberal policies, fear is being spread across societies by a wide array of political actors, more often than not including forces of the institutional Left. This paves the way for emerging combinations of neoliberalism, authoritarianism, and nationalism, as well as for a closure of migration routes that is epitomized by the predicament of migrants and refugees living in camps in Greece and elsewhere. These are the two sides of the same dynamic that is emptying out the very notion of a European democracy capable of drawing expansive force from the challenges of the global present. It is important in this regard to stress the continuity between the "debt crisis" in Greece and the ways in which the crisis of the border regime has been managed by the European institutions. The threat of being kicked out of the Eurozone (the single currency space) before the "deal" of July 2015 was immediately mirrored at the end of that year by the threat of exclusion from the Schengen zone of passport-free travel should the Greek government refuse the extended deployment of Frontex (the EU agency for border control) at its borders and more generally should it refuse to comply with a reorganization of the European border regime that basically assigned to the country the role of a giant holding zone for thousands of migrants and refugees (see Heller and Pezzani 2016; Kasparek 2016).

The spectacle of migrants held in Greek camps, spatial and political formations that blur the boundary between detention facilities and refugee camps across the world, should be understood with respect to a complex set of governmental practices that target migrants—from the roles increasingly played by financial institutions in the management of refugees (a recent report of the Office of the United Nations High Commissioner for Refugees [UNHCR 2017] presents it as the "next financial inclusion frontier") to the experimentation of new, flexible recruitment schemes in a country like Germany (see Altenried et al. 2018). This is just to say that, while an experience of "abandonment" definitely shapes the reality of thousands of migrants and refugees, migration continues to be a crucial factor in weaving the social and productive fabric of many parts of Europe, and it will definitely continue to be so in the future. At stake today, even in the "spectacle" of border fortification (see De Genova 2013), are, first of all, the terms of migrants' inclusion and the forms of management of their presence within Europe. These terms and forms are becoming more and more violent, enabling and prompting social subordination and economic exploitation, processes that directly target migrants and refugees while carrying with them implications that go well beyond those migrants and refugees. These processes foreshadow a society permeated by fear, violence, and competition, where spaces of equality and solidarity are steadily erased and cooperation only takes place insofar as it is directly exploitatable by capital. It is not by accident, therefore, that migration continues in many European countries to be a crucial field of struggle, where heterogeneous coalitions of social movements do not merely fight against racism and exclusion but rather reinvent freedom, equality, and solidarity on a daily basis.

It may be useful to provide a sketch of some of the main practices and struggles that crisscross and politicize migration in Europe today. The sketch will be necessarily schematic but it will nonetheless give an idea of experiences that are widespread across different countries and regions, although they may take different forms and intensity here and there. First, there is a need to stress that migrants themselves continue to be at the forefront of several struggles, both through the challenge that their sheer movement posits to external and internal borders and through their participation in established social movements, ranging from the topic of housing to labor unionism and feminism. In the wake of the long summer of migration there has moreover been a significant shift in the migratory landscape in several European countries, with the presence of a huge number of people fleeing from zones of war (in Syria and beyond) that have further blurred the structurally arbitrary boundaries between migrants and refugees and established new fronts of struggle. Second, since 2015 in several European countries— say, from Greece to Germany—practices of spontaneous and often amazing solidarity have cultivated the blossoming of "welcoming" initiatives that have involved tens of thousands of common European citizens and have often become stabilized after the "emergency." An active citizenry has emerged, and though it exists beyond the boundaries and the languages of activists' circles, it has been capable in many cases of staging productive dialogues and encounters with the antiracist movement. Third, a new generation of NoBorder activists has committed with extreme passion and generosity to support migrants' challenges to European borders, struggling to facilitate passage both at "external frontiers" (for instance across the "Balkan route") and at the multiple internal borders encountered by migrants in Europe (say, from Calais to Ventimiglia, but also around railway stations and squares in several cities and countries). The radical practices of NoBorder activists have simultaneously fostered various projects of activism at sea, such as the WatchTheMed AlarmPhone, a kind of hotline for migrants crossing maritimes borders toward Europe (Stierl 2016), while the multiplication of clashes between European institutions and NGOs regarding rescue operations at sea has led in many cases to a politicization of "humanitarian" assistance and of human rights activists.

The Best Hotel in Europe

The sketch I just provided is schematic and quite partial, but it should help convey the specificity of the City Plaza Hotel within the landscape of migrants' struggles and migration related activism in Europe. What distinguishes City Plaza is indeed the fact that it combines the experiences, claims, and languages of all the struggles I have just mentioned. City Plaza would be of course unimaginable without the several hundreds of migrants that have traversed its space in the last two years. But it is also a site of solidarity, nurtured and made possible by the support of myriad initiatives and individuals in Athens and beyond, in turn nurturing the further spread of such practices. In addition, NoBorder activism is a constitutive component of City Plaza, where it intermingles with more mundane practices of self-organization at the level of everyday life.

In a way, one can say that the occupation of the Hotel on April 22, 2016, started a political experience that has been able to refer back both to the Greek spring and to an older history of migrants' struggles in the country while simultaneously responding to the reorganization of the European border regime that had a month previously culminated in the EU-Turkey deal. The occupation of a seven-floor building by hundreds of activists and migrants radically raised the question of private property in a political conjuncture that was shaped by the surrender of the Greek Left government and by the ensuing spread of political disenchantment among activists. Yet, over the last two years, the City Plaza Hotel has been a point of reference not only for migrants' struggles and self-organization but also more generally for all attempts to rethink political activism and projects of social transformation in Athens. Meanwhile, the involvement in past experiences of networking at the European level has helped to spark wide transnational solidarity around the slogan "No pool, no minibar, no room service, but still: the best hotel in Europe!" In the wake of the occupation, hundreds of activists from Europe and beyond visited City Plaza, and many of them decided to live there and be part of its "community of struggle."

Other articles in this section dwell on the meaning and labor of self-organization within a space like the City Plaza Hotel, on the specific politics of coalition that they are developing to support migrants' claims for social and political rights, and on other questions raised by these two years of occupation and struggle. Rooted in Athens, traversed by the imaginaries, desires, and needs of migrants coming from Afghanistan, Syria, Kurdistan, and Iran, as well as by those of transnational activists from across and beyond Europe, the City Plaza Hotel instantiates what can be called a counter-geography of struggle and resistance. At the same time, intermingling languages and cultures, it foreshadows the laborious reinvention of freedom and equality that is needed to create a new world. The City Plaza slogan "Create homes! Smash the borders!" effectively grasps the combination of resistance and constitutive politics that makes up its specificity and accounts for its extraordinary value.

References

Altenried, Moritz, et al. 2018. "Logistical Borderscapes. Politics and Mediation of Mobile Labor in Germany after the 'Summer of Migration'." In "Rethinking Migration and Autonomy from within the Crises," edited by Martina Tazzioli, Glenda Garelli, and Nicholas De Genova. *South Atlantic Quarterly* 117, no. 2: 291–312.

Arampatzi, Athina. 2017. "The Spatiality of Counter-Austerity Politics in Athens, Greece: Emergent 'Urban Solidarity Spaces'." *Urban Studies* 54, no. 9: 2155–71.

Bojadžijev, Manuela, and Sandro Mezzadra. 2015. "'Refugee Crisis' or Crisis of European Migration Policies?" *Focaalblog.com*, November 2015. www.focaalblog.com/2015/11/12/manuela-bojadzijev-and-sandro-mezzadra-refugee-crisis-or-crisis-of-european-migration-policies/.

Cappuccini, Monia. 2017. *Austerity and Democracy in Athens. Crisis and Community in Exarchia*. London: Palgrave Macmillan.

De Genova, Nicholas. 2013. "Spectacles of Migrants' Illegality: The Scene of Exclusion, the Obscene of Inclusion." *Ethnic and Racial Studies* 36, no. 7: 1180–98.

Garelli, Glenda, and Martina Tazzioli. 2016. "Beyond Detention: Spatial Strategies of Dispersal and Channels of Forced Transfer." *Society and Space*, November 8. societyandspace.org/2016/11/08/hotspot-beyond-detention-spatial-strategy-of-dispersal-and-channels-of-forced-transfer/.

Heller, Charles, and Lorenzo Pezzani. 2016. "Ebbing and Flowing: The EU's Shifting Practices of (Non-)Assistance and Bordering in a Time of Crisis." *Near Futures Online* 1. nearfuturesonline.org/ebbing-and-flowing-the-eus-shifting-practices-of-non-assistance-and-bordering-in-a-time-of-crisis/.

Hess, Sabine, et al. 2017. *Der lange Sommer der Migration. Grenzregime III* (*The Long Summer of Migration: Border Regime III*). Berlin: Assoziation A.

Kasparek, Bernd. 2016. "Routes, Corridors, and Spaces of Exception: Governing Migration and Europe." *Near Futures Online* 1. nearfuturesonline.org/routes-corridors-and -spaces-of-exception-governing-migration-and-europe/.

Kasparek, Bernd, and Marc Speer. 2015. "Of Hope. Ungarn und der lange Sommer der Migration" ("Hungary and the Long Summer of Migration"). *Bordermonitoring.eu*, September 7. bordermonitoring.eu/ungarn/2015/09/of-hope/.

Mezzadra, Sandro, and Brett Neilson. 2013. *Border as Method, or, the Multiplication of Labor.* Durham, NC: Duke University Press.

Nasioka, Katerina. 2014. "Communities of Crisis: Ruptures as Common Ties during Class Struggles in Greece, 2011–2012." *South Atlantic Quarterly* 113, no. 2: 285–97.

Stierl, Maurice. 2016. "A Sea of Struggles: Activist Border Interventions in the Mediterranean Sea." *Citizenship Studies* 20, no. 5: 561–78.

Traynor, Ian, Jennifer Rankin, and Helena Smith. 2015. "Greek Crisis: Surrender Fiscal Sovereignty in Return for Bailout, Merkel Tells Tsipras." *Guardian.com*, July 12. theguardian .com/business/2015/jul/12/greek-crisis-surrender-fiscal-sovereignty-in-return-for-bailout -merkel-tells-tsipras.

UNHCR (Office of the United Nations High Commissioner for Refugees). 2017. *Serving Refugee Populations. The Next Financial Inclusion Frontier.* Geneva: UNHCR and Social Performance Task Force. https://sptf.info/images/Guidelines-for-FSPs-on-serving-refugee -populations-March2017.pdf.

Notes on Contributors

Fadi A. Bardawil is an assistant professor of contemporary Arab cultures and global studies in the Department of Asian Studies and adjunct assistant professor of French and Francophone studies at the University of North Carolina, Chapel Hill. His research examines the international circulation of social theory and the traditions of critical inquiry of contemporary Arab intellectuals, both at home and in the diaspora. His writings have appeared in *boundary 2*, *Journal of Palestine Studies* (Arabic edition), *Comparative Studies of South Asia, Africa and the Middle East, Kulturaustausch, Jadaliyya, al-Akhbar* (2006–11), *Ma3azef.com*, and the Syrian ezine *Al-Jumhuriya*. He is completing a book currently titled "Emancipation Binds: Arab Revolutionary Marxism, Disenchantment, Critique."

Benjamin Y. Fong is an Honors Faculty Fellow at Barrett, the Honors College, at Arizona State University and the author of *Death and Mastery: Psychoanalytic Drive Theory and the Subject of Late Capitalism* (2016).

Samantha Rose Hill is the assistant director of the Hannah Arendt Center for Politics and Humanities and visiting assistant professor of political studies at Bard College. She is also associate faculty at the Brooklyn Institute for Social Research, where she teaches courses on critical theory. She is finishing a manuscript of Arendt's poetry. Her writing can be found in *Theory and Event, Contemporary Political Theory, Amor Mundi*, and *openDemocracy*, among other venues.

Robert Hullot-Kentor is the chair of the Critical Theory and the Arts graduate program at the School of Visual Arts in New York City.

Loukia Kotronaki is a postdoctoral researcher in the department of political science and history at Panteion University (Athens, Greece). She has conducted extensive research on transnational collective action, social movements, party politics, and democratization processes in Europe. Having published several academic articles and book chapters, she is presently completing a monograph, titled "Another World is Possible: Social Movements and Political Parties in Neoliberal Times." Her current research focuses on forms of protest and cultures of solidarity during the financial and refugee crisis in Greece.

Olga Lafazani is a postdoctoral researcher in the Department of Geography in Harokopion University, Athens. She currently holds a scholarship from State's Scholarship Foundation (IKY). Her research interests revolve around issues of borders, migration, urban space, and everyday life. She has published in several academic journals and collective volumes. She has been an active member of antiracist collectives for more than fifteen years.

Giorgos Maniatis is a social anthropologist and has been active in the antiracist movement in Greece for the last twenty years.

Robyn Marasco is an associate professor of political science at Hunter College, CUNY. She is the author of *The Highway of Despair: Critical Theory after Hegel* (2015).

Sandro Mezzadra teaches political theory at the University of Bologna and is an adjunct research fellow at the Institute for Culture and Society of Western Sydney University. With Brett Neilson, he is the author of *Border as Method, or, the Multiplication of Labor* (2013) and *The Politics of Operations: Excavating Contemporary Capitalism* (forthcoming).

Andrew Poe teaches political theory at Amherst College, where he is an assistant professor of political science and a member of the coordinating committee of the Amherst Program in Critical Theory. His research engages problems of democratic theory, especially modes of resistance, rhetoric, belief, extremism, and political affect. Currently, he is completing a book manuscript that traces a critical genealogy of democratic enthusiasm, titled "The Contest for Political Enthusiasm."

Michael Stein is a PhD candidate in the Department of Political Science at the University of Massachusetts Amherst and a member of the Coordinating Committee of the Amherst Program in Critical Theory.

Christian Thorne is a professor of English at Williams College. He is the author of *The Dialectic of Counter-Enlightenment* (2009).

Barbara Umrath teaches gender studies at the Technische Hochschule Köln (University of Applied Sciences Cologne), Germany. In her work, she combines contemporary feminist theory with critical social theory in the Frankfurt School tradition.

DOI 10.1215/00382876-2862784

EXTENT AND NATURE OF CIRCULATION: Average number of copies of each issue published during the preceding twelve months; (A) total number of copies printed, 429.5; (B.1) paid/requested mail subscriptions, 132.75; (B.4) Paid distribution by other classes, 8 (C) total paid/requested circulation, 140.75.; (D.1) samples, complimentary, and other nonrequested copies, 43.75; (D.4) nonrequested copies distributed through outside the mail, 35.5; (E) total nonrequested distribution (sum of D.1 & D.4), 79.25; (F) total distribution (sum of C & E), 220.; (G) copies not distributed (office use, leftover, unaccounted, spoiled after printing, returns from news agents), 209.5; (H) total (sum of F & G), 429.5.

Actual number of copies of a single issue published nearest to filing date: (A) total number of copies printed, 482; (B.1) paid/requested mail subscriptions, 210; (B.4) Paid distribution by other classes, 8(C) total paid/requested circulation, 218 (D.1) samples, complimentary, and other nonrequested copies, 0; (D.4) nonrequested copies distributed through outside the mail, 37; (E) total nonrequested distribution (sum of D.1 & D.4), 37; (F) total distribution (sum of C & E), 255; (G) copies not distributed (office use, leftover, unaccounted, spoiled after printing, returns from news agents), 227 (H) total (sum of F & G), 482.

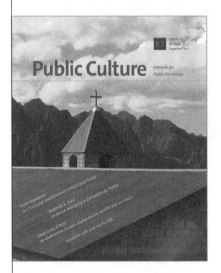

Keep up to date on new scholarship

Issue alerts are a great way to stay current on all the cutting-edge scholarship from your favorite Duke University Press journals. This free service delivers tables of contents directly to your inbox, informing you of the latest groundbreaking work as soon as it is published.

To sign up for issue alerts:

1. Visit **dukeu.press/register** and register for an account. You do not need to provide a customer number.

2. After registering, visit **dukeu.press/alerts**.

3. Go to "Latest Issue Alerts" and click on "Add Alerts."

4. Select as many publications as you would like from the pop-up window and click "Add Alerts."

read.dukeupress.edu/journals